ANSI/ISO C++ Professional Programmer's Handbook

Danny Kalev

ANSI/ISO C++ Professional Programmer's Handbook

Danny Kalev

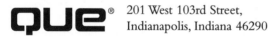 201 West 103rd Street,
Indianapolis, Indiana 46290

ANSI/ISO C++ Professional Programmer's Handbook

International Standard Book Number: 0-7897-2022-1

Library of Congress Catalog Card Number: 99-62146

Printed in the United States of America

First Printing: June 1999

01   00   99   4   3   2

Trademarks

Warning and Disclaimer

Executive Editor
Tracy Dunkelberger

Acquisitions Editor
Michelle Newcomb

Development Editor
Bryan Morgan

Managing Editor
Brice Gosnell

Project Editor
Sara Bosin

Copy Editor
JoAnna Kremer

Indexer
Aamir Burki

Proofreader
Benjamin Berg

Technical Editor
Sivaramakrishnan J.

Software Development Specialist
Adam Swetnam

Interior and Cover Design
Gary Adair

Layout Technicians
Brandon Allen
Stacey DeRome
Tim Osborn
Staci Somers

Table of Contents

About the Author

Danny Kalev is a certified system analyst and software engineer with more than 10 years of experience, specializing in C++ and object-oriented analysis and design. He is now finishing his M.A. in applied linguistics at the University of Tel Aviv, Israel. He is a hi-fi enthusiast and likes all kinds of music. He is also interested in natural languages and philology.

His technical interests involve generic programming, networking, compiler technology, artificial intelligence, and embedded systems. He has contributed several articles to C++ magazines and Web publishers, and is one of the co-authors of *C++ How To*. He is also a member of the ANSI C++ standardization Standards committee.

Dedication

I dedicate this book to my dear parents, Rachel and Samuel.

Danny Kalev

Acknowledgments

I thank the staff at Macmillan Computer Publishing for their immeasurable assistance and utmost professionalism. In particular, I want to thank Michelle Newcomb for just about everything—speediest deliveries, late at night emails, and clockwork coordination among team members from various continents. I also want to thank Tracy Dunkelberger for the insightful ideas and advice-laden suggestions. Special thanks go to Bryan Morgan: Working with you is a real pleasure. I thank JoAnna Kremer and Sara Bosin for patiently working with me. Shiva did an outstanding job reviewing my manuscripts and provided many invaluable comments.

Another big "thank you" goes to Dr. Outi Bat-El, who long ago convinced me that English is the ultimate language for writing—you were right all along. I thank Bjarne Stroustrup for the lightning-speed replies to my emails and for allowing me to quote from his book. Other members of the ANSI C++ Standards committee who have contributed to this book are Josee Lajoie, David Vandevoorde, and David Abrahams.

Most importantly, I would like to thank my family, my friends and my colleagues (and in particular, to Kay Keppler) for their support and encouragement in writing this book.

Danny Kalev

Tell Us What You Think!

As the reader of this book, you are our most important critic and commentator. We value your opinion and want to know what we're doing right, what we could do better, what areas you'd like to see us publish in, and any other words of wisdom you're willing to pass our way.

As a publisher for Que, I welcome your comments. You can fax, email, or write me directly to let me know what you did or didn't like about this book—as well as what we can do to make our books stronger.

Please note that I cannot help you with technical problems related to the topic of this book, and that due to the high volume of mail I receive, I might not be able to reply to every message.

When you write, please be sure to include this book's title and author as well as your name and phone or fax number. I will carefully review your comments and share them with the author and editors who worked on the book.

Fax:	317-581-4666
Email:	programming@mcp.com
Mail:	Associate Publisher at Que
	201 West 103rd Street
	Indianapolis, IN 46290 USA

Now the whole earth used the same language and the same words.
—Genesis 11:1

Preface

Of all the programming languages I've ever used, I enjoy writing in C++ the most. It certainly has a few wrinkles and dark corners that can baffle even experienced programmers, but the expressiveness and the sense of control that C++ gives you are unparalleled among other high-level programming languages. The flexibility of C++ has a price, though: Although learning Visual Basic is only a matter of days, a C++ novice needs a few good months to become productive. Nonetheless, most C++ programmers today have at least some basic knowledge of the language, and many of them are also ex-C programmers. C++ tutorials usually describe the language from the basics, providing lengthy introductory discussions on topics about which the majority of C++ programmers already know. Consequently, it is not unusual to find C++ books that well exceed 1000 pages. This book uses a different approach: I have attempted to focus on the core issues, while avoiding explaining the obvious. I do not discuss the fundamental types of C++, nor do I explain what variables, pointers, structs, and functions are. Instead, the emphasis is on topics that intermediate-to advanced-level programmers will find useful. The intent is to give you a concise, clear, and advice-laden account of the various features of the language as they are specified in the current ANSI/ISO Standard. Many of the discussions dig deep into the underlying mechanisms of C++. Thus, instead of just explaining the constructs of RTTI and how they are used, I also discuss how a typical implementation of the RTTI mechanism might look, and how the implementation affects performance. This approach has two advantages: By knowing what is actually going on behind the scenes, you can avoid common pitfalls and inefficiencies; furthermore, you can refute some of the myths and hearsay about C++.

The code samples in the book are fully-compliant with the Standard and were tested on two different compilers: MS Visual C++ 6.0 (Service Pack 1) and EGCS 1.1. Some code samples were also tested on Borland's C++ Builder 4.0. Note, however, that as of the time of this writing, a 100% ANSI-compliant compiler is still unavailable; exported templates are not yet supported by any commercial compilers, as far as I know; and compilers that support function `try` blocks and in-class initialization of static constants are also rather rare these days. For this reason, you might encounter compilation errors in code samples that use these features or any other features that were recently added to the Standard. Hopefully, Standard-compliant compilers will appear soon.

The Source Code listings that appear in the book are also available at `http://mcp.com`.

The ANSI/ISO Standard is now available for downloading from the ANSI Web site at `http://www.ansi.org`. The downloadable PDF format costs $18. Note that the Standard is copyrighted, and that other national standardization bodies might sell it at different prices. Remember also that the Standard is not written in plain English, and it is definitely not a tutorial of the language.

I hope that by reading this book, you will gain broader understanding of the language, better design and programming skills, and, eventually, that you will find C++ as enjoyable as I do. If you have comments or questions about the book, you can email me at `dannykk@inter.net.il`.

Thank You!

Que Professional would like to thank the following contributors for submitting comments and feedback on this book prior to its publication. In an unprecedented move to ensure quality, all Que Professional titles are posted for peer review and comment prior to publication on professional.quecorp.com. Thanks to the contributors' technical suggestions and personal perspectives we move closer to our goal of creating high-quality, solutions-oriented educational material.

Que Professional Publishing

Online Reviewers & Contributors

Oscar Esteban
Madrid, Spain

Eugene Girard
Kingston, Ontario, Canada

Roger Gullhaug
Norway

David Huang
Wheaton, IL, USA

Jonathan H. Lundquist
Spokane, WA

Gamaliel Masters
Council, Idaho, USA

John Seybold
China Lake, CA, USA

Tiaan Wessels
South Africa

Michael Goldshteyn

Ronald Ledford

Edward Jason Riedy

Michael S. Sage

John Tobler

Mike Haspert

Acknowledgements

I

What's New in C++?

1

Introduction

THE PRECURSORS OF OBJECT-ORIENTED PROGRAMMING can be traced back to the late 1960s: classes, inheritance, and virtual member functions were integral features of Simula67, a programming language that was mainly used for writing event-driven simulations. When Smalltalk first appeared back in 1972, it offered a pure object-oriented programming environment. In fact, Smalltalk defined object-oriented programming. This style of programming was so innovative and revolutionary at the time that it took more than a decade for it to become a standard in the software industry. Undoubtedly, the emergence of C++ in the early 1980s provided the most considerable contribution to this revolution.

The Origins of C++

In 1979, a young engineer at Bell Labs, Bjarne Stroustrup, started to experiment with extensions to C to make it a better tool for implementing large-scale projects. In those days, an average project consisted of tens of thousands of lines of code (LOC).

Today, Microsoft's Windows 2000 (formerly NT 5.0) consists of more than 30 million lines of code (and counting).

When projects leaped over the 100,000 LOC count, the shortcomings of C became noticeably unacceptable. Efficient teamwork is based, among other things, on the capability to decouple development phases of individual teams from one another—something that was difficult to achieve in C.

C with Classes

By adding classes to C, the resultant language—"C with classes"—could offer better support for encapsulation and information hiding. A class provides a distinct separation between its internal implementation (the part that is more likely to change) and its external interface. A class object has a determinate state right from its construction, and it bundles together the data and operations that manipulate it.

Enter C++

In 1983, several modifications and extensions had already been made to C with classes. In that year, the name "C++" was coined. Ever since then, the ++ suffix has become a synonym for object-orientation. It was also in that year that C++ was first used outside AT&T Bell Labs. The number of users was doubling every few months—and so was the number of compilers and extensions to the language.

The Late 1980s: Opening the Floodgates

Between 1985 and 1989, C++ underwent a major reform. Protected members, protected inheritance, templates, and a somewhat controversial feature called multiple inheritance were added to the language. It was clear that C++ needed to become standardized.

ANSI Committee Established

In 1989, the *American National Standards Institution (ANSI)* committee for the standardization of C++ was established. The official name of the committee was X3J16, and later it was changed to J16. Generally, standardization committees don't write a standard from scratch; rather, they adopt an existing de facto reference and use it as their baseline. The ANSI C committee used *The C Programming Language* by Kernighan and Ritchie as a starting point. Likewise, the ANSI C++ committee used the *Annotated C++ Reference Manual (ARM)* by Ellis and Stroustrup as its base document. The ARM provided a clear and detailed starting point for the committee's work. The committee's policy was to not rush into establishing a half-baked standard that would become obsolete in a year or two. Instead, the policy was to allow the demands for changes to emerge from the users of the language, the C++ community. Nonetheless, the committee also initiated extensible modifications and changes to the language, such as *runtime type information (RTTI)* and the new cast notation.

Maturation

By that time, hundreds of thousands of people were using the language. C++ compilers were available for almost every platform. New C++-based frameworks, such as MFC and OWL, had emerged. The committee had to face enormous pressure from several directions. Some organizations were advocating new features and extensions to the language that were borrowed from other object-oriented languages, while other parties strove to keep it as efficient as possible. On top of this, C++ had to retain its backward compatibility with C, including the support of eight different flavors for integral types, cumbersome pointer syntax, structs, unions, global functions, and many other features that don't exactly go hand in hand with object-oriented programming.

International Standardization

C++ standardization was a joint international endeavor in which national standardization bodies from all over the world were intensively involved. This is different from the standardization of C. C standardization was first carried out by ANSI as an American standard and was later adopted, with some modifications (mainly internationalization issues), as an international standard by the *International Standardization Organization (ISO)*. The international venture of C++ guaranteed a worldwide acceptance of the standard, albeit at the price of somewhat more complicated procedures. Thus, the committee's meetings were actually joint meetings of both the ANSI working group and the ISO working group. Officially, the ANSI working group served as an advisor to ISO. Therefore, two votes were taken on every technical issue: an ANSI vote, to decide what the ANSI recommendation was, and a subsequent ISO vote, to actually make the decision. Some important changes were made in order to meet the criteria for ISO approval, including the addition of wchar_t as a built-in type, the templatization of the `iostream` library, the templatization of class `string`, and the introduction of the *locale library*, which encapsulates cultural-dependent differences.

Committee Drafts and Public Review

The committee's initial task was to produce a draft of the Standard, known as the *Committee Draft (CD)*. For that purpose, the committee convened three times a year, one week at a time, in different places in the world. The first CD received several disapproving votes, as well as many comments from ISO. The committee resolved these technical issues and addressed the comments in the second CD. The second CD was approved by ISO; however, there were still five "nay" votes and accompanying comments. Following the ISO balloting, the CDs were made available to the public. The public review process enabled C++ users from all over the world to comment on the proposed CD and point out contradictions and omissions.

Feature Freeze and Finalization

After the approval of the second CD in November 1996, the committee's task was mainly to respond to the five "nay" votes and their accompanying comments and turn them into "aye" votes. The resultant document was the *Final Draft International Standard*, or the *FDIS*. At the meeting of the standardization committee in November, 1997 at Morristown, New Jersey, the FDIS was unanimously approved. In 1998, after a few minor changes, the FDIS was approved by ISO and became an international standard. In accordance with ISO rules, after it was approved, the Standard entered a freeze period of five years; during this time, the only modifications that are allowed are error fixes. People who find such defects can submit a Defect Report to the committee for consideration.

C++ as Opposed to Other Object-Oriented Languages

C++ differs from other object-oriented languages in many ways. For instance, C++ is not a root-based language, nor does it operate on a runtime virtual machine. These differences significantly broaden the domains in which C++ can be used.

Backward Compatibility with Legacy Systems

The fact that legacy C code can be combined seamlessly with new C++ code is a major advantage. Migration from C to C++ does not force you to throw away good, functional C code. Many commercial frameworks, and even some components of the Standard Library itself, are built upon legacy C code that is wrapped in an object-oriented interface.

Performance

Interpreted languages allow easier code porting, albeit at the cost of significant performance overhead. C++, on the other hand, uses the compile-and-link model it inherited from C. One of the goals of C++ designers has been to keep it as efficient as possible; a compile-and-link model enables very efficient code generation and optimization. Another performance factor is the use of a garbage collector. This feature is handy and prevents some common programming bugs; however, garbage collected languages are disqualified from time-critical application development, where determinacy is paramount. For that reason, C++ does not have a garbage collector.

Object-Orientation and Other Useful Paradigms

In addition to object-oriented programming, C++ supports other useful programming styles, including procedural programming, object-based programming, and generic programming—making it a multi-paradigm, general-purpose programming language.

Procedural Programming

Procedural programming is not very popular these days. However, there are some good reasons for C++ to support this style of programming, even today.

Gradual Migration of C Programmers to C++

C programmers who make their first steps in C++ are not forced to throw all their expertise away. Many primitives and fundamental concepts of C++ were inherited from C, including built-in operators and fundamental types, pointers, the notion of dynamic memory allocation, header files, preprocessor, and so on. As a transient phase, C programmers can still remain productive when the shift to C++ is made.

Bilingual Environments

C++ and C code can work together. Under certain conditions, this combination is synergetic and robust.

Machine-Generated Code

Many software tools and generators generate C code as an intermediate stage of application build. For example, SQL queries on most relational databases are translated into C code, which is in turn compiled and linked. There's not much point in forcing these generators to produce C++ code (although some do so) when the generated code is not going to be used by human programmers. Furthermore, many early C++ compilers were not really compilers in the true meaning of the word; they are better described as translators because they translated C++ code into intermediate C code that was later compiled and linked. In fact, any valid C++ programs can be translated directly into pure C code.

Object-Oriented Programming

This is the most widely used style of programming in C++. The intent of this book is to deliver useful guidelines and rules of thumb for efficient, reliable, reusable, and easy to maintain object-oriented code. But there is no universal consensus as to what object-oriented really is; the definitions vary among schools, languages, and users. There *is*, however, a consensus about a common denominator—a combination of encapsulation, information hiding, polymorphism, dynamic binding, and inheritance. Some maintain that advanced object-oriented programming consists of generic programming support and multiple inheritance. These concepts will be discussed in depth in the chapters that follow.

Generic Programming

Generic programming proceeds one step beyond object-oriented programming in pursuing reusability. Two important features of C++, templates and operator overloading, are the basis of generic programming. STL, a collection of generic algorithms and containers, is probably the most impressive manifestation of this paradigm.

Aim of the Book

This book is aimed at experienced C++ developers who seek a guide for enhancing their design and programming proficiency. It discloses facts and techniques and provides a knowledge base for advanced, Standard-compliant, and efficient use of C++. In addition, the book also explains the underlying mechanism behind the high-level features of the language, and it explains the philosophy behind the design and evolution of C++.

Target Audience

The target audience is intermediate and advanced level C++ developers who want to improve their proficiency by acquiring new programming techniques and design idioms. On top of adding many new features to the language, the standardization committee has deprecated several features and library components. In this book, readers who want to develop long-lasting, future-proof C++ software can find a comprehensive list of deprecated features and their recommended alternatives.

Organization of the Book

Chapter 2, "Standard Briefing: The Latest Addenda to ANSI/ISO C++," presents some of the key terms that are used in the C++ Standard, and which are used extensively in this book. Following this, the recent changes and extensions to C++ are described. Finally, Chapter 2 gives an overview of the deprecated features that are listed in the Standard, and suggests standard-compliant replacements for them.

Chapter 3, "Operator Overloading," explores the benefits as well as the potential problems of operator overloading. It discusses the restrictions that apply to operator overloading and explains how to use conversion operators.

Chapter 4, "Special Member Functions: Default Constructor, Copy Constructor, Destructor, and Assignment Operator," explains the semantics of the special member functions and their role in class design. It also demonstrates several techniques and guidelines for effective use of these special member functions.

Chapter 5, "Object-Oriented Programming and Design," provides a brief survey of the various programming styles that are supported by C++, focusing on the principles of object-oriented design and programming.

Chapter 6, "Exception Handling," first describes traditional error handling methods and their disadvantages, and then presents standard exception handling. A brief historical account of the design of exception handling is provided and, finally, exception handling-related performance issues are discussed.

Chapter 7, "Runtime Type Information," discusses the three components of runtime type information, namely `typeid`, `dynamic_cast`, and class `type_info`. In addition, it explains when the use of RTTI is necessary. Finally, it discusses the performance overhead associated with runtime type information.

Chapter 8, "Namespaces," elucidates the rationale behind the addition of namespaces to the language and the problems that namespaces solve. Then it demonstrates how namespaces are used in practice, and how they interact with other language features.

Chapter 9, "Templates," discusses various aspects of designing and implementing templates, including class templates, function templates, and template issues that are of special concern (such as pointers to members, virtual member functions within a template class, inheritance relations, and explicit instantiations).

Chapter 10, "STL and Generic Programming," is an introduction to the Standard Template Library and to generic programming in general. It discusses the principles of generic programming, focusing on STL as an exemplary framework of generic programming. This chapter also demonstrates the use of STL components: containers, algorithms, iterators, allocators, adapters, binders, and function objects. The most widely used STL components, `std::vector` and `std::string`, are explored in detail.

Chapter 11, "Memory Management," explains the memory model of C++. It describes the three types of data storage: static, automatic, and free store. This chapter also delves into the semantics of operators `new` and `delete` and their underlying implementation. In addition, it demonstrates the use of advanced memory management techniques and guides you in avoiding common memory-related errors.

Chapter 12, "Optimizing Your Code," is dedicated to code optimization. It provides useful guidelines and tips for writing more efficient code, and it proceeds toward more aggressive optimization techniques for minimizing space and accelerating runtime speed.

Chapter 13, "C Language Compatibility Issues," demonstrates how to migrate from C to C++ and, in particular, how to migrate from procedural programming to object-orientation. It lists the differences between the C subset of C++ and ISO C. Finally, it delves into the underlying representation of C++ objects in memory and their compatibility with C structs.

Chapter 14, "Concluding Remarks and Future Directions," seals this book. It describes the principles and guidelines in the design and evolution of C++ throughout the last two decades, and compares it to the evolution of other, less successful programming languages. Then it lists features that almost made it into the Standard. Next, it discusses possible future extensions, including automated garbage collection, object persistence, and concurrency. Other hypothetical future extensions that are described are dynamically linked libraries, rule-based programming, and extensible member functions.

2

Standard Briefing: The Latest Addenda to ANSI/ISO C++

Introduction

C++ today is very different from what it was in 1983, when it was first named "C++". Many features have been added to the language since then; older features have been modified, and a few features have been deprecated or removed entirely from the language. Some of the extensions have radically changed programming styles and concepts. For example, downcasting a base to a derived object was considered a bad and unsafe programming practice before the standardization of Runtime Type Information. Today, downcasts are safe, and sometimes even unavoidable. The list of extensions includes `const` member functions, exception handling, templates, new cast operators, namespaces, the Standard Template Library, `bool` type, and many more. These have made C++ the powerful and robust multipurpose programming language that it is today.

The evolution of C++ has been a continuous and progressive process, rather than a series of brusque revolutions. Programmers who learned C++ only three or five years ago and haven't caught up with the extensions often discover that the language slips through their fingers: Existing pieces of code do not compile anymore, others compile with a plethora of compiler warnings, and the source code listings in object-oriented magazines seem substantially different from the way they looked not so long ago. "Namespaces? Never heard of these before," and "What was wrong with C-style cast? Why shouldn't I use it anymore?" are some of the frequently asked questions in various C++ forums and conferences.

Understanding the ANSI/ISO Standard

But even experienced C++ programmers who have kept up with changes by subscribing to newsgroups, reading magazines and books, or exchanging emails with the company's guru might still find that the C++ nomenclature in professional literature is sometimes unclear. The ANSI/ISO Standard is written in a succinct and technical jargon that is jocularly called *standardese*—which is anything but plain English. For instance, the *One Definition Rule* (article 3.2 in the Standard), which defines under what conditions separate definitions of the same entity are valid, is explained in textbooks in a simpler—although sometimes less accurate—manner, when compared to the Standard text. The use of standardese ensures the accuracy that is needed for writing compilers and checking the validity of programs. For this purpose, the Standard defines numerous specific terms that are used extensively throughout the volume; for instance, it distinguishes between a *template id* and a *template name*, whereas an average programmer simply refers to both as templates. Familiarity with these specific terms is the key to reading and interpreting the Standard correctly.

Purpose and Structure of This Chapter

The purposes of this chapter are threefold. First, it presents some of the key terms that are used extensively throughout the Standard and throughout this book, for example, *undefined behavior* and *deprecated features*. (Note that topic-specific terms such as *argument-dependent lookup* and *trivial constructor* are presented in their relevant chapters rather than here.) Then, the new features that have been added to C++—such as `bool` type, new typecast operators, and `mutable` data members—are discussed. Because these topics are not explained elsewhere in this book, they are presented here in detail, along with code samples. After that comes a list of other newly added features that are covered extensively in other chapters of the book.

   These topics are presented here only briefly. The intent is to provide you with an *executive summary*—a panorama of the latest addenda to the ANSI/ISO C++ Standard—that you can use as a checklist of topics. When reading the brief topics overview, you might come across an unfamiliar topic; in these instances, you are always referred to the chapter that discusses the topic in further detail. Finally, there is an overview of the deprecated features and a list of suggested replacements for them.

The Standard's Terminology

This part explains some of the key terms in the Standard that are used throughout the book. These terms appear in italics when they are presented for the first time. Note that these definitions are not exact quotations from the Standard; rather, they are interpretive definitions.

Arguments and Parameters

The words *arguments* and *parameters* are often used interchangeably in the literature, although the Standard makes a clear distinction between the two. The distinction is chiefly important when discussing functions and templates.

Argument

An argument is one of the following: an expression in the comma-separated list that is bound by the parentheses in a function call; a sequence of one or more preprocessor tokens in the comma-separated list that is bound by the parentheses in a function-like macro invocation; the operand of a throw-statement or an expression, type, or template-name in the comma-separated list that is bound by the angle brackets in a template instantiation. An argument is also called an *actual parameter*.

Parameter

A parameter is one of the following: an object or reference that is declared in a function declaration or definition (or in the catch clause of an exception handler); an identifier from the comma-separated list that is bound by the parentheses immediately following the macro name in a definition of a function-like macro; or a template-parameter. A parameter is also called a *formal parameter.*

The following example demonstrates the difference between a parameter and an argument:

```
void func(int n, char * pc); //n and pc are parameters
template <class T> class A {}; //T is a a parameter

int main()
{
  char c;
  char *p = &c;
  func(5, p); //5 and p are arguments
  A<long> a; //'long' is an argument
  A<char> another_a; //'char' is an argument
  return 0;
}
```

Translation Unit

A *translation unit* contains a sequence of one or more declarations. The Standard uses the term *translation unit* rather than *source file* because a single translation unit can be assembled from more than a single source file: A source file and the header files that are #included in it are a single translation unit.

Program

A *program* consists of one or more translation units that are linked together.

Well-Formed Program

A *well-formed program* is one that is constructed according to the Standard's syntax and semantic rules and that obeys the One Definition Rule (explained in the following section). An *ill-formed program* is one that does not meet these requirements.

lvalues and rvalues

An *object* is a contiguous region of storage. An *lvalue* is an expression that refers to such an object. The original definition of lvalue referred to an object that can appear on the left-hand side of an assignment. However, `const` objects are lvalues that cannot be used in the left side of an assignment. Similarly, an expression that can appear in the right side of an expression (but not in the left side of an expression) is an *rvalue*. For example

```
#include <string>
using namespace std;
int& f();
void func()
{
  int n;
  char buf[3];
  n = 5; // n is an lvalue; 5 is an rvalue
  buf[0] = 'a'; // buf[0] is an lvalue, 'a' is an rvalue
  string s1 = "a", s2 = "b", s3 = "c"; // "a", "b", "c" are rvalues
  s1 =  // lvalue
      s2 +s3; //s2 and s3 are lvalues that are implicitly converted to rvalues
  s1 = //lvalue
      string("z"); //temporaries are rvalues
  int * p = new int; //p is an lvalue; 'new int' is an rvalue
  f() = 0; //a function call that returns a reference is an lvalue
  s1.size(); //otherwise, a function call is an rvalue expression
}
```

An lvalue can appear in a context that requires an rvalue; in this case, the lvalue is implicitly converted to an rvalue. An rvalue cannot be converted to an lvalue. Therefore, it is possible to use every lvalue expression in the example as an rvalue, but not vice versa.

Behavior Types

The Standard lists several types of program behaviors, which are detailed in the following sections.

Implementation-Defined Behavior

Implementation-defined behavior (for a well-formed program and correct data) is one that depends on the particular implementation; it is a behavior that each implementation must document. For example, an implementation documents the size of fundamental types, whether a char can hold negative values, and whether the stack is unwound in the case of an uncaught exception. Implementation-defined behavior is also called *implementation-dependent behavior*.

Unspecified Behavior

Unspecified behavior (for a well-formed program and correct data) is one that depends on the particular implementation. The implementation is not required to document which behavior occurs (but it is allowed to do so). For example, whether operator new calls to the Standard C library function malloc() is unspecified. Following is another example: The storage type for the temporary copy of an exception object is allocated in an unspecified way (however, it cannot be allocated on the free store).

Implementation-defined behavior and unspecified behavior are similar. Both refer to consistent behavior that is implementation-specific. However, unspecified behavior usually refers to the underlying mechanism of the implementation, which users generally do not access directly. Implementation-dependent behavior refers to language constructs that can be used directly by users.

Undefined Behavior

Undefined behavior is one for which the Standard imposes no requirements. This definition might sound like an understatement because undefined behavior indicates a state that generally results from an erroneous program or erroneous data. Undefined behavior can be manifested as a runtime crash or as an unstable and unreliable program state—or it might even pass unnoticed. Writing to a buffer past its boundary, accessing an out-of-range array subscript, dereferencing a dangling pointer, and other similar operations result in undefined behavior.

Conclusions

Unspecified behavior and implementation-defined behavior are consistent—albeit nonportable—behaviors that are left intentionally unspecified by the C++ Standard, usually to allow efficient and simple compiler implementation on various platforms. Conversely, undefined behavior is always undesirable and should never occur.

The One Definition Rule

A class, an enumeration, an inline function with external linkage, a class template, a nonstatic function template, a member function template, a static data member of a class template, or a template specialization for which some template parameters are not specified can be defined more than once in a program—provided that each definition appears in a different translation unit, and provided that the definitions meet the requirements that are detailed in the following sections.

Token-by-Token Identity

Each definition must contain the same sequence of tokens. For example

```
//file fisrt.cpp
inline int C::getVal () { return 5; }
```

```
//file sec.cpp
typedef int I;
inline I C::getVal () { return 5; } // violation of ODR,
                                    // I and int are not identical tokens
```

On the other hand, white spaces and comments are immaterial:

```
//file fisrt.cpp
inline int C::getVal () { return 5; }
  //file sec.cpp
inline int C::getVal () { /*complies with the ODR*/
return 5; }
```

Semantic Equivalence

Each token in the identical sequences of the separate definitions has the same semantic contents. For example

```
//file first.cpp
typedef int I;
inline I C::getVal () { return 5; }
```

```
//file second.cpp
typedef unsigned int I;
inline I C::getVal () { return 5; } //error; different semantic content for I
```

Linkage Types

A name that refers to an object, reference, type, function, template, namespace, or value that is declared in another scope is said to have *linkage*. The linkage can be either *external* or *internal*. Otherwise, the name has no linkage.

External Linkage

A name that can be referred to from other translation units or from other scopes of the translation unit in which it was defined has *external linkage*. Following are some examples:

```
void g(int n) {} //g has external linkage
int glob; //glob has external linkage
extern const int E_MAX=1024; //E_MAX has external linkage
namespace N
{
  int num;  //N::num has external linkage
```

```
    void func();//N::func has external linkage
}
class C {}; //the name C has external linkage
```

Internal Linkage

A name that can be referred to by names from other scopes in the translation unit in which it was declared, but not from other translation units, has *internal linkage*. Following are some examples:

```
static void func() {} //func has internal linkage
union //members of a non-local anonymous union have internal linkage
{
   int n;
   void *p;
};
const int MAX=1024; //non-extern const variables have internal linkage
typedef int I; //typedefs have internal linkage
```

Names with No Linkage

A name that can only be referred to from the scope in which it is declared has no linkage. For example

```
void f()
{
   int a; //a has no linkage
   class B {/**/}; //a local class has no linkage
}
```

Side Effect

A *side effect* is a change in the state of the execution environment. Modifying an object, accessing a `volatile` object, invoking a library I/O function, and calling a function that performs any of these operations are all side effects.

Addenda

This part details the new features—and extensions to existing features—that have been adopted by the C++ Standard in recent years.

New Typecast Operators

C++ still supports C-style cast, as in

```
int i = (int) 7.333;
```

Nonetheless, C-style cast notation is problematic for several reasons. First, the operator () is already used excessively in the language: in a function call, in precedence reordering of expressions, in operator overloading, and in other syntactic constructs.

Second, C-style cast carries out different operations in different contexts—so different that you can hardly tell which is which. It can perform an innocuous standard cast, such as converting an `enum` value to an `int`; but it can also cast two nonrelated types to one another. In addition, a C-style cast can be used to remove the `const` or `volatile` qualifiers of an object (and in earlier stages of C++, the language was capable of performing dynamic casts as well).

Because of these multiple meanings, the C-style cast is opaque. Sometimes it is very difficult for a reader to clearly understand the intent of the code author who uses a C-style cast operation. Consider the following example:

```
#include <iostream>
using namespace std;
void display(const unsigned char *pstr)
{
  cout<<pstr<<endl;
}

void func()
{
  const char * p = "a message";
  display( (unsigned char*) p); //signed to unsigned cast is required
                                // but const is also removed. was that
                                // intentional or a programmer's oversight?
}
```

The new cast operators make the programmer's intention clearer and self-documenting. In addition, they enable the compiler to detect mistakes that cannot be detected with C-style cast. The new cast operators are intended to replace C-style cast; C++ programmers are encouraged to use them instead of C-style cast notation. These operators are detailed in the following sections.

static_cast

`static_cast <Type> (Expr)` performs well-behaved and reasonably well-behaved casts. One of its uses is to indicate explicitly a type conversion that is otherwise performed implicitly by the compiler.
For example

```
class Base{};
class Derived : public Base {};
void func( Derived * pd)
{
 Base * pb = static_cast<Base *> (pd); //explicit
}
```

A pointer to a derived object can be automatically converted to a pointer to a public base. The use of an explicit cast makes the programmer's intent clearer.

`static_cast` can be used to document user-defined conversion. For example

```
class Integer
{
  public: operator int ();
```

```
};
void func(Integer& integer)
{
 int num = static_cast<int> (integer); //explicit
}
```

Narrowing conversions of numeric types can also be performed explicitly by a
static_cast. For example

```
void func()
{
   int num = 0;
   short short_num = static_cast<short> (num);
}
```

This conversion is somewhat riskier than the previous conversions. A short might
not represent all the values that an int can hold; an explicit cast is used here, instead of
an implicit conversion, to indicate that a type conversion is performed. Casting an
integral value to an enum is also a dangerous operation because there is no guarantee
that the value of an int can be represented in an enum. Note that in this case, an
explicit cast is necessary:

```
void func()
{
   enum status {good, bad};
   int num = 0;
   status s = static_cast<status> (num);
}
```

You can use static_cast to navigate through class hierarchies. Unlike
dynamic_cast, however, static_cast relies solely on the information that is available at
compile time—so don't use it instead of dynamic_cast. Using static_cast for this
purpose is safer than using C-style cast because it does not perform conversions
between nonrelated classes. For example

```
class A{};
class B{};
A *pa;
B * pb = static_cast<B *> (pa); //error, pointers are not related
```

const_cast

const_cast <T> (Expr) removes only the const or volatile qualifiers of Expr and
converts them to type T. T must be the same type of Expr, except for the missing
const or volatile attributes. For example

```
#include <iostream>
using namespace std;
void print(char *p) //parameter should have been declared as const; alas,
{
   cout<<p;
}
void f()
{
```

```
    const char msg[] = "Hello World\n";
    char * p = const_cast<char *> (msg); //remove constness
    print(p);
}
```

const_cast can also convert an object to a const or volatile one:

```
void read(const volatile int * p);
int *p = new int;
read( const_cast<const volatile int *> (p) ); //explicit
```

Note that the removal of the const qualifier of an object does not guarantee that its value can be modified; it only guarantees that it can be used in a context that requires a non-const object. So that you understand these limitations, the following sections examine const semantics in further detail.

const Semantics

There are actually two types of const: *true* const and *contractual* const. A true const object is an lvalue that was originally defined as const. For example

```
const int cn = 5; // true const
const std::string msg("press any key to continue"); // true const
```

On the other hand, an object with contractual const quality is one that was defined without the const qualifier, but that is treated as though it were const. For example

```
void ReadValue(const int& num)
{
  cout<<num;   // num may not be modified in ReadValue()
}
int main()
{
  int n =0;
  ReadValue(n); //contractual const, n is treated as if it were const
}
```

When a true const variable is explicitly cast to a non-const variable, the result of an attempt to change its value is undefined. This is because an implementation can store true const data in the read-only memory, and an attempt to write to it usually triggers a hardware exception. (Using an explicit cast to remove constness does not change the physical memory properties of a variable.) For example

```
const int cnum = 0; //true const, may be stored in the machine's ROM
const int * pci = &cnum;
int *pi = const_cast<int*> (pci); // brute force attempt to unconst a variable
cout<< *pi; //OK, value of cnum is not modified
*pi = 2;  //undefined, an attempt to modify cnum which is a true const variable
```

On the other hand, casting away the contractual constness of an object makes it possible to modify its value safely:

```
int num = 0;
const int * pci = &num;  // *pci is a contractual const int
int *pi = const_cast<int*> (pci);   // get rid of contractual const
*pi = 2;    // OK, modify num's value
```

To conclude, const_cast is used to remove the const or volatile qualities of an object. The resultant value can be used in a context that requires a non-const or volatile object. The cast operation is safe as long as the resultant value is not modified. It is possible to modify the value of the resultant object only if the original operand is not truly const.

reinterpret_cast

reinterpret_cast <to> (from) is used in low-level, unsafe conversions. reinterpret_cast merely returns a low-level reinterpretation of the bit pattern of its operand. Note, however, that reinterpret_cast cannot alter the const or volatile qualification of its operand. The use of reinterpret_cast is dangerous and highly non-portable—use it sparingly. Following are examples of reinterpret_cast uses.

reinterpret_cast can be used to convert two pointers of completely nonrelated types, as in

```
#include <cstdio>
using namespace std;
void mem_probe()
{
  long n = 1000000L; long *pl = &n;
  unsigned char * pc = reinterpret_cast <unsigned char *> (pl);
  printf("%d %d %d %d", pc[0], pc[1], pc[2], pc[3]); //memory dump
}
```

reinterpret_cast can cast integers to pointers, and vice versa. For example

```
void *pv = reinterpret_cast<void *> (0x00fffd);
int ptr = reinterpret_cast<int> (pv);
```

reinterpret_cast can also be used for conversions between different types of function pointers. The result of using the resultant pointer to call a function with a non-matching type is undefined.

Do not use reinterpret_cast instead of static_cast—the results might be undefined. For example, using reinterpret_cast to navigate through the class hierarchy of a multiply-inherited object is likely to yield the wrong result. Consider the following:

```
class A
{
private:
  int n;
};
class B
{
private:
  char c;

};

class C: public A, public B
{};
```

```
void func(B * pb)
{
  C *pc1 = static_cast<C*> (pb); //correct offset adjustment
  C *pc2 = reinterpret_cast<C*> (pb); //no offset calculated
}
int main()
{
 B b;
 func(&b);
}
```

On my machine, pc1 is assigned the value 0x0064fdf0, whereas pc2 is assigned 0x0064fdf4. This demonstrates the difference between the two cast operators. Using the information that is available at compile time, static_cast converts a pointer to B to a pointer to C. It does so by causing pc1 to point at the start of C by subtracting the offset of the subobject B. On the other hand, reinterpret_cast simply assigns the binary value of pb to pc2, without any further adjustments; for this reason, it yields the wrong result.

dynamic_cast

In pre-standard C++, as was noted earlier, C-style cast was used to perform a dynamic cast as well. The cast was either static or dynamic, depending on the type of the operand. The Standardization committee, however, opposed this approach. An expensive runtime operation that looked exactly like a static cast (that is, penalty-free) can mislead the users. For this purpose, a new operator was introduced to the language: dynamic_cast (dynamic_cast is discussed in further detail in Chapter 7, "Runtime Type Information"). The name and the syntax of dynamic_cast were chosen to look markedly different from C-style cast. All other new typecast operators follow this model. Following is an example of dynamic_cast:

```
Derived *p = dynamic_cast<Derived *> (&base); //pointer form
Derived & rd = dynamic_cast<Derived &> (base); //reference form
```

Conclusions

The new typecasting operators are clearer and more explicit in their intended purpose. A name such as dynamic_cast warns its users about its incurred runtime overhead. Most importantly, though, the new cast operators are safer because they give the compiler a chance to detect the programmer's mistakes.

Users might find the proliferation of cast operators somewhat confusing. In particular, the choice between static_cast and reinterpret_cast might not seem immediately clear. How to choose? As a rule, static_cast is the first choice. If the compiler refuses to accept it, use reinterpret_cast instead.

Built-in bool Type

The built-in bool data type was added to the Standard after consideration of several other proposals. None of these was found satisfactory. Following is an overview of some of these proposals, which is in turn followed by a discussion of the characteristics of the bool type.

typedef Boolean

One suggestion was to use a typedef for a Boolean data type:

```
typedef int bool;
```

However, a typedef that relies on another built-in type of the language renders the Boolean type unusable with some language features. For example, using it in function overloading can result in ambiguities:

```
void f(bool);
void f(int);//error, redefinition of void f(bool);
```

In addition, a typedef is not strongly typed. Consequently, it is impossible to ensure that only Boolean values are assigned to it in a context that requires Boolean values.

enum Type

An alternative solution was to use an enum type:

```
enum bool { false, true};
```

enums are strongly typed. However, the committee wanted to ensure backward compatibility with old code that used int values as a Boolean data type. For example

```
#include <ctype.h>
enum bool {false, true};
void f()
{
  enum bool b;
  b = islower('a'); //compile time error, int assigned to an enum
}
```

Class bool

A third suggestion was to use a class such as the following:

```
class bool
{
private:
  int val;
public:
  operator int();
};
```

Such a class guarantees type uniqueness, so it can be used to overload functions and to specialize templates. In addition, it is backward compatible with Boolean integers. There are, however, several drawbacks to the class approach. First, users are required to #include a dedicated header and to link their programs with the compiled code of the class. Worse yet, the conversion operator might interfere with user-defined conversion operators that are defined in other classes. Finally, a full-blown class that defines constructors and conversion operators is significantly less efficient than a fundamental type. For these reasons, the Standardization committee decided to add a new built-in type.

A Built-in Type bool

bool is an implementation-dependent integral type that can hold either a true or a false value. A standardized Boolean type has several advantages:

- **Portability**—All Standard compliant compilers support bool type. When code is ported to different platforms, it will work as expected.
- **Readability**—The use of explicit keywords such as true, false, and bool is self-documenting and is more evident than the use of int values.
- **Type Distinctness**—Because bool is a distinct type, the following functions are now also distinct:
  ```
  void f(bool b);
  void f(int n);
  ```
- **Performance**—Memory usage can be optimized by the implementation, which is allowed to use a single byte to represent a bool instead of an int. In addition, the use of a built-in type rather than a class also ensures the highest performance.

With the introduction of the bool data type, built-in operators were modified accordingly to work with bool values. The logical operators &&, ¦¦, and ! now take bool values as arguments and return bool results. Similarly, the relational operators <, >, <=, >=, ==, and != return bool results. In addition, iostream classes were adjusted to support the new type.

Viewing bool Variables as Literals

By default, iostream objects display bool variables as 0 and 1. It is possible to override the default setting by inserting the formatting flag boolalpha to the stream object. Subsequently, the symbolic representations false and true are displayed instead of 0 and 1. For example

```
#include <iostream>
using namespace std;
int main()
{
  bool b = true;
  cout<<b;  // default setting; display 1
  cout<<boolalpha; //henceforth, display 'true' and 'false' instead of 1 and 0
  cout<<b;  // output: true
  cout<<!b;  // output: false
  return 0;
}
```

Exception Handling

Exception handling is used to report and handle runtime errors. Supplementary features, namely *exception specifications* and *function* try *blocks*, were added to the Standard in recent years. The following sections provide a brief overview of these features. (Exception handling and the supplementary features are discussed in more detail in Chapter 6, "Exception Handling.")

Exception Specification

A function can indicate the potential exceptions it can throw by specifying a list of these exceptions. Exception specifications are particularly useful when users of such a function can only view its prototype but cannot access its source file. Following is an example of specifying an exception:

```
class Zerodivide{/*..*/};
int divide (int, int) throw(Zerodivide);   //function may throw an exception
                                           //of type Zerodivide, but no other
```

Function try Blocks

A *function* try *block* is a function whose body consists of a try block and its associated handlers. A function try block enables you to catch exceptions that might be thrown by a base class constructor or by a constructor of a member object. The original specification of exception handling did not enable users to handle exceptions thrown from a constructor or a member initialization list locally; a function try block fixes this loophole. Following is an example of a function try block:

```
class Err{};
A::A(const string& s) throw (Err);   //allowed to throw only
                                     //an exception of type Err

  try
    : str(s) //str's constructor might throw a bad_alloc
             //exception, which violates C's exception specification

    {
      // constructor function body
    }
    catch (...) //we get here when an exception is thrown
                //during the construction of str or C
    {
      throw Err(); //replace bad_alloc exception with an Err exception
    }
```

Memory Management

The Standard now defines three different versions of operator new: plain new, nothrow new, and placement new. Each of these operators has an array version as well. The Standard also defines six matching types of operator delete that correspond the specific versions of new. Memory management and the recently added versions of new and delete are discussed in further detail in Chapter 11, "Memory Management."

Operator new Throws an Exception in Case of a Failure

In earlier stages of C++, operator new returned a NULL pointer when it failed to allocate the requested amount of memory. The C++ standardization committee changed the specification of operator new so that it throws an exception of type std::bad_alloc, rather than returning a NULL pointer, when it fails. A program that uses operator new directly or indirectly has to handle a potential std::bad_alloc exception. For example

```
void f(int size) //standard-conforming usage of operator new
{
  char *p = new char [size];
  //...use p safely
  delete [] p;
  return;
}
#include <stdexcept>
#include <iostream>
using namespace std;
const int BUF_SIZE = 1048576L;
int main()
{
  try
  {
    f(BUF_SIZE);
  }
  catch(bad_alloc& ex)   //handle exception thrown from f()
  {
    cout<<ex.what()<<endl;
    //...other diagnostics and remedies
  }
  return -1;
}
```

nothrow new

The Standard also defines an exception-free version of operator new, which returns a NULL pointer in case of a failure rather than throwing an exception. This version of new takes an additional argument named nothrow. For example

```
#include <new>
#include <string>
using namespace std;

void f(int size) // demonstrating nothrow new
{
  char *p = new (nothrow) char [size]; //array nothrow new
  if (p == 0)
  {
    //...use p
    delete p;
  }
```

```
  string *pstr = new (nothrow) string; //plain nothrow new
  if (pstr == 0)
  {
    //...use pstr
    delete [] pstr;
  }
  return;
}
```

Placement new

An additional version of operator new enables the user to construct an object at a pre-determined memory position. This version is called placement new. Following is an example of using placement new:

```
#include <new>
#include <iostream>
using namespace std;

void placement()
{
  int   *pi = new int;       //plain new
  int   *p = new (pi) int (5);  //placement new
  //...use p
  delete pi;
}
```

Constructors and Destructors

Fundamental types can be initialized by a special constructor. In addition, the Standard also defines a pseudo destructor for each of these types (see Chapter 4, "Special Member Functions: Default Constructor, Copy Constructor, Destructor, and Assignment Operator").

Constructors of Fundamental Types

Variables of fundamental types can be initialized by invoking their constructor explicitly. For example

```
  void f()
  {
    int n = int(); // zero initialized
    char c = char(); // also zero initialized
    double d = double(0.5); //other initializers are allowed
  }
```

This language extension enables uniform treatment in templates for fundamental types and user-defined types.

Explicit Constructors

A constructor that takes a single argument is, by default, an implicit conversion operator that converts its argument to an object of its class. In order to avoid such implicit conversions, a constructor that takes one argument can be declared `explicit`. For example

```
class C
{
public:
  explicit C(int size);  // disallow implicit conversion
};
```

Pseudo Destructors

A *pseudo destructor* is a syntactic construct whose sole purpose is to satisfy the need for generic algorithms and containers. It is a no-op code, and has no real effect on its object. For example

```
typedef int N;
void f()
{
  N i = 0;
  i.N::~N();  // pseudo destructor invocation
  i = 1;  // i was not affected by the invocation of the pseudo destructor
}
```

Local Definitions and Scoping Rules

The scoping rules for a variable that is defined in a `for` statement were changed. Additionally, it is now possible to define and initialize variables inside an `if` condition.

The Scope of a Local Loop Counter

C++ allows declaration of variables wherever they are needed, enabling immediate initializations. A good example is a loop counter, which can be declared inside a `for` statement. For example

```
void f()
{
  for (int i = 0; i < 10; i++) // i declared and initialized
                               // inside a for-statement
  {
    cout << i <<endl; //output 0 to 9
  }
  int n = i; //compilation error, i not in scope
}
```

In earlier stages of C++, a local variable declared in this way remained accessible in its enclosing block. This was a source for bugs and name hiding. Consequently, the standard has been revised to fix this loophole, so to speak; local variables that are created this way are inaccessible outside their `for` statement. In the preceding example, the variable i goes out of scope when the loop is exited.

Declaring Variables Inside an **if** Condition

You can define and initialize a variable inside the condition of an if statement. For example

```
class Base {/*..*/};
class Derived: public Base {/*..*/};
void func (Base& b)
{
  if ( Derived *pd = dynamic_cast < Derived* > (&b) ) //declaration
                                           // inside an if-condition
  {
    //dynamic_cast was successful; use pd here
    return;
  }//pd goes out of scope at this point

  //otherwise dynamic_cast failed; variable pd is not in scope
}
```

The advantage of declaring the pointer pd locally is obvious: It is always initialized with an appropriate value, and it isn't visible to other parts of the program that are not to use it (see Chapter 12, "Optimizing Your Code").

Namespaces

Namespaces were the latest feature to be added to the language. Namespaces are used to prevent name conflicts and to facilitate configuration management and version control in large-scale projects. Most of the components of the Standard Library are grouped under namespace std. There are three methods for injecting namespace members into a scope: a using directive, a using declaration, or a fully qualified name. Argument-dependent lookup, or Koenig lookup, simplifies the use of namespaces by automating the name lookup process. Namespaces are discussed in more detail in Chapter 8, "Namespaces."

Templates

A *template* is a mold from which related functions or classes are instantiated. Templates have come a long way since they were first introduced to the language in 1991. Back then, they were merely clever macros. However, the adoption of STL required considerable extensions to this feature. An overview of these extensions is provided in the following sections. Templates are discussed in detail in Chapter 9, "Templates."

Template-Template Argument

A template can now take a template as an argument. For example

```
int send(const std::vector<char*>& );
int main()
{
```

```
std::vector <std::vector<char*> > msg_que(10);
//...fill msg_que

for (int i =0; i < 10; i++) //transmit messages
  send(msg_que[i]);
return 0;
}
```

Default Type Arguments

Templates can have default type arguments. For example
```
template <class T, class S = size_t > class C  //using a default type
{/**/};
```

Member Templates

Templates can be nested; a template can be declared within another class or a class template. Such a template is called a *member template*. Following is an example:
```
template<class T> class C
{
public:
  template<class T2> int func(const T2&); //declaration of a member template
  //...
};

template<class T> template<class T2> int C<T>::func(const T2& s) // definition
{
   //...
}
```

The typename Keyword

To support member templates and template inheritance, the keyword typename was added to the language. By default, the compiler assumes that a qualified name refers to a non-type. The typename keyword instructs the compiler to supersede this default interpretation and resolve the ambiguity in favor of a typename instead.

Exported Templates

It is possible to compile a template definition only once, and to subsequently use only the template's declaration in other translation units. To compile a template separately and then use its declaration, the template has to be *exported*. This is done by preceding the template's definition with the keyword export.

The Standard Template Library

According to Bjarne Stroustrup, the most important change in C++ since 1991 is not a language change; it is the addition of the Standard Library. The *Standard Template*

Library, or *STL*, comprises a substantial part of the Standard Library. STL is collection of generic containers—such as vector, list, and stack—and a rich collection of generic algorithms for sorting, finding, merging, and transforming these containers. Chapter 10, "STL and Generic Programming," is dedicated to STL.

Internationalization and Localization

The current C++ Standard is an international Standard approved by ISO. To qualify as such, Standard C++ has been fully internationalized. Internationalization consists of several modifications and extensions. These include the addition of the keyword wchar_t (wchar_t was already defined in ISO C as a typedef but it wasn't a reserved keyword). In addition, the standard stream and string classes have been templatized to support both narrow and wide characters. Finally, the <locale> library defines template classes and declares functions that encapsulate and manipulate locale-related information such as monetary, numeric, and time conventions. The locale feature sets are encapsulated in classes (or *facets*) that the users can extend.

Wide Character Streams

C++ provides four standard I/O streams that are automatically instantiated before a program's outset. They are defined in the header <iostream>:

```
cin    // standard input stream of char
cout   // standard output stream of char
cerr   // standard unbuffered output stream for error messages
clog   // standard output stream for error messages
```

Each of these four streams now has a corresponding wide-character version:

```
wcin
wcout
wcerr
wclog
```

Miscellaneous

Two additional extensions were recently added to the Standard: the initialization of const static data members inside the class body and the mutable storage specifier. Both of these extensions are discussed in the following sections.

Initialization of const static Data Members

const static data members of an integral type can now be initialized inside their class. In this case, the initialization is also a definition, so no further definitions are required outside the class body. For example

```
#include <string>
class Buff
{
private:
```

```
static const int MAX = 512; // initialization +definition
static const char flag = 'a'; // initialization +definition
static const std::string msg; //non-integral type; must be defined outside
                             //the class body
//..
};
const std::string Buff::msg = "hello";
```

A `mutable` Object Member

A `const` member function cannot modify the state of its object. However, auxiliary data members (flags, reference counters) sometimes have to be modified by a `const` member function. Such data members can be declared `mutable`. A `mutable` member is never `const`, even if its object is `const`; therefore, it can be modified by a `const` member function. The following example demonstrates the use of this feature:

```
class Buffer
{
private:
  void * data;  //raw data buffer to be transmitted on some network
  size_t size;
  mutable int crc;//used to verify that no errors occurred during transmission
public:
  int GetCrc() const;
  void Transmit() const; //computation of crc is done here
};
void f()
{
  Buffer buffer;
  //...fill buffer with data
  buffer.Transmit(); //crc can be modified here; non-mutable members may not
}
```

There is no point in calculating the `crc` value every time a few more bytes are appended to `buffer`. Instead, it is computed by the member function `Transmit()` right before `buffer` is sent. However, `Transmit()` is not supposed to modify its object's state; therefore, it is declared as a `const` member function. In order to allow assignment of the correct `crc` value, the data member `crc` is declared `mutable`; hence, it can be modified by a `const` member function.

Deprecated Feature

A *deprecated feature* is one that the current edition of the Standard regards as normative, but that is not guaranteed to be part of the Standard in future revisions. Again, this is somewhat understating the intent of this definition. One of the consequences of the evolution and standardization of a programming language is the gradual removal of undesirable, dangerous, or redundant features and constructs. By deprecating a feature, the standardization committee expresses the desire to have the feature removed from the language. Removing it from the language altogether is impractical because existing code will not compile anymore. The deprecation gives the user sufficient time to replace a deprecated feature with a Standard-endorsed feature. The Standard lists the features that are discussed in the following sections as deprecated.

Use of an Operand of Type **bool** with the Postfix ++ Operator

Applying postfix ++ to a variable of type bool is still allowed for backward compatibility with old code that uses plain int or some typedef, as in

```
bool done = false;
while(!done)
{
  if(condition)
    //...do something
  else done++; //deprecated
}
```

Incrementing a bool always yields true, regardless of the original value. However, this practice is deprecated; therefore, it might not be supported in the future. Remember that applying -- (decrement operator) to a bool variable is illegal.

Use of **static** to Declare Objects in a File Scope

The use of the keyword static to declare a function or an object local to a translation unit is deprecated. Instead, use an *unnamed namespace* for that purpose (more on this in Chapter 8).

Access Declarations

The access of a member of a base class can be changed in a derived class by an *access declaration*. For example

```
class A
{
public:
 int k;
 int l;
};

class D : public A
{
private:
   A::l; // access declaration changes access of A::l to private; deprecated
};
```

The use of access declarations is deprecated. Use a using *declaration* instead:

```
class D : public A // using-declaration version
{
private:
   using A::l; // using declaration changes the access of A::l to private
};
```

```
void func()
{
  D d;
  d.l = 0; //error; cannot access private member
}
```

Implicit Conversion from const to non-const Qualification for String Literals

A string literal can be implicitly converted from type pointer to const char to type pointer to char. Similarly, a wide string literal can be implicitly converted from type pointer to const wchar_t to pointer to wchar_t. For example

```
char *s = "abc"; //string literal implicitly converted to non-const; deprecated
```

The type of the literal "abc" is const char[], but s is a pointer to non-const char. Such implicit conversions from const to non-const qualifications for string literals are deprecated because they might lead to the following erroneous code:

```
strcpy(s, "cde"); //undefined behavior
```

The preferred form is

```
const char *s = "abc"; //OK
```

Standard C Headers in the form <name.h>

For compatibility with the Standard C library, C++ still supports the naming convention of C headers in the form <xxx.h>—but this naming convention is now deprecated (this is discussed in more detail in Chapter 8). For example

```
#include <stdlib.h> //deprecated
```

Use the newer naming convention, <cxxx>, instead:

```
#include <cstdlib> //OK,  'c' prefixed and ".h" omitted
```

The reason for this is that ".h" headers inject all their names into the global namespace, whereas the newer convention headers, <cname>, keep their names in namespace std.

Implicit int Declarations

The default type for missing declarations such as the following is int:

```
static k =0; //'int' type deduced; deprecated
const c =0; //'int' type deduced; deprecated
```

This convention is now considered deprecated. Instead, use explicit type names:

```
static int k =5;
const int c = 0;
```

Other Deprecated Features

The Standard deprecates some of the members of old `iostream` classes (article 4.6). In addition, it deprecates three types in the header `<strstream>` that associate stream buffers with character array objects (article 4.7).

From a user's point of view, deprecated features are not to be used in new code because future versions of the language will flag it as an error. In the interim period, compilers can issue a warning about its use.

Conclusions

As you have seen, standard C++ is quite different from what it used to be four, five, or ten years ago. Many of the changes and modifications have been initiated by software vendors (the `bool` data type, for instance). Others have been initiated by the Standardization committee (for example, the new cast operators and STL). During the hectic standardization process, complaints about "randomly accepted changes" on the one hand, and "missing features" on the other hand, were often heard. However, the Standardization committee has been very thoughtful and prudent in selecting these extensions and modifications. Fortunately, the approval of the Standard by ISO in 1998 ensures its stability for at least five years. This freeze period enables both compiler vendors and language users to digest the current Standard and use it effectively. In doing so, one usually finds that C++ is better today than it ever was.

II

OO Design and Programming

3

Operator Overloading

A BUILT-IN OPERATOR CAN BE extended to support user-defined types. Such an extension *overloads* the predefined meaning of an operator rather than overrides it. Although ordinary functions can offer the same functionality, operator overloading provides a uniform notational convention that is clearer than the ordinary function call syntax. For example

```
Monday < Tuesday; //overloaded <
Greater_than(Monday, Tuesday);
```

The history of operator overloading can be traced back to the early days of Fortran. Fortran, the first high-level programming language, presented the concept of operator overloading in a way that was revolutionary back in the mid-1950s. For the first time, built-in operators such as + or - could be applied to various data types: integers, real and complex. Until then, assembly languages—which didn't even support operator notation—had been the only choice for programmers. Fortran's operator overloading was limited to a fixed set of built-in data types; they could not be extended by the programmer. Object-based programming languages offered user-defined overloaded operators. In such languages, it is possible to associate a set of operators with a user-defined type. Object-oriented languages usually incorporate operator overloading as well.

The capability to redefine the meaning of a built-in operator in C++ was a source of criticism. People—mostly C programmers making the migration to C++—felt that overloading an operator was as dangerous as enabling the programmer to add, remove, or change keywords of the language. Still, notwithstanding the potential Tower of Babel that might arise as a result, operator overloading is one of the most fundamental features of C++ and is mandatory for generic programming (generic programming is discussed in Chapter 10, "STL and Generic Programming"). Today, even languages that tried to make do without operator overloading are in the process of adding this feature.

This chapter explores the benefits as well as the potential problems of operator overloading. It also discusses the few restrictions that apply to operator overloading. Finally, it presents conversion operators, which are a special form of overloaded operators.

An overloaded operator is essentially a function whose name is an operator preceded by the keyword `operator`. For example

```
class Book
{
private:
  long ISBN;
public:
//...
  long get_ISBN() const { return ISBN;}
};

bool operator < (const Book& b1, const Book& b2) // overload operator <
{
  return b1.get_ISBN() < b2.get_ISBN();
}
```

Operator Overloading Rules of Thumb

C++ enforces few restrictions on operator overloading. For instance, it does not prohibit a programmer from overloading the operator ++ in order to perform a decrement operation on its object (to the dismay of its users, who would instead expect operator ++ to perform an increment operation). Such misuses and puns can lead to a cryptic coding style that is almost unintelligible. Often, the source code that contains the definition of an overloaded operator is not accessible to its users; therefore, overloading an operator in an unexpected, nonintuitive manner is not recommended.

The other extreme, avoiding operator overloading altogether, is not a practical choice either because it means giving up an important tool for data abstraction and generic programming. When you are overloading an operator to support a user-defined type, therefore, it is recommended that you adhere to the basic semantics of the corresponding built-in operator. In other words, an overloaded operator has the same side effects on its operands and manifests the same interface as does the corresponding built-in operator.

Members and Nonmembers

Most of the overloaded operators can be declared either as nonstatic class members or as nonmember functions. In the following example, the operator == is overloaded as a nonstatic class member:

```
class Date
{
private:
  int day;
  int month;
  int year;
public:
  bool operator == (const Date & d ); // 1: member function
};
```

Alternatively, it can be declared as a friend function (the criteria for choosing between a member and a friend will be discussed later in this chapter):

```
bool operator ==( const Date & d1, const Date& d2); // 2: nonmember function
class Date
{
private:
  int day;
  int month;
  int year;
public:
  friend bool operator ==( const Date & d1, const Date& d2);
};
```

Nonetheless, the operators [ ], ( ), =, and -> can only be declared as nonstatic member functions; this ensures that their first operand is an lvalue.

Operator's Interface

When you overload an operator, adhere to the interface of its built-in counterpart. The interface of an operator consists of the number of operands to which it applies, whether any of these operands can be altered by the operator, and the result that is returned by the operator. For example, consider operator ==. Its built-in version can be applied to a wide variety of fundamental types, including int, bool, float, and char, and to pointers. The underlying computation process that is required for testing whether the operands of operator == are equal is an implementation detail. However, it can be generalized that the built-in == operator tests its left and right operands for equality and returns a bool value as its result. It is important to note also that operator == does not modify any of its operands; in addition, the order of the operands is immaterial in the case of operator ==. An overloaded operator == should conform to this behavior, too.

Operator Associativity

Operator == is binary and symmetrical. An overloaded version of == conforms to these qualities. It takes two operands, which are of the same type. Indeed, one can use operator == to test the equality of two operands of distinct fundamental types, for example char and int. However, C++ automatically applies *integral promotion* to the operands in this case; as a result, the seemingly distinct types are promoted to a single common type before they are compared. The symmetrical quality implies that an overloaded operator == is to be defined as a friend function rather than a member function. So that you can see why, here's a comparison of two different versions of the same overloaded operator ==:

```
class Date
{
private:
  int day;
  int month;
  int year;
public:
  Date();
  bool  operator == (const Date & d) const;  // 1 asymmetrical
  friend bool operator ==(const Date& d1, const Date& d2); //2 symmetrical
};

bool operator ==(const Date& d1, const Date& d2);
```

The overloaded operator == that is declared as a member function in (1) is inconsistent with the built-in operator == because it takes two arguments of different types. The compiler transforms the member operator == into the following:

```
bool  Date::operator == (const Date *const,  const Date&) const;
```

The first argument is a const this pointer that points to a const object (remember that this is always a const pointer; it points to a const object when the member function is also const). The second argument is a reference to const Date. Clearly, these are two distinct types for which no standard conversion exists. On the other hand, the friend version takes two arguments of the same type. There are practical implications to favoring the friend version over the member function. STL algorithms rely on a symmetrical version of the overloaded operator ==. For example, containers that store objects that do not have symmetrical operator == cannot be sorted.

Another example, built-in operator +=, which also takes two operands, modifies its left operand but leaves the right operand unchanged. The interface of an overloaded += needs to reflect the fact that it modifies its object but not its right operand. This is reflected by the declaration of the function parameter as const, whereas the function itself is a non-const member function. For example

```
class Date
{
private:
```

```
    int day;
    int month;
    int year;
public:
    Date();
    //built-in += changes its left operand but not its right one
    //the same behavior is maintained here
    Date & operator += (const Date & d);
};
```

To conclude, it can be said that every overloaded operator must implement an interface that is similar to the one that is manifested by the built-in operator. The implementer is free to define the underlying operation and hide its details—as long as it conforms to the interface.

Restrictions on Operator Overloading

As was previously noted, an overloaded operator is a function that is declared with the operator keyword, immediately followed by an *operator id*. An operator id can be one of the following:

```
new   delete   new[]    delete[]
+     -    *    /    %    ^    &    |    ~
!     =    <    >    +=   -=   *=   /=   %=
^=    &=   |=   <<   >>   >>=  <<=  ==   !=
<=    >=   &&   ||   ++   --   ,    ->*  ->
()    []
```

In addition, the following operators can be overloaded both in their unary and binary forms:

```
+     -    *    &
```

Overloaded operators are inherited in the same manner as other base class functions. Note that these rules do not apply to the assignment operator, which is implicitly declared for a class if it is not declared by the user. Therefore, a base class assignment operator is always hidden by the copy assignment operator of the derived class. (The assignment operator is discussed in Chapter 4, "Special Member Functions: Default Constructor, Copy Constructor, Destructor, and Assignment Operator.")

Operators Can Only Be Overloaded for User-Defined Types

An overloaded operator must take at least one argument of a user-defined type (operators new and delete are an exception—see Chapter 11, "Memory Management," for more details). This rule ensures that users cannot alter the meaning of expressions that contain only fundamental types. For example

```
int i,j,k;
k = i + j; //always uses built-in = and +
```

Invention of New Operators Is Not Allowed

An overloaded operator extends a built-in one, so you cannot introduce new operators into the language (conversion operators differ from ordinary overloaded operators in this respect). The following example attempts to overload the @ operator, but does not compile for that reason:

```
void operator @ (int); //illegal, @ is not a built-in operator or a type name
```

Precedence and Argument Number

Neither the precedence nor the number of arguments of an operator can be altered. For example, an overloaded && must have exactly two arguments—as does the built-in && operator. In addition, the precedence of an operator cannot be altered when it is overloaded. A sequence of two or more overloaded operators, for instance t2<t1/t2, is evaluated according to the precedence rules of the built-in operators. Because the division operator ranks higher than the less than operator, the expression is always interpreted as t2<(t1/t2).

Default Parameters

Unlike ordinary functions, overloaded operators cannot declare a parameter with a default value (operator () is the exception to this rule; it is discussed later).

```
class Date
{
private:
  int day;
  int month;
  int year;
public:
  Date & operator += (const Date & d = Date() ); //error, default argument
};
```

This rule might seem arbitrary, but it captures the behavior of built-in operators, which never have default operands either.

Operators That Cannot Be Overloaded

There are several operators that cannot be overloaded. They are characterized by the fact that they take a name, rather than an object, as their right operand. These operators are:

- Direct member access, operator .
- Dereference pointer to class member, operator .*
- Scope resolution, operator ::
- Size of, operator sizeof

The conditional operator ?: cannot be overloaded either.

Additionally, the new type cast operators—`static_cast<>`, `dynamic_cast<>`, `reinterpret_cast<>`, and `const_cast<>`—and the # and ## preprocessor tokens cannot be overloaded.

Conversion Operators

It is not uncommon to find C++ and C code used together. For instance, legacy systems that were originally written in C can be wrapped by an object-oriented interface. Such bilingual systems often need to support a dual interface at the same time—one that caters to an object-oriented environment and another that caters to a C environment. Classes that implement specific numeric entities—such as complex numbers and binary numbers—and nibbles also tend to use conversion operators to enable smoother interaction with fundamental types.

Strings are a classic example of the need for a dual interface. A string object might have to be used in contexts that support only null-terminated `char` arrays. For example

```
class Mystring
{
private:
  char *s;
  int size;
public:
  Mystring(const char *);
  Mystring();
//...
};

#include <cstring>
#include "Mystring.h"
using namespace std;
int main()
{
  Mystring str("hello world");
  int n = strcmp(str, "Hello");  //compile time error:
                                 //str is not of  type const char *

  return 0;
}
```

C++ offers an automatic means of type conversion for such cases. A conversion operator can be thought of as a user-defined typecasting operator; it converts its object to a different type in contexts that require that specific type. The conversion is done automatically. For example

```
class Mystring    //now with conversion operator
{
private:
  char *s;
  int size;
```

```
public:
  Mystring();
  operator const char * () {return s; } //convert Mystring  to a C-string
//...
};
```

```
int n = strcmp(str, "Hello"); //OK, automatic conversion of str to const char *
```

Conversion operators differ from ordinary overloaded operators in two ways. First, a conversion operator does not have a return value (not even void). The return value is deduced from the operator's name.

Secondly, a conversion operator takes no arguments.

Conversion operators can convert their objects to any given type, fundamental and user-defined alike:

```
struct DateRep  //legacy C code
{
  char day;
  char month;
  short year;
};
```

```
class Date // object-oriented wrapper
{
private:
  DateRep dr;
public:
  operator DateRep () const { return dr;} // automatic conversion to DateRep
};
```

```
extern "C" int transmit_date(DateRep);  // C-based communication API function


int main()
{
  Date d;
  //...use d

  //transmit date object as a binary stream to a remote client
  int ret_stat = transmit_date(d); //using legacy communication API
  return 0;
}
```

Standard Versus User-Defined Conversions

The interaction of a user-defined conversion with a standard conversion can cause undesirable surprises and side effects, and therefore must be used with caution. Examine the following concrete example.

A non-explicit constructor that takes a single argument is also a conversion operator, which casts its argument to an object of this class. When the compiler has to resolve an overloaded function call, it takes into consideration such user-defined conversions in addition to the standard ones. For example

```
class Numeric
{
private:
  float f;
public:
  Numeric(float ff): f(ff) {} //constructor is also a float-to-Numeric
                              // conversion operator
};

void f(Numeric);

Numeric num(0.05);
f(5.f);  //OK, calls void f(Numeric). Numeric's constructor
         //converts argument to a Numeric object
```

Suppose you add at a later stage another overloaded version of f():

```
void f (double);
```

Now the same function call resolves differently:

```
f(5.f); // now calls f(double), not f(Numeric)
```

This is because float is promoted to double automatically in order to match an overloaded function signature. This is a standard type conversion. On the other hand, the conversion of float to Numeric is a user-defined conversion. User-defined conversions rank lower than standard conversions in overload resolution; as a result, the function call resolves differently.

Because of this phenomenon and others, conversion operators have been severely criticized. Some programming schools ban their usage altogether. However, conversion operators are a valuable—and sometimes inevitable—tool for bridging between dual interfaces, as you have seen.

Postfix and Prefix Operators

For primitive types, C++ distinguishes between ++x; and x++; as well as between --x; and x--;. Under some circumstances, objects have to distinguish between prefix and postfix overloaded operators as well (for example, as an optimization measure; see Chapter 12, "Optimizing Your Code"). Postfix operators are declared with a dummy int argument, whereas their prefix counterparts take no arguments. For example

```
class Date
{
public:
  Date& operator++(); //prefix
  Date& operator--(); //prefix
  Date& operator++(int unused); //postfix
  Date& operator--(int unused); //postfix
```

```
};

void f()
{
Date d, d1;
d1 = ++d;//prefix: first increment d and then assign to d1
d1 = d++; //postfix; first assign, increment d afterward
}
```

Using Function Call Syntax

An overloaded operator call is merely "syntactic sugar" for an ordinary function call.
You can use the explicit function call instead of the operator syntax as follows:

```
bool operator==(const Date& d1, const Date& d2);

void f()
{
  Date d, d1;
  bool equal;
  d1.operator++(0); // equivalent to: d1++;
  d1.operator++(); // equivalent to: ++d1;
  equal = operator==(d, d1);// equivalent to: d==d1;
  Date&(Date::*pmf) (); //pointer to member function
  pmf = & Date::operator++;
}
```

Consistent Operator Overloading

Whenever you overload operators such as + or -, it might become necessary to support the corresponding += and -= operators as well. The compiler does not do that for
you automatically. Consider the following example:

```
class Date
{
public:
  Date& operator + (const Date& d);  //note: operator += not defined
};

Date d1, d2;
d1 = d1 + d2; //fine; uses overloaded + and default assignment operator
d1 += d2; //compile time error: 'no user defined operator += for class Date'
```

Theoretically, the compiler could synthesize a compound operator += by combining
the assignment operator and the overloaded + operator so that the expression d1 +=
d2; is automatically expanded into d1 = d1+d2;. However, this is undesirable because
the automatic expansion might be less efficient than a user-defined version of the
operator. An automated version creates a temporary object, whereas a user-defined
version can avoid it. Moreover, it is not difficult to think of situations in which a class
has an overloaded operator +, but does not have operator += intentionally.

Returning Objects by Value

For the sake of efficiency, large objects are usually passed to—or returned from—a function by reference or by their addresses. There are, however, a few circumstances in which the best choice is still to return an object by value. Operator + is an example of this situation. It has to return a result object, but it cannot modify any of its operands. The seemingly natural choice is to allocate the result object on the free store and return its address. Nevertheless, this is not such a good idea. Dynamic memory allocation is significantly slower than local storage. It also might fail and throw an exception, which then has to be caught and handled. Even worse, this solution is error prone because it is unclear who is responsible for deleting this object—the creator or the user?

Another solution is to use a static object and return it by reference. For example

```
class Year
{
private:
  int year;
public:
  Year(int y = 0) : year(y) {}
  Year& operator + (const Year& other) const; //returns a reference to
                                              //a local static Year

  int getYear() const;
  void setYear(int y);
};

Year& Year::operator + (const Year& other) const
{
  static Year result;
  result = Year(this->getYear() + other.getYear() );
  return result;
}
```

Static objects solve the ownership problem, but they are still problematic: On each invocation of the overloaded operator, the same instance of the static object is being modified and returned to the caller. The same object can be returned by reference to several more users, who do not know that they are holding a shared instance that has just been modified behind their back.

Finally, the safest and most efficient solution is still to return the result object by value:

```
class Year
{
private:
  int year;
public:
  Year(int y = 0) : year(y) {}
  Year operator + (const Year& other) const; //return Year object by value
  int getYear() const;
  void setYear(int y);
```

```
};

Year Year::operator + (const Year& other) const
{
  return Year(this->getYear() + other.getYear() );
}
```

Multiple Overloading

Overloaded operators obey the rules of function overloading. Therefore, it is possible to overload an operator more than once. When is it useful? Consider the following Month class and its associated operator ==:

```
class Month
{
private:
  int m;
public:
  Month(int m = 0);
};

bool operator == (const Month& m1, const Month &m2);
```

It is possible to use the overloaded operator == to compare a plain int value and a Month object due to the implicit conversion of int to Month. For example

```
void f()
{
  int n = 7;
  Month June(6);
  bool same =
    (June == n); //calls bool operator == (const Month& m1, const Month &m2);
}
```

This works fine, but it's inefficient: The argument n is first converted to a temporary Month object, which is then compared with the object June. You can avoid the unnecessary construction of a temporary object by defining additional overloaded versions of operator ==:

```
bool operator == (int m, const Month& month);
bool operator == (const Month& month, int m);
```

Consequently, the expression June == n will now invoke the following overloaded operator:

```
bool operator == (const Month& month, int m);
```

This overloaded version does not create a temporary object, so it's more efficient. The same performance considerations led the C++ Standardization committee to define three distinct versions of operator == for std::string (see Chapter 10, "STL and Generic Programming") and other classes of the Standard Library.

Overloading Operators for Other User-Defined Types

You can overload an operator for enum types as well. For example, it may be useful to overload operators such as ++ and -- so that they can iterate through the enumerator values of a given enum type. You can do it like this:

```
#include <iostream>
using namespace std;

enum Days
{
  Monday,
  Tuesday,
  Wednesday,
  Thursday,
  Friday,
  Saturday,
  Sunday
};

Days& operator++(Days& d, int)  // postfix ++
{
  if (d == Sunday)
    return d = Monday; //rollover
  int temp = d; //convert to an int
  return d = static_cast<Days> (++temp);
}

int main()
{
 Days day = Monday;
 for (;;) //display days as integers
 {
   cout<< day <<endl;
   day++;
   if (day == Sunday)
     break;
 }
 return 0;
}
```

If you prefer to view the enumerators in their symbolic representation rather than as integers, you can overload the operator << as well:

```
ostream& operator<<(ostream& os, Days d) //display Days in symbolic form
{
  switch(d)
  {
  case Monday:
    return os<<"Monday";
  case Tuesday:
```

```
        return os<<"Tuesday";
      case Wednesday:
        return os<<"Wednesday";
      case Thursday:
        return os<<"Thursady";
      case Friday:
        return os<<"Friday";
      case Saturday:
        return  os<<"Satrurday";
      case Sunday:
        return os<<"Sunday";
      default:
        return os<<"Unknown";
      }
    }
```

Overloading the Subscript Operator

For various classes that contain arrays of elements, it's handy to overload the subscript operator to access a single element. Remember always to define two versions of the subscript operator: a const version and a non-const version. For example

```
class Ptr_collection
{
private :
 void **ptr_array;
 int elements;
public:
  Ptr_collection() {}
  //...
  void * operator [] (int index) { return ptr_array[index];}
  const void * operator [] (int index) const { return ptr_array[index];}
};

void f(const Ptr_collection & pointers)
{
  const void *p = pointers[0]; //calls const version of operator []
  if ( p == 0)
    return;
  else
  {
    //...use p
  }
}
```

Function Objects

A function object is implemented as a class that contains an overloaded version of the function call operator. An instance of such a class can be used just like a function.

Ordinary functions can have any number of arguments; therefore, operator () is exceptional among other operators because it can have an arbitrary number of parameters. In addition, it can have default arguments. In the following example, a function object implements a generic increment function:

```
#include <iostream>
using namespace std;

class increment
{
  //a generic increment function
  public : template < class T > T operator()  (T t) const { return ++t;}
};

void f(int n, const increment& incr)
{
  cout << incr(n); //output 1
}

int  main()
{
  int i = 0;
  increment incr;
  f(i, incr);
  return 0;
}
```

Conclusions

The concept of operator overloading is neither new nor C++ exclusive. It is one of the most fundamental facilities for implementing abstract data types and compound classes. In many ways, overloaded operators in C++ behave like ordinary member functions: They are inherited, they can be overloaded more than once, and they can be declared as either nonstatic members or as nonmember functions. However, several restrictions apply to overloaded operators. An overloaded operator has a fixed number of parameters, and it cannot have default arguments. In addition, the associativity and the precedence of an operator cannot be altered. Built-in operators have an interface, consisting of the number of operands to which the operator can be applied, whether the operator modifies any of its operands, and the result that is returned by the operator. When you are overloading an operator, it is recommended that you conform to its built-in interface.

Conversion operators are a special type of overloaded operators. They differ from ordinary overloaded operators in two respects: They do not have a return value and they do not take any arguments.

4

Special Member Functions: Default Constructor, Copy Constructor, Destructor, and Assignment Operator

O BJECTS ARE THE FUNDAMENTAL UNIT of abstraction in object-oriented programming. An object, in the broader sense, is a region of memory storage. Class objects have properties that are determined when the object is created. Conceptually, every class object has four *special member functions*: default constructor, copy constructor, assignment operator, and destructor. If these members are not explicitly declared by the programmer, the implementation implicitly declares them. This chapter surveys the semantics of the special member functions and their role in class design and implementation. This chapter also examines several techniques and guidelines for effective use of the special member functions.

Constructors

A constructor is used to initialize an object. A default constructor is one that can be invoked without any arguments. If there is no user-declared constructor for a class, and if the class does not contain const or reference data members, the implementation implicitly declares a default constructor for it.

An implicitly-declared default constructor is an inline public member of its class; it performs the initialization operations that are needed by the implementation to create an object of this type. Note, however, that these operations do not involve initialization of user-declared data members or allocation of memory from the free store. For example

```
class C
{
private:
  int n;
  char *p;
public:
  virtual ~C() {}
};

void f()
{
  C obj;  // 1 implicitly-defined constructor is invoked
}
```

The programmer did not declare a constructor in class C—an implicit default constructor was declared and defined by the implementation in order to create an instance of class C in the line numbered 1. The synthesized constructor does not initialize the data members n and p, nor does it allocate memory for the latter. These data members have an indeterminate value after obj has been constructed.

This is because the synthesized default constructor performs only the initialization operations that are required by the implementation—not the programmer—to construct an object. In this case, C is a polymorphic class. An object of this type contains a pointer to the virtual function table of its class. The virtual pointer is initialized by the implicitly-defined constructor.

Other implementation-required operations that are performed by implicitly-defined constructors are the invocation of a base class constructor and the invocation of the constructor of embedded objects. The implementation does not declare a constructor for a class if the programmer has defined one. For example

```
class C
{
private:
  int n;
  char *p;
public:
  C() : n(0), p(NULL) {}
  virtual ~C() {}
};

void f2()
{
  C obj;  // 1 user-defined constructor is invoked
}
```

Now the data members of the object obj are initialized because the user-defined constructor was invoked to create it. Note, however, that the user-defined constructor only initializes the data members n and p. Obviously, the virtual pointer must have been initialized as well—otherwise, the program will be ill-formed. But when did the initialization of the virtual pointer take place? The compiler augments the user-defined constructor with additional code, which is inserted into the constructor's body before any user-written code, and performs the necessary initialization of the virtual pointer.

Calling an Object's Member Function from Its Constructor

Because the virtual pointer is initialized in the constructor before any user-written code, it is safe to call member functions (both virtual and nonvirtual) of an object from its constructor. It is guaranteed that the invoked virtual is the one that is defined in the current object (or of the base class, if it has not been overridden in the current object). However, virtual member functions of objects that are derived from the one whose constructor is executing are not called. For example

```
class A
{
public:
  virtual void f() {}
  virtual void g() {}
};

class B: public  A
{
public:
  void f () {} // overriding A::f()
  B()
  {
    f();   // calls B::f()
    g();  // g() was not overriden in B, therefore calling A::g()
  }
};
class C: public B
{
public:
  void f () {} //overriding B::f()
  };
```

Please note that if the object's member functions refer to data members of the object, it is the programmer's responsibility to initialize these data members first—most preferably with a *member-initialization list* (member-initialization lists are discussed next). For example

```
class C
{
private:
  int n;
  int  getn() const { cout<<n<<endl; }
public:
  C(int j) : n(j) { getn(); } //Fine: n initialized before getn() is called
};
```

Trivial Constructors

As you have observed, compilers synthesize a default constructor for every class or struct, unless a constructor was already defined by the user. However, in certain conditions, such a synthesized constructor is redundant:

```
class Empty {}; //class has no base classes, virtual member functions
                //or embedded objects
```

```
struct Person
{
  int age;
  char name[20];
  double salary;
};
int main()
{
  Empty e;
  Person p;
  p.age = 30;
  return 0;
}
```

An implementation can instantiate `Empty` and `Person` objects without a constructor. In such cases, the explicitly-declared constructor is said to be *trivial*, which means that the implementation does not need it in order to create an instance of its class. A constructor is considered trivial when all the following hold true:

- Its class has no virtual member functions and no virtual base classes.
- All the direct base classes of the constructor's class have trivial constructors.
- All the member objects in the constructor's class have trivial constructors.

You can see that both `Empty` and `Person` fulfill these conditions; therefore, each of them has a trivial constructor. The compiler suppresses the automatic synthesis of a trivial constructor, thereby producing code that is as efficient in terms of size and speed as that which is produced by a C compiler.

Avoid Reduplicating Identical Pieces of Constructors' Code

It is very common to define a class that has more than one constructor. For instance, a `string` class can define one constructor that takes `const char *` as an argument, another that takes an argument of type `size_t` to indicate the initial capacity of the string, and a default constructor.

```
class string
{
private:
  char * pc;
  size_t capacity;
  size_t length;
```

```
    enum { DEFAULT_SIZE = 32};
public:
    string(const char * s);
    string(size_t initial_capacity );
    string();
//...other member functions and overloaded operators
};
```

Each of the three constructors performs individual operations. Nonetheless, some identical tasks—such as allocating memory from the free store and initializing it, or assigning the value of capacity to reflect the size of the allocated storage—are performed in every constructor. Instead of repeating identical pieces of code in each of the constructors, it is better to move the recurring code into a single nonpublic member function. This function is called by every constructor. The results are shorter compilation time and easier future maintenance:

```
class string
{
private:
    char * pc;
    size_t capacity;
    size_t length;
    enum { DEFAULT_SIZE = 32};
    // the following function is called by every user-defined constructor
    void init( size_t cap = DEFAULT_SIZE);
public:
    string(const char * s);
    string(size_t initial_capacity );
    string();
//...other member functions and overloaded operators
};

void string::init( size_t cap)
{
    pc = new char[cap];
    capacity = cap;
}


string::string(const char * s)
{
    size_t size = strlen (s);
    init(size + 1); //make room for null terminating character
    length = size;
    strcpy(pc, s);
}
string::string(size_t initial_capacity )
{
    init(initial_capacity);
    length=0;
}
```

```
string::string()
{
  init();
  length = 0;
}
```

Is a Default Constructor Always Necessary?

A class might have no default constructor. For example

```
class File
{
private:
  string path;
  int mode;
public:
  File(const string& file_path, int open_mode);
  ~File();
};
```

Class `File` has a user-defined constructor that takes two arguments. The existence of a user-defined constructor blocks the synthesis of an implicitly-declared default constructor. Because the programmer did not define a default constructor either, class `File` does not have a default constructor. A class with no default constructor limits its users to a narrower set of allowed uses. For instance, when an array of objects is instantiated, the default constructor—and only the default constructor—of each array member is invoked. Therefore, you cannot instantiate arrays thereof unless you use a complete initialization list:

```
File folder1[10]; //error, array requires default constructor

File folder2[2] = { File("f1", 1)}; //error, f2[1] still requires
                                     //a default constructor

File folder3[3] = { File("f1", 1), File("f2",2), File("f3",3) }; //OK,
                                     //fully initialized array
```

Similar difficulties arise when you attempt to store objects that have no default constructor in STL containers:

```
#include <vector>
using namespace std;
void f()
{
  vector <File> fv(10); //error, File has no default constructor
  vector <File> v; //OK
  v.push_back(File("db.dat", 1)); //OK
  v.resize(10); //error, File has no default constructor
  v.resize(10, File("f2",2)); //OK
}
```

Was the lack of a default constructor in class `File` intentional? Maybe. Perhaps the implementer considered an array of `File` objects undesirable because each object in the array needs to somehow acquire its path and open mode. However, the lack of a default constructor imposes restrictions that are too draconian for most classes.

Eligibility for STL Containment

In order to qualify as an element in an STL container, an object must possess a copy constructor, an assignment operator, and a destructor as public members (more on this in Chapter 10, "STL and Generic Programming").

A default constructor is also required for certain STL container operations, as you saw in the preceding example.

Many operating systems store the files in a directory as a linked list of file objects. By omitting a default constructor from `File`, the implementer severely compromises the capability of its users to implement a file system as a `std::list<File>`.

For a class such as `File`, whose constructor must initialize its members with user-supplied values, it might still be possible to define a default constructor. Instead of supplying the necessary path and open mode as constructor arguments, a default constructor can read them from a sequential database file.

When Are Default Constructors Undesirable?

Still, a default constructor can be undesirable in some cases. One such case is a singleton object. Because a singleton object must have one and only one instance, it is recommended that you block the creation of built-in arrays and containers of such objects by making the default constructor inaccessible. For example

```cpp
#include<string>
using namespace std;

int API_getHandle(); //system API function

class Application
{
private:
  string name;
  int handle;
  Application(); // make default constructor inaccessible
public:
  explicit Application(int handle);
  ~Application();
};

int main()
{
  Application theApp( API_getHandle() ); //ok
  Application apps[10]; //error, default constructor is inaccessible
}
```

Class `Application` does not have a default constructor; therefore, it is impossible to create arrays and containers of `Application` objects. In this case, the lack of a default constructor is intentional. (Other implementation details are still required to ensure that a single instance—and only a single instance—of `Application` is created. However, making the default constructor inaccessible is one of these details.)

Constructors of Fundamental Types

Fundamental types such as `char`, `int`, and `float` have constructors, as do user-defined types. You can initialize a variable by explicitly invoking its default constructor:

```
int main()
{
  char c = char();
  int n = int ();
  return 0;
}
```

The value that is returned by the explicit invocation of the default constructor of a fundamental type is equivalent to casting 0 to that type. In other words,

```
char c = char();
```

is equivalent to

```
char c = char(0);
```

Of course, it is possible to initialize a fundamental type with values other than **0**:

```
float f = float (0.333);
char c = char ('a');
```

Normally, you use the shorter notation:

```
char c = 'a';
float f = 0.333;
```

However, this language extension enables uniform treatment in templates for fundamental types and user-defined types. Fundamental types that are created on the free store using the operator `new` can be initialized in a similar manner:

```
int *pi= new int (10);
float *pf = new float (0.333);
```

explicit Constructors

A constructor that takes a single argument is, by default, an implicit conversion operator, which converts its argument to an object of its class (see also Chapter 3, "Operator Overloading"). Examine the following concrete example:

```
class string
{
private:
  int size;
```

```
    int capacity;
    char *buff;
public:
    string();
    string(int size);   // constructor and implicit conversion operator
    string(const char *); // constructor and implicit conversion operator
    ~string();
};
```

Class `string` has three constructors: a default constructor, a constructor that takes `int`, and a constructor that constructs a string from `const char *`. The second constructor is used to create an empty `string` object with an initial preallocated buffer at the specified size. However, in the case of class `string`, the automatic conversion is dubious. Converting an `int` into a string object doesn't make sense, although this is exactly what this constructor does. Consider the following:

```
int main()
{
    string s = "hello"; //OK, convert a C-string into a string object
    int ns = 0;
    s = 1; // 1 oops, programmer intended to write ns = 1,
}
```

In the expression `s = 1;`, the programmer simply mistyped the name of the variable ns, typing s instead. Normally, the compiler detects the incompatible types and issues an error message. However, before ruling it out, the compiler first searches for a user-defined conversion that allows this expression; indeed, it finds the constructor that takes `int`. Consequently, the compiler interprets the expression `s = 1;` as if the programmer had written

```
s = string(1);
```

You might encounter a similar problem when calling a function that takes a `string` argument. The following example can either be a cryptic coding style or simply a programmer's typographical error. However, due to the implicit conversion constructor of class `string`, it will pass unnoticed:

```
int f(string s);
int main()
{
  f(1); // without an explicit constructor,
        //this call is expanded into:  f ( string(1) );
        //was that intentional or merely a programmer's typo?
}
```

In order to avoid such implicit conversions, a constructor that takes one argument needs to be declared `explicit`:

```
class string
{
//...
public:
    explicit string(int size);   // block implicit conversion
```

```
string(const char *); //implicit conversion
~string();
};
```

An `explicit` constructor does not behave as an implicit conversion operator, which enables the compiler to catch the typographical error this time:

```
int main()
{
  string s = "hello"; //OK, convert a C-string into a string object
  int ns = 0;
  s = 1; // compile time error ; this time the compiler catches the typo
}
```

Why aren't all constructors automatically declared `explicit`? Under some conditions, the automatic type conversion is useful and well behaved. A good example of this is the third constructor of `string`:

```
string(const char *);
```

The implicit type conversion of `const char *` to a string object enables its users to write the following:

```
string s;
s = "Hello";
```

The compiler implicitly transforms this into

```
string s;
//pseudo C++ code:
s = string ("Hello"); //create a temporary and assign it to s
```

On the other hand, if you declare this constructor `explicit`, you have to use explicit type conversion:

```
class string
{
//...
public:
  explicit string(const char *);
};
int main()
{
  string s;
  s = string("Hello");   //explicit conversion now required
  return 0;
}
```

Extensive amounts of legacy C++ code rely on the implicit conversion of constructors. The C++ Standardization committee was aware of that. In order to not make existing code break, the implicit conversion was retained. However, a new keyword, `explicit`, was introduced to the language to enable the programmer to block the implicit conversion when it is undesirable. As a rule, a constructor that can be invoked with a single argument needs to be declared `explicit`. When the implicit type conversion is intentional and well behaved, the constructor can be used as an implicit conversion operator.

Blocking Undesirable Object Instantiation

Sometimes it might be useful to disallow programmers from instantiating an object of a certain class, for example, a class that is meant to be used only as a base class for others. A `protected` constructor blocks creation of class instances, yet it does so without disallowing derived objects' instantiation:

```
class CommonRoot
{
protected:
  CommonRoot(){}//no objects of this class should be instantiated
  virtual  ~CommonRoot ();
};

class Derived: public CommonRoot
{
public:
  Derived();
};

int main()
{
  Derived d;    // OK, constructor of d has access to
                //any protected member in its base class

  CommonRoot cr;  //compilation error: attempt to
                  //access a protected member of CommonRoot
}
```

The same effect of blocking instantiation of a class can be achieved by declaring pure virtual functions. However, these add runtime and space overhead. When pure virtual functions aren't needed, you can use a `protected` constructor instead.

Using Member Initialization Lists

A constructor might have a member initialization (mem-initialization for short) list that initializes the data members of the class. For example

```
class Cellphone //1: mem-init
{
private:
  long number;
  bool on;
public:
  Cellphone (long n, bool ison) : number(n), on(ison) {}
};
```

The constructor of `Cellphone` can also be written as follows:

```
Cellphone (long n, bool ison) //2 initialization within constructor's body
{
  number = n;
  on = ison;
}
```

There is no substantial difference between the two forms in the case of `Cellphone`'s constructor. This is due to the way mem-initialization lists are processed by the compiler. The compiler scans the mem-initialization list and inserts the initialization code into the constructor's body before any user-written code. Thus, the constructor in the first example is expanded by the compiler into the constructor in the second example. Nonetheless, the choice between using a mem-initialization list and initialization inside the constructor's body is significant in the following four cases:

- Initialization of `const` members
- Initialization of reference members
- Passing arguments to a constructor of a base class or an embedded object
- Initialization of member objects

In the first three cases, a mem-initialization list is mandatory; in the fourth case, it is optional. Consider the concrete examples that are discussed in the following paragraphs.

const Data Members

const data members of a class, including `const` members of a base or embedded subobject, must be initialized in a mem-initialization list.

```
class Allocator
{
private:
  const int chunk_size;
public:
  Allocator(int size) : chunk_size(size) {}
};
```

Reference Data Members

A reference data member must be initialized by a mem-initialization list.

```
class Phone;
class Modem
{
private:
  Phone & line;
public:
  Modem(Phone & ln) : line(ln) {}
};
```

Invoking a Constructor of a Base or a Member Object with Arguments

When a constructor has to pass arguments to the constructor of its base class or to the constructor of an embedded object, a mem-initializer must be used.

```
class base
{
private:
  int num1;
  char * text;
public:
  base(int n1, char * t) {num1 = n1; text = t; } //no default constructor
};

class derived : public base
{
private:
  char *buf;
public:
  derived (int n, char * t) : base(n, t) //pass arguments to base constructor
  { buf = (new char[100]);}
};
```

Embedded Objects

Consider the following example:

```
#include<string>
using std::string;
class Website
{
private:
  string URL
  unsigned int IP
public:
  Website()
  {
    URL = "";
    IP = 0;
  }
};
```

Class `Website` has an embedded object of type `std::string`. The syntax rules of the language do not force the usage of mem-initialization to initialize this member. However, the performance gain in choosing mem-initialization over initialization inside the constructor's body is significant. Why? The initialization inside the constructor's body is very inefficient because it requires the construction of the member `URL`; a temporary `std::string` object is then constructed from the value `""`, which is in turn assigned to `URL`. Finally, the temporary object has to be destroyed. The use of a mem-initialization list, on the other hand, avoids the creation and destruction of a temporary object (the performance implications of mem-initialization lists are discussed in further detail in Chapter 12, "Optimizing Your Code").

The Order of a Mem-Initialization List Must Match the Order of Class Member Declarations

Due to the performance difference between the two forms of initializing embedded objects, some programmers use mem-initialization exclusively—even for fundamental types. It is important to note, however, that the order of the initialization list has to match the order of declarations within the class. This is because the compiler transforms the list so that it coincides with the order of the declaration of the class members, regardless of the order specified by the programmer. For example

```
class Website
{
private:
  string URL; //1
  unsigned int IP; //2
public:
  Website() : IP(0), URL("") {} // initialized in reverse order
};
```

In the mem-initialization list, the programmer first initializes the member IP, and then URL, even though IP is declared after URL. The compiler transforms the initialization list to the order of the member declarations within the class. In this case, the reverse order is harmless. When there are dependencies in the order of initialization list, however, this transformation can cause unexpected surprises. For example

```
class string
{
private:
  char *buff;
  int capacity;
public:
  explicit string(int size) :
  capacity(size), buff (new char [capacity]) {} undefined behavior
};
```

The mem-initialization list in the constructor of string does not follow the order of declaration of string's members. Consequently, the compiler transforms the list into

```
explicit string(int size) :
buff  (new char [capacity]), capacity(size) {}
```

The member capacity specifies the number of bytes that new has to allocate; but it has not been initialized. The results in this case are undefined. There are two ways to avert this pitfall: Change the order of member declarations so that capacity is declared before buff, or move the initialization of buff into the constructor's body.

The Exception Specification of an Implicitly-Declared Default Constructor

An implicitly-declared default constructor has an *exception specification* (exception specifications are discussed in Chapter 6, "Exception Handling"). The exception specification of an implicitly declared default constructor contains all the exceptions of every other special member function that the constructor invokes directly. For example

```
struct A
{
  A(); //can throw any type of exception
};
struct B
{
  B() throw(); //not allowed to throw any exceptions
};
struct C : public B
{
  //implicitly-declared C::C() throw;
}
struct D: public A, public B
{
  //implicitly-declared D::D();
};
```

The implicitly declared constructor in class C is not allowed to throw any exceptions because it directly invokes the constructor of class B, which is not allowed to throw any exceptions either. On the other hand, the implicitly declared constructor in class D is allowed to throw any type of exception because it directly invokes the constructors of classes A and B. Since the constructor of class A is allowed to throw any type of exception, D's implicitly declared constructor has a matching exception specification. In other words, D's implicitly declared constructor allows all exceptions if any function that it directly invokes allows all exceptions; it allows no exceptions if every function that it directly invokes allows no exceptions either. As you will see soon, the same rules apply to the exception specifications of other implicitly declared special member functions.

Copy Constructor

A *copy constructor* is used to initialize its object with another object. A constructor of a class C is a copy constructor if its first argument is of type C&, const C&, volatile C&, or const volatile C&, and if there are no additional arguments or if all other arguments have default values. If there is no user-defined copy constructor for a class, the implementation implicitly declares one. An implicitly declared copy constructor is an inline public member of its class, and it has the form

```
C::C(const C&);
```

if each base class of C has a copy constructor whose first argument is a reference to a const object of the base class type, and if all the nonstatic embedded objects in C also have a copy constructor that takes a reference to a const object of their type. Otherwise, the implicitly declared copy constructor is of the following type:

```
C::C(C&);
```

An implicitly declared copy constructor has an exception specification. The exception specification contains all the exceptions that might be thrown by other special functions that the copy constructor invokes directly.

Implicitly Defined Copy Constructors

A copy constructor is said to be *trivial* if it is implicitly declared, if its class has no virtual member functions and no virtual base classes, and if its entire direct base classes and embedded objects have trivial copy constructors. The implementation implicitly defines an implicitly-declared, nontrivial copy constructor to initialize an object of its type from a copy of an object of its type (or from one derived from it). The implicitly defined copy constructor performs a memberwise copy of its subobjects, as in the following example:

```
#include<string>
using std::string;
class Website //no user-defined copy constructor
{
private:
  string URL;
  unsigned int IP;
public:
  Website() : IP(0), URL("") {}
};
int main ()
{
  Website site1;
  Website site2(site1); //invoke implicitly-defined copy constructor
}
```

The programmer did not declare a copy constructor for class Website. Because Website has an embedded object of type std::string, which happens to have a user-defined copy constructor, the implementation implicitly defines a copy constructor for class Website and uses it to copy construct the object site2 from site1. The synthesized copy constructor first invokes the copy constructor of std::string, and then performs a bitwise copying of the data members of site1 into site2.

Novices are sometimes encouraged to define the four special member functions for every class they write. As can be seen in the case of the Website class, not only is this unnecessary, but it is even undesirable under some conditions. The synthesized copy constructor (and the assignment operator, as you are about to see) already do the "right thing". They automatically invoke the constructors of base and member subobjects, they initialize the virtual pointer (if one exists), and they perform a bitwise copying of fundamental types. In many cases, this is exactly the programmer's intention anyway. Furthermore, the synthesized constructor and copy constructor enable the implementation to create code that is more efficient than user-written code because it can apply optimizations that are not always possible otherwise.

Implementation-Required Initializations

Like ordinary constructors, copy constructors—either implicitly defined or user-defined—are augmented by the compiler, which inserts additional code into them to invoke the copy constructors of direct base classes and embedded objects. It is guaranteed, however, that virtual base subobjects are copied only once.

Simulating Virtual Constructors

Unlike ordinary member functions, a constructor has to know the exact type of its object at compile time in order to construct it properly. Consequently, a constructor cannot be declared `virtual`. Still, creating an object without knowing its exact type is useful in certain conditions. The easiest way to simulate virtual construction is by defining a virtual member function that returns a constructed object of its class type. For example

```
class Browser
{
public:
  Browser();
  Browser( const Browser&);
  virtual Browser* construct()
    { return new Browser; } //virtual default constructor
  virtual Browser* clone()
    { return new Browser(*this); } // virtual copy constructor
  virtual ~Browser();
//...
};

class HTMLEditor: public Browser
{
public:
  HTMLEditor ();
  HTMLEditor (const HTMLEditor &);
  HTMLEditor * construct()
    { return new HTMLEditor; }//virtual default constructor
  HTMLEditor * clone()
    { return new HTMLEditor (*this); } //virtual copy constructor
  virtual ~HTMLEditor();
  //...
};
```

The polymorphic behavior of the member functions `clone()` and `construct()` enables you to instantiate a new object of the right type, without having to know the exact type of the source object.

```
void create (Browser& br)
{
  br.view();
  Browser* pbr  = br.construct();
```

```
//...use pbr and br
delete pbr;
}
```

pbr is assigned a pointer to an object of the right type—either Browser or any class publicly derived from it. Note that the object br does not delete the new object it has created; this is the user's responsibility. If it did, the lifetime of the reproduced objects would depend on the lifetime of their originator—which would significantly compromise the usability of this technique.

Co-variance of Virtual Member Functions

The implementation of virtual constructors relies on a recent modification to C++, namely virtual functions' covariance. An overriding virtual function has to match the signature and the return type of the function it overrides. This restriction was recently relaxed to enable the return type of an overriding virtual function to co-vary with its class type. Thus, the return type of a public base can be changed to the type of a derived class. The co-variance applies only to pointers and references.

Assignment Operator

A user-declared assignment operator of class C is a nonstatic, nontemplate member function of its class, taking exactly one argument of type C, C&, const C&, volatile C&, or const volatile C&.

Implicitly Defined Assignment Operator

If there is no user-defined assignment operator for a class, the implementation implicitly declares one. An implicitly declared assignment operator is an inline public member of its class, and it has the form

```
C& C::operator=(const C&);
```

if each base class of C has an assignment operator whose first argument is a reference to a const object of base class type, and if all the nonstatic embedded objects in C also have an assignment operator that takes a reference to a const object of their type. Otherwise, the implicitly declared assignment operator is of the following type:

```
C& C::operator=(C&);
```

Caution
Please note that some compilers do not support virtual member functions' covariance yet.

An implicitly-declared assignment operator has an exception specification. The exception specification contains all the exceptions that might be thrown by other special functions that the assignment operator invokes directly. An assignment operator is said to be *trivial* if it is implicitly declared, if its class has no virtual member functions or virtual base classes, and if its direct base classes and embedded objects have a trivial assignment operator.

Simulating Inheritance of Assignment Operator

Because an assignment operator is implicitly declared for a class if it is not declared by the programmer, the assignment operator of a base class is always hidden by the assignment operator of a derived class. In order to extend—rather than override—the assignment operator in a derived class, you must first invoke the assignment operator of the base explicitly, and then add the operations that are required for the derived class. For example

```cpp
class B
{
private:
  char *p;
public:
  enum {size = 10};
  const char * Getp() const {return p;}
  B() : p ( new char [size] ) {}
  B& operator = (const C& other);
  {
    if (this != &other)
      strcpy(p, other.Getp() );
    return *this;
  }
 };
class D : public B
{
private:
  char *q;
public:
  const char * Getq() const {return q;}
  D(): q  ( new char [size] ) {}
  D& operator = (const D& other)
  {
    if (this != &other)
    {
     B::operator=(other);  //first invoke base's assignment operator explicitly
     strcpy(q, (other.Getq()));  //add extensions here
    }
    return *this;
  }
};
```

When Are User-Written Copy Constructors and Assignment Operators Needed?

The synthesized copy constructor and assignment operator perform a memberwise copy. This is the desirable behavior for most uses. However, it can be disastrous for classes that contain pointers, references, or handles. In such cases, you have to define a copy constructor and assignment operator to avoid *aliasing*. Aliasing occurs when the same resource is used simultaneously by more than one object. For example

```cpp
#include <cstdio>
using namespace std;
class Document
{
private:
  FILE *pdb;
public:
  Document(const char *filename) {pdb = fopen(filename, "t");}
  Document(FILE *f =NULL) : pdb(f){}
  ~Document() {fclose(pdb);} //bad, no copy constructor
                             //or assignment operator defined
};

void assign(Document& d)
{
  Document temp("letter.doc");
  d = temp;  //Aliasing; both d and temp are pointing to the same file
}//temp's destructor is now called and closes file while d is still using it

int main()
{
  Document doc;
  assign(doc);
  return 0;
  //doc now uses a file which has just been closed. disastrous
}}//OOPS! doc's destructor is now invoked and closes 'letter.doc' once again
```

Because the implementer of class Document did not define a copy constructor and assignment operator, the compiler defined them implicitly. However, the synthesized copy constructor and assignment operator result in aliasing because the same file can be shared by more than one object. An attempt to open or close the same file twice yields undefined behavior. One way to solve this problem is to define an appropriate copy constructor and assignment operator. Please note, however, that the aliasing results from the reliance on low-level language constructs (file pointers in this case), whereas an embedded fstream object can perform the necessary checks automatically. In that case, a user-written copy constructor and assignment operator are unnecessary.

The same problem occurs when bare pointers to char are used as data members instead of as string objects. If you use a pointer to char rather than std::string in class Website, you face an aliasing problem as well.

Implementing Copy Constructor and Assignment Operator

Another conclusion that can be drawn from the preceding example is that whenever you define a copy constructor, you must also define the assignment operator. When you define only one of the two, the compiler creates the missing one—but it might not work as expected.

The "Big Three Rule" or the "Big Two Rule"?

The famous "Big Three Rule" says that if a class needs any of the Big Three member functions (copy constructor, assignment operator, and destructor), it needs them all. Generally, this rule refers to classes that allocate memory from the free store. However, many other classes require only that the Big Two (copy constructor and assignment operator) be defined by the user; the destructor, nonetheless, is not always required. Examine the following example:

```
class Year
{
private:
  int y;
  bool cached; //has the object been cached?
public:
  //...
  Year(int y);
  Year(const Year& other) //cached should not be copied
  {
    y = other.getYear();
  }
  Year& operator =(const Year&other) //cached should not be copied
  {
    y = other.getYear();
    return *this;
  }
  int getYear() const { return y; }
};//no destructor required for class Year
```

Class Year does not allocate memory from the free store, nor does it acquire any other resources during its construction. A destructor is therefore unnecessary. However, the class needs a user-defined copy constructor and assignment operator to ensure that the value of the member cached is not copied because it is calculated for every individual object separately.

When a user-defined copy constructor and assignment operator are needed, it is important to implement them in a way that prevents self-assignment or aliasing. Usually, it is sufficient to fully implement only one of the two, and then define the other by means of the first.

```
#include <cstring>
using namespace std;
class Person
{
private:
  int age;
  char * name;
public:
  int getAge () const { return age;}
  const char * getName() const { return name; }
  //...
  Person (const char * name = NULL, int age =0) {}
  Person & operator= (const Person & other);
  Person (const Person& other);
};
Person & Person::operator= (const Person & other)
{
  if (&other  !=  this) //guard from self assignment
  {
     size_t len = strlen( other.getName());
     if (strlen (getName() ) < len)
     {
        delete [] name; //release current buffer
        name = new char [len+1];
     }
     strcpy(name, other.getName());
     age = other.getAge();
  }
  return *this;
}

Person::Person (const Person & other)
{
 *this=other; //OK, use user-defined assignment operator is invoked
}
```

Blocking Object Copying

There are situations in which enabling the user to copy or assign a new value to an object is undesirable. You can disable both by explicitly declaring the assignment operator and copy constructor as private:

```
class NoCopy
{
private:
  NoCopy&  operator = (const NoCopy& other) { return *this; }
```

```
  NoCopy(const NoCopy& other) {/*..*/}
public:
  NoCopy() {}
//...
};

void f()
{
  NoCopy nc;  // fine, default constructor called
  NoCopy nc2(nc);  //error; attempt to call a private copy constructor
  nc2 = nc; //also a compile time error; operator= is private
}
```

Destructors

A destructor destroys an object of its class type. It takes no arguments and has no
return type (not even void). const and volatile qualities are not applied on an object
under destruction; therefore, destructors can be invoked for const, volatile, or const
volatile objects. If there is no user-defined destructor for a class, the implementation
implicitly declares one. An implicitly declared destructor is an inline public member
of its class and has an exception specification. The exception specification contains all
the exceptions that might be thrown by other special functions that the destructor
invokes directly.

A destructor is trivial if it is implicitly declared and if its entire direct base classes
and embedded objects have trivial destructors. Otherwise, the destructor is nontrivial.
A destructor invokes the destructors of the direct base classes and member objects of
its class. The invocation occurs in the reverse order of their construction. All destructors are called with their qualified name, ignoring any possible virtual overriding
destructors in more derived classes. For example

```
#include <iostream>
using namespace std;

class A
{
public:
  virtual ~A() { cout<<"destroying A"<<endl;}
};

class B: public A
{
public:
  ~B() { cout<<"destroying B"<<endl;}
};

int main()
{
  B b;
  return 0;
};
```

This program displays

```
destroying B
destroying A
```

This is because the compiler transforms the user-defined destructor of class B into

```
~B()
{
    //user-written code below
  cout<<"destroying B"<<endl;
    //pseudo C++ code inserted by the compiler below
  this->A::~A(); // destructor called using its qualified name
}
```

Although the destructor of class A is virtual, the qualified call that is inserted into the destructor of class B is resolved statically (calling a function with a qualified name bypasses the dynamic binding mechanism).

Explicit Destructor Invocation

Destructors are invoked implicitly in the following cases:

- For static objects at program termination
- For local objects when the block in which the object is created exits
- For a temporary object when the lifetime of the temporary object ends
- For objects allocated on the free store using new, through the use of `delete`
- During stack unwinding that results from an exception

A destructor can also be invoked explicitly. For example

```
class C
{
public:
~C() {}
};

void destroy(C& c)
{
  c.C::~C(); //explicit destructor activation
}
```

A destructor can also be explicitly invoked from within a member function of its object:

```
void C::destroy()
{
  this->C::~C();
}
```

In particular, explicit destructor invocation is necessary for objects that were created by the placement new operator (`placement new` is discussed in Chapter 11, "Memory Management").

Pseudo Destructors

Fundamental types have constructors, as you have seen. In addition, fundamental types also have a *pseudo destructor*. A pseudo destructor is a syntactic construct whose sole purpose is to satisfy the need of generic algorithms and containers. It is a no-op code that has no real effect on its object. If you examine the assembly code that your compiler produces for a pseudo destructor invocation, you might discover that the compiler simply ignored it. A pseudo destructor invocation is shown in the following example:

```
typedef int N;
int main()
{
  N i = 0;
  i.N::~N(); //pseudo destructor invocation
  i = 1; //i  was not affected by the invocation of the pseudo destructor
  return 0;
}
```

The variable i is defined and initialized. In the following statement, the pseudo destructor of the non-class type N is explicitly invoked but it has no effect on its object. Like the constructors of fundamental types, pseudo destructors enable the user to write code without having to know if a destructor actually exists for a given type.

Pure Virtual Destructors

Unlike ordinary member functions, a virtual destructor is not overridden when it is redefined in a derived class. Rather, it is extended. Consequently, when you try to declare a pure virtual destructor, you might encounter compilation errors, or worse—a runtime crash. In this respect, pure virtual destructors are exceptional among pure virtual functions—they have to be defined. You can refrain from declaring a destructor with the pure specifier, making it only virtual. However, this is an unnecessary design compromise. You can enjoy both worlds by forcing an interface whose members are all pure virtual, including the destructor—and all this without experiencing runtime crashes. How is it done?

First, the abstract class contains only a declaration of a pure virtual destructor:

```
class Interface
{
public:
  virtual void Open() = 0;
  virtual ~Interface() = 0;
};
```

Somewhere outside the class declaration, the pure virtual destructor has to be defined as follows:

```
Interface::~Interface()
{} //definition of a pure virtual destructor; should always be empty
```

Constructors and Destructors Should Be Minimal

When you are designing a class, remember that it might serve as a base for other subclasses. It can also be used as a member object in a larger class. As opposed to ordinary member functions, which can be overridden or simply not called, the base class constructor and destructor are automatically invoked. It is not a good idea to force users of a derived and embedded object to pay for what they do not need, but are forced to accept. In other words, constructors and destructors should contain nothing but the minimal functionality needed to construct an object and destroy it. A concrete example can demonstrate that: A `string` class that supports serialization should not open/create a file in its constructor. Such operations need to be left to a dedicated member function. When a new derived class—such as `ShortString`, which holds a fixed length string—is created, its constructor is not forced to perform superfluous file I/O that is imposed by the constructor of its base class.

Conclusions

The constructor, copy constructor, assignment operator, and destructor automate most of the tedium that is associated with creating, copying, and destroying objects. The symmetry between a constructor and a destructor in C++ is rare among object-oriented programming languages, and it serves as the basis for advanced design idioms (as you will see in the next chapter, "Object-Oriented Programming and Design").

Each C++ object possesses the four member functions, which can be declared by the programmer or declared implicitly by the implementation. An implicitly declared special member function can be trivial, which means that the implementation does not have to define it. The synthesized special member functions perform only operations that are required by the implementation. User-written special member functions are automatically augmented by the compiler—to ensure the proper initialization of base and embedded subobjects—and the virtual pointer. Fundamental types have constructors and pseudo destructors, which facilitate generic programming.

In many cases, the synthesized special member functions do the "right thing". When the default behavior is unfitted, the programmer has to define the special functions explicitly. Often, however, the need for user-written code derives from combining low-level data structures with a high-level interface, and might indicate a design flaw. Declaring a constructor `explicit` ensures that it will not serve as an implicit conversion operator.

A mem-initialization list is necessary for the initialization of `const` and reference data members, as well as to pass arguments to a base or embedded subobject. In all other cases, a mem-initialization list is optional but can enhance performance. Constructors and assignment operators can be used in several ways to control instantiation and copying of objects. Destructors can be invoked explicitly. Destructors that are declared pure virtual have to be defined.

5

Object-Oriented Programming and Design

Introduction

C++ is the most widely used object-oriented programming language today. The success of C++ has been a prominent factor in making object-oriented design and programming a de facto standard in today's software industry. Yet, unlike other object-oriented programming languages (some of them have been around for nearly 30 years), C++ does not enforce object-oriented programming—it can be used as a "better C", as an *object-based* language, or as a generic programming language. This flexibility, which is unparalleled among programming languages, makes C++ a suitable programming language in any domain area—real-time, embedded systems, data processing, numerical computation, graphics, artificial intelligence, or system programming.

This chapter begins with a brief survey of the various programming styles that are supported by C++. Next, you will focus on various aspects of object-oriented design and programming.

Programming Paradigms

A programming paradigm defines the methodology of designing and implementing software, including the building blocks of the language, the interaction between data structures and the operations applied to them, program structure, and how problems are generally analyzed and solved. A programming language provides the linguistic means (keywords, preprocessor directives, program structure) as well as the extra-linguistic capabilities, namely standard libraries and programming environment, to support a specific programming paradigm. Usually, a given programming language is targeted for a specific application domain, for example, string manipulation, mathematical applications, simulations, Web programming, and so on. C++, however, is not confined to any specific application domain. Rather, it supports many useful programming paradigms. The following sections discuss these paradigms and their characteristics.

Procedural Programming

C++ is a superset of ISO C. As such, it can be used as a procedural programming language, albeit with tighter type checking and several enhancements that improve design and coding: reference variables, inline functions, default arguments, and `bool` type. Procedural programming is based on separation between functions and the data that they manipulate. In general, functions rely on the physical representation of the data types that they manipulate. This dependency is one of the most problematic aspects in the maintenance and extensibility of procedural software.

Procedural Programming Is Susceptible to Design Changes

Whenever the definition of a type changes (as a result of porting the software to a different platform, changes in the customer's requirement, and so on), the functions that refer to that type have to be modified accordingly. The opposite is also true: When a function is being changed, its arguments might be affected as well; for instance, instead of passing a `struct` by value, it might be passed by address to optimize performance. Consider the following:

```
struct Date //pack data in a compact struct
{
  char day;
  char month;
  short year;
};
bool isDateValid(Date d); //pass by value
void getCurrentDate(Date * pdate); //changes its argument, address needed
void initializeDate (Date* pdate); //changes its argument, address needed
```

Data structures, such as `Date`, and the group of associated functions that initialize, read, and test them are very common in software projects in which C is the predominant programming language. Now suppose that due to a change in the design, `Date` is required to also hold the current time stamp in seconds. Consequently, a change in the definition of `Date` is made:

```
struct Date
{
  char day;
  char month;
  short year;
```

```
   long seconds;
}; //now less compact than before
```

All the functions that manipulate `Date` have to be modified to cope with change. An additional change in the design adds one more field to store millionths of a second in order to make a unique timestamp for database transactions. The modified `Date` is now

```
struct Date
{
  char day;
  char month;
  short year;
  long seconds;
  long millionths;
};
```

Once more, all the functions that manipulate `Date` have to be modified to cope with the change. This time, even the interface of the functions changes because `Date` now occupies at least 12 bytes. Functions that are passed a `Date` by value are modified to accept a pointer to `Date`.

```
bool isDateValid(Date* pd); // pass by address for efficiency
```

Drawbacks of Procedural Programming

This example is not fictitious. Such frequent design changes occur in almost every software project. The budget and time overhead that are produced as a result can be overwhelming; indeed, they sometimes lead to the project's discontinuation. The attempt to avoid—or at least to minimize—these overheads has led to the emergence of new programming paradigms.

Procedural programming enables only a limited form of code reuse, that is, by calling a function or using a common user-defined data structure. Nonetheless, the tight coupling between a data structure and the functions that manipulate it considerably narrows their reusability potential. A function that computes the square root of a `double` cannot be applied to a user-defined `struct` that represents a `complex`, for example. In general, procedural programming languages rely on static type checking, which ensures better performance than dynamic type checking—but it also compromises the software's extensibility.

Procedural programming languages provide a closed set of built-in data types that cannot be extended. User-defined types are either unsupported or they are "second class citizens" in the language. The user cannot redefine built-in operators to support them. Furthermore, the lack of abstraction and information hiding mechanisms force users to expose the implementation details. Consider the standard C functions `atof()`, `atoi()`, and `atol()`, which convert a C-string to `double`, `int`, and `long`, respectively. Not only do they force the user to pay attention to the physical data type of the return value (on most machines these days, an `int` and a `long` are identical anyway), they also prohibit the use of other data types.

Why Procedural Programming Still Matters

In spite of its noticeable drawbacks, procedural programming is still the preferred programming paradigm in some specific application domains, such as embedded and time critical systems. Procedural programming is also widely used in machine generated code because code reuse, extensibility, and maintenance are immaterial in this case. Many SQL interpreters, for example, translate the high-level SQL statements into C code that is then compiled.

Procedural programming languages—such as C, Pascal, or Fortran—produce the most efficient machine code among high-level programming languages. In fact, development teams that are reluctant to adopt object orientation often point to performance degradation as the major deterring factor.

The evolution of C++ is unique among programming languages. The job of its creators might have been a lot easier had they chosen to design it from scratch, without guaranteeing backward compatibility with C. Yet this backward compatibility is one of the its strengths: It enables organizations and programmers to benefit from C++ without having to trash hundreds of millions of lines of working C code. Furthermore, C programmers can easily become productive in C++ even before they have fully mastered object-oriented programming.

Object-Based Programming

The limitations of procedural programming have led researchers and developers alike to find better methods of separating implementation details from interfaces. Object-based programming enables them to create user-defined types that behave like first class citizens. User-defined types can bundle data and meaningful operations in a single entity—a *class*. Classes also support information hiding, thereby separating implementation details such as physical representation and underlying bookkeeping from the set of services that a class provides, or its *interface*. Users of a class are allowed to access its interface, but they cannot access its implementation details. The separation between the implementation—which might vary rather frequently due to design changes, portability, and efficiency—and the stable interface is substantial. This separation ensures that changes in the design are localized to a single entity—the class implementation; the class users, on the other hand, are not affected. To assess the importance of object-based programming, examine a simple-minded `Date` class:

```
class Date
{
private:
  char day;
  char month;
  short year;
public:
  bool isValid();
  Date getCurrent();
  void initialize();
};
```

Object-Based Programming Localizes Changes in Implementation Details

Now suppose that you have to change the definition of `Date` to support time:

```
class Date
{
private:
  char day;
  char month;
  short year;
  long secs;
public:
  bool isValid();
  Date getCurrent();
  void initialize ();
};
```

The addition of a new data member does not affect the interface of `Date`. The users of `Date` don't even know that a new field has been added; they continue to receive the same services from the class as before. Of course, the implementer of `Date` has to modify the code of the member functions to reflect the change. Therefore, `Date::initialize()` has to initialize one more field. Still, the change is localized only to the definition of `Date::initialize()` because users cannot access the underlying representation of `Date`. In procedural programming, however, users can access the data members of `Date` directly.

Abstract Data Types

Classes such as `Date` are sometimes called *concrete types*, or *abstract data types* (not to be confused with *abstract classes*; see the sidebar titled "Abstract Data Types Versus Abstract Classes" later in this chapter).

These classes can meet a vast variety of needs in clean and easy-to-maintain capsules that separate implementation from interface. C++ provides the necessary mechanisms for data abstraction in the form of classes, which bundle data with a full set of associated operations. Information hiding is achieved by means of the `private` access specifier, which restricts the access to data members to class members exclusively.

Operator Overloading

In object-based languages, the user can extend the definition of a built-in operator to support a user-defined type (operator overloading is discussed in Chapter 3, "Operator Overloading"). This feature provides a higher level of abstraction by rendering user-defined types a status of built-in types. For example

```
class Date
{
private:
  char day;
  char month;
  short year;
  long secs;
```

```
public:
  bool operator < (const Date& other);
  bool operator == (const Date& other);
  //...other member functions
};
```

Characteristics of Object–Based Programming

In a way, object-based programming can be thought of as a subset of object-oriented programming; that is, some common principles are adhered to in both paradigms. Unlike object-oriented programming, however, object-based programming does not use inheritance. Rather, each user-defined class is a self-contained entity that is neither derived from a more general type, nor does it serve as a base for other types. The lack of inheritance in this paradigm is not coincidental. Proponents of object-based programming claim that inheritance complicates design, and that it might propagate bugs and deficiencies in a base class to its subclasses. Furthermore, inheritance also implies polymorphism, which is a source for additional design complexities. For instance, a function that takes a base object as an argument also knows how to handle any object that is publicly derived from that base.

Advantages of Object–Based Programming

Object-based programming overcomes most of the shortcomings of procedural programming. It localizes changes, it decouples implementation details from the interface, and it supports user-defined types. The Standard Library provides a rich set of abstract data types, including `string`, `complex`, and `vector`. These classes are designed to provide an abstraction for very specific uses, for example, character manipulations and complex numbers arithmetic. They are not derived from a more general base class, and they are not meant to be used as a base for other classes.

Abstract Data Types Versus Abstract Classes

The terms *abstract data type* and *abstract class* refer to two entirely different concepts, although both of them use the word *abstract* due to a historical accident. An abstract data type (also called a *concrete type*) is a self-contained, user-defined type that bundles data with a set of related operations. It behaves in the same way as does a built-in type. However, it is not extensible nor does it exhibit dynamic polymorphism. In contrast, an abstract class is anything but an abstract data type. It is not a data type (normally, abstract classes do not contain any data members), nor can you instantiate an object thereof. An abstract class is merely a skeletal interface, that specifies a set of services or operations that other (non-abstract) classes implement. Unfortunately, the distinction between the two concepts is often confused. Many people erroneously use the term *abstract data type* when they are actually referring to an abstract class.

Limitations of Object-Based Programming

Object-based programming is advantageous for specific uses. However, it cannot capture real-world relationships that exist among objects. The commonality that exists among a floppy disk and a hard disk, for instance, cannot be expressed directly in an object-based design. A hard disk and a floppy disk can both store files; they can contain directories and subdirectories, and so on. However, the implementer has to create two distinct and autonomous entities in this case, without sharing any common features that the two have.

Object-Oriented Programming

Object-oriented programming overcomes the limitations of object-based programming by providing the necessary constructs for defining *class hierarchies*. A class hierarchy captures the commonality among similar—and yet distinct—types. For example, the classes `Mouse` and a `Joystick` are two distinct entities, yet they share many common features that can be factored out into a common class, `PointingDevice`, which serves as a base class for both. Object-oriented programming is based on the foundations of object-based programming such as information hiding, abstract data typing, and encapsulation. In addition, it supports inheritance, polymorphism, and dynamic binding.

Characteristics of Object-Oriented Programming

Object-oriented programming languages differ from one another, sometimes considerably. Smalltalk programmers who migrate to C++, for instance, find the differences between the two languages somewhat daunting. The same can be said, of course, for C++ programmers who migrate to Smalltalk or Eiffel. However, several common characteristics that exist in all object-oriented programming languages distinguish them from non–object-oriented ones. These characteristics are presented in the following sections.

Inheritance

Inheritance enables a derived class to *reuse* the functionality and interface of its base class. The advantages of reuse are enormous: faster development time, easier maintenance, and simpler extensibility. The designer of class hierarchies captures the generalizations and commonality that exist among related classes. The more general operations are located in classes that appear higher in the derivation graph. Often, the design considerations are application-specific. For instance, the classes `Thesaurus` and `Dictionary` might be treated differently in an online ordering system of a bookstore and a computerized library of the linguistics department in some university. In the bookstore's online ordering system, the classes `Thesaurus` and `Dictionary` can inherit from a common base class called `Item`:

```
#include <string>
#include <list>
```

```
using namespace std;

class Review{/*...*/};
class Book
{
private:
  string author;
  string publisher;
  string ISBN;
  float list_price;
  list<Review> readers_reviews;
public:
  Book();
  const string& getAuthor() const;
  //...
};
```

Classes Dictionary and Thesaurus are defined as follows:

```
class Dictionary : public Book
{
private:
 int languages; //bilingual, trilingual etc.
 //...
};


class Thesaurus: public Book
{
private:
 int no_of_entries;
//...
};
```

However, the computerized library of the linguistics department might use a different hierarchy:

```
class Library_item
{
private:
  string Dewey_classification;
  int copies;
  bool in_store;
  bool can_be_borrowed;
  string author;
  string publisher;
  string ISBN;
public:
  Library_item();
  const string& getDewey_classification() const;
  //...
};


class Dictionary : public Library_item
```

```
{
private:
 int languages;
 bool phonetic_transciption;
 //...
};

class Thesaurus: public Library_item
{
private:
 int entries;
 int century; //historical period of the language, e.g., Shakespeare's era
 //...
};
```

These two hierarchies look different because they serve different purposes. However, the crucial point is that the common functionality and data are "elevated" to the base class that is extended by more specialized classes. Introducing a new class, for example Encyclopedia, to either the bookstore ordering system or the computerized library of the linguistics department is much easier in an object-oriented environment. That is because most of the functionality of the new class already exists in the base class, whatever it might be. On the other hand, in an object-based environment, every new class has to be written from scratch.

Polymorphism

Polymorphism is the capability of different objects to react in an individual manner to the same message. Polymorphism is widely used in natural languages. Consider the verb *to close*: It means different things when applied to different objects. Closing a door, closing a bank account, or closing a program's window are all different actions; their exact meaning depends on the object on which the action is performed. Similarly, polymorphism in object-oriented programming means that the interpretation of a message depends on its object. C++ has three mechanisms of static (compile-time) polymorphism: operator overloading, templates, and function overloading.

Operator Overloading   Applying operator +=, for example, to an int or a string is interpreted by each of these objects in an individual manner. Intuitively, however, you can predict what results will be, and you can find some similarities between the two. Object-based programming languages that support operator overloading are, in a limited way, polymorphic as well.

Templates   A vector<int> and a vector<string> react differently; that is, they execute a different set of instructions when they receive the same message. However, you can expect similar behavior (templates are discussed in detail in Chapter 9, "Templates"). Consider the following example:

```
vector < int > vi;  vector < string > names;
string name("Bjarne");
vi.push_back( 5 ); // add an integer at the end of the vector
names.push_back (name); //add a string at the end of the vector
```

Function Overloading Function overloading is a third form of polymorphism. In order to overload a function, a different list of parameters is used for each overloaded version. For example, a set of valid overloaded versions of a function named f() might look similar to the following:

```
void f(char c, int i);
void f(int i, char c); //order of parameters is significant
void f(string & s);
void f();
void f(int i);
void f(char c);
```

Note, however, that a function that differs only by its returned type is illegal in C++:

```
int f();  //error; differs from void f(); above only by return type
int f(float f);  //fine - unique signature
```

Dynamic Binding

Dynamic binding takes the notion of polymorphism one step further. In dynamic binding, the meaning of a message depends on the object that receives it; yet, the exact type of the object can be determined only at runtime. Virtual member functions are a good example of this. The specific version of a virtual function might not be known at compile time. In this case, the call resolution is delayed to runtime, as in the following example:

```
#include <iostream>
using namespace std;

class base
{
  public: virtual void f() { cout<< "base"<<endl;}
};

class derived : public base
{
  public: void f() { cout<< "derived"<<endl;} //overrides base::f
};

void identify(base & b) // the argument can be an instance
                        // of base or any object derived from it
{
  b.f(); //base::f or derived::f? resolution is delayed to runtime
}
//a separate translation unit
int main()
{
  derived d;
  identify(d); // argument is an object derived from base
  return 0;
}
```

The function `identify` can receive any object that is publicly derived from class `base`—even objects of subclasses that were defined after `identify` was compiled.

Dynamic binding has numerous advantages. In this example, it enables the user to extend the functionality of `base` without having to modify `identify` in any way. In procedural and object-based programming, such flexibility is nearly impossible. Furthermore, the underlying mechanism of dynamic binding is automatic. The programmer doesn't need to implement the code for runtime lookup and dispatch of a virtual function, nor does he or she need to check the dynamic type of the object.

Techniques Of Object-Oriented Programming

Up until now, the discussion has focused on the general characteristics of object-oriented programming and design. This part presents C++-specific practical techniques and guidelines of object-oriented programming.

Class Design

Classes are the primary unit of abstraction in C++. Finding the right classes during analysis and design is perhaps the most important phase in the lifetime of an object-oriented software system. The common guidelines for finding classes state that a class should represent a real-world object; others maintain that nouns in natural languages should represent classes. This is true to some extent, but nontrivial software projects often have classes that exist nowhere except the programming domain. Does an exception represent a real-world object? Do function objects (which are discussed in Chapter 10, "STL and Generic Programming") and smart pointers have an equivalent outside the programming environment? Clearly, the relationship between real-world entities and objects is not 1:1.

Finding the Classes

The process of finding the right classes is mostly derived from the functional requirements of the application domain. That is, a designer can decide to represent a concept as a class (rather than, for example, a member function within a different class or a global function) when it serves the needs of the application. This is usually done by means of CRC (Class, Responsibility, Collaboration) cards or any other method.

Common Design Mistakes with Classes

No two object-oriented languages are alike. The programming language also affects the design. As you learned in Chapter 4, "Special Member Functions: Default Constructor, Copy Constructor, Destructor, and Assignment Operator," C++ has a distinct symmetry between constructors and destructors that most other object-oriented languages do not have. Objects in C++ can automatically clean up after themselves. C++ also enables you to create local objects with automatic data storage. In other languages, objects can only be created on heap memory. C++ is also one of just a few languages that support multiple inheritance. C++ is a strongly-typed language with static type checking. As much as design gurus insist on separating pure design from implementation artifacts (that is, language-specific behavior), such language-specific features do affect the overall design.

Object-orientation is not a panacea. Some common pitfalls can lead to monstrous applications that need constant maintenance, that perform unsatisfactorily, and that only eventually—or never—reach production. Some of these design mistakes are easy to detect.

Gigantic Classes

There are no standardized methods for measuring the size of a class. However, many small specialized classes are preferred to a bulky single class that contains hundreds of member functions and data members. But such bulky classes do get written. Class `std::string` has a fat interface of more than 100 member functions; clearly, this is an exception to the rule and, to be honest, many people consider this to be a compromise between conflicting design approaches. Still, ordinary programs rarely use all these members. More than once I've seen programmers extending a class with additional member functions and data members instead of using more plausible object-oriented techniques such as subclassing. As a rule, a class that exceeds a 20–30 member function count is suspicious.

Gigantic classes are problematic for at least three reasons: Users of such classes rarely know how to use them properly; the implementation and interface of such classes tend to undergo extensive changes and bug-fixes; and they are not good candidates for reuse because the fat interface and intricate implementation details can fit only a very limited usage. In a sense, large classes are very similar to large functions—they are non-cohesive and difficult to maintain.

Exposing Implementation Details

Declaring data members with public access is, almost without exception, a design flaw. Still, even vendors of popular frameworks resort to this deprecated programming style. It might be tempting to use public data members because it saves the programmer the bother of writing trivial *accessors* and *mutators* (*getters* and *setters*, respectively). This approach cannot be recommended, however, because it results in maintenance difficulties and it compromises the class's reliability. Users of such classes tend to rely heavily on their implementation details; even if they normally avoid such dependencies, they might feel that the exposure of the implementation details implies that they are not supposed to change. Sometimes there is no other choice—the class implementer has not defined any other method of accessing data members of a class. The process of modifying or extending such classes becomes a maintenance nightmare. Infrastructure components, such as `Date` or `string` classes, can be used dozens of times within a single source file. It is not hard to imagine what it is like when dozens of programmers, each producing dozens of source files, have to chase every source line that refers to any one of these classes. This is exactly what caused the notorious Year 2000 Bug. If, on the other hand, data members are declared `private`, users cannot access them directly. When the implementation details of the class are modified, only accessors and mutators need to be modified, but the rest of the code remains intact.

There is another danger in exposing implementation details. Due to indiscriminate access to data members and helper functions, users can inadvertently tamper with the object's internal data members. They might delete memory (which is supposed to be deleted by the destructor), or they might change the value of a file handle, and so on, with disastrous results. Therefore, it is always a better design choice to hide implementation details of an object.

The "Resource Acquisition Is Initialization" Idiom

Many objects of various kinds share a similar characterization: They must be acquired by means of initialization prior to their usage; then they can be used, and then they have to be released explicitly. Objects such as `File`, `CommunicationSocket`, `DatabaseCursor`, `DeviceContext`, `OperatingSystem`, and many others have to be opened, attached, initialized, constructed, or booted, respectively, before you can use them. When their job is done, they have to be flushed, detached, closed, released, or logged out, respectively. A common design mistake is to have the user request explicitly for the initialization and release operations to take place. A much better choice is to move all initialization action into the constructor and all release actions into the destructor. This technique is called *resource acquisition is initialization* (*The C++ Programming Language, 3rd ed.*, page 365). The advantage is a simplified usage protocol. Users can start using the object right after it has been created, without bothering with whether the object is valid or whether further arbitrary initialization actions have to be taken. Furthermore, because the destructor also releases all its resources, users are free from that hassle too. Please note that this technique usually requires an appropriate exception handling code to cope with exceptions that are thrown during construction of the object.

Classes and Objects

Unlike some other object-oriented programming languages, C++ makes a clear distinction between a class, which is a user-defined type, and an object, which is an instance thereof. There are several features for manipulating the state of a class rather than the state of individual objects. These features are discussed in the following sections.

Static Data Members

A static member is shared by all instances of its class. For that reason, it is sometimes termed a *class variable*. Static members are useful in synchronization objects. For example, a file lock can be implemented using a `static` data member. An object that is trying to access this file has to check first whether the file is being processed by another user. If the file is available, the object turns the flag on and the user can process the file safely. Other users are not allowed to access the file until the flag is reset to false. When the object that is processing the file is finished, it has to turn off the flag, enabling another object to access it.

```
class fileProc
{
private:
  FILE *p;
  static bool Locked;
public:
  //...
  bool isLocked () const;
  //...
};

bool fileProc::Locked;
```

Static Member Functions

A static member function in a class can access only other static members of its class. Unlike ordinary member functions, a static member function can be invoked even when no object instance exists. For example

```
class stat
{
private:
  int num;
public:
  stat(int n = 0) {num=n;}
  static void print() {cout <<"static member function" <<endl;
};

int main()
{
  stat::print(); //no object instance required
  stat s(1);
  s.print();//still, a static member function can be called from an object
  return 0;
}
```

Static members are used in the following cases:

- When all other data members of an object are also static
- When the function does not depend on any other object member (like `print()`, in the previous example)
- As a wrapper of a global function

A Pointer to Member Cannot Refer to a Static Member Function

It is illegal to assign the address of a static class member to a pointer to member. However, you can take the address of a static member function of a class and treat it as if it were an ordinary function. For example

```
class A
{
public:
  static  void f();
};
int main()
{
  void (*p) () = &A::f; //OK, ordinary pointer to function
}
```

You can do this because a static member function is essentially an ordinary function, which doesn't take an implicit this argument.

Defining a Class Constant

When you need a constant integer member in a class, the easiest way to create one is by using a const static member of an integral type; unlike other static data members, such a member can be initialized within the class body (see also Chapter 2, "Standard Briefing: The Latest Addenda to ANSI/ISO C++"). For example

```
class vector
{
private:
  int v_size;
  const static int MAX= 1024; //a single MAX is shared by all vector objects
  char *p;
public:
  vector() {p = new char[MAX]; }
  vector( int size)
  {
    if (size <= MAX)
      p = new char[size] ;
    else
      p = new char[MAX];
  }
};
```

Designing Class Hierarchies

After identifying a set of potential classes that might be required for the application, it is important to correctly identify the interactions and relationships among the classes to specify inheritance, containment, and ownership. The design of class hierarchies, as opposed to designing concrete types, requires additional considerations that are discussed in this section.

Private Data Members Are Preferable to Protected Ones

Data members of a class are usually a part of its implementation. They can be replaced when the internal implementation of the class is changed; therefore, they need to be hidden from other classes. If derived classes need to access these data members, they need to use accessor methods instead of directly accessing data members of a base class. Consequently, no modification is required for derived classes when a change is made in the base class.

Here's an example:

```
class Date
{
private:
  int d,m,y //how a date is represented is an implementation detail
public:
  int Day() const {return d; }
};
class DateTime : public Date
{
private:
  int hthiss;
  int minutes;
  int seconds;
public:
//...additional member functions
};
```

Now assume that class Date is used mostly on display devices, so it has to supply some method of converting its d,m,y members into a displayable string. In order to enhance performance, a design modification is made: Instead of the three integers, a single string now holds the date representation. Had class DateTime relied on the internal implementation of Date, it would have had to be modified as well. But because it can access Date's data members only through access methods, all that is required is a small change in the Date::Day() member function. Please note that accessor methods are usually inlined anyway, so their use does not incur additional runtime overhead.

Declaring Virtual Base Class Destructors

A base class needs to have its destructor declared virtual. In doing so, you ensure that the correct destructor is always called, even in the following case:

```
class Base
{
private:
  char *p;
public:
  Base() { p = new char [200]; }
  ~ Base () {delete [] p; } //non virtual destructor, bad
};
```

```
class Derived : public Base
{
private:
  char *q;
public:
  Derived() { q = new char[300]; }
  ~Derived() { delete [] q; }
  //...
};

void destroy (Base & b)
{
  delete &b;
}

int main()
{
  Base *pb = new Derived(); //200 + 300 bytes allocated
  //... meddle with pb
  destroy (*pb); //OOPS! only the destructor of Base is called
  //were Base's destructor virtual, the correct destructor would be called
  return 0;
}
```

Virtual Member Functions

Virtual member functions enable subclasses to extend or override the behavior of a base class. Deciding which members in a class can be overridden by a derived class is not a trivial issue. A class that overrides a `virtual` member function is only committed to adhere to the prototype of the overridden member function—not to its implementation. A common mistake is to declare all member functions as `virtual` "just in case". In this respect, C++ makes a clear-cut distinction between abstract classes that provide pure interfaces as opposed to base classes that provide implementation as well as an interface.

Extending a Virtual Function in a Derived Class

There are cases in which you want a derived class to extend a virtual function defined in its base class rather than override it altogether. It can be done quite easily in the following way:

```
class shape
{
  //...
public:
  virtual void draw();
  virtual void resize(int x, int y) { clearscr(); /*...*/ }};

class rectangle: public shape
{
```

```
    //...
public:
  virtual void resize (int x, int y)
  {
    shape::resize(x, y);  //explicit call to the base's virtual function
    //add functionality
    int size = x*y;
    //...
  }
};
```

The overriding function in a derived class should invoke an overridden function of its base class using its fully-qualified name.

Changing Access Specification of a Virtual Function

The access specification of a virtual member function that is defined in a base class can be changed in a derived class. For example

```
class Base
{
public:
  virtual void Say() { cout<<"Base";}
};
class Derived : public Base
{
private: //access specifier changed; legal but not a good idea
  void Say() {cout <<"Derived";} // overriding Base::Say()
};
```

Although this is legal, it does not work as expected when pointers or references are used; a pointer or reference to Base can also be assigned to any object that is publicly derived from Base:

```
Derived d;
Base *p = &d;
p->Say(); //OK, invokes Derived::Say()
```

Because the actual binding of a virtual member function is postponed to runtime, the compiler cannot detect that a nonpublic member function will be called; it assumes that p points to an object of type Base, in which Say() is a public member. As a rule, do not change the access specification of a virtual member function in a derived class.

Virtual Member Functions Should Not Be Private

As you saw previously, it is customary to extend virtual functions in a derived class by first invoking the base class's version of that function; then extend it with additional functionality. This can't be done when a virtual function is declared private.

Abstract Classes and Interfaces

An abstract class is one that has at least one *pure virtual member function,* that is, a non-implemented placeholder that must be implemented by its derived class. Instances of an abstract class cannot be created because it is intended to serve as a design skeleton for concrete classes that are derived from it, and not as an independent object. See the following example:

```
class File  //abstract class; serves as interface
{
public:
  int virtual open() = 0;  //pure virtual
  int virtual close() = 0; //pure virtual
};


class diskFile: public File
{
private:
  string filename;
  //...
public:
  int open() {/*...*/}
  int close () {/*...*/}
};
```

Use Derivation Instead of Type-Fields

Suppose that you have to implement an internationalization helper class that manages the necessary parameters of every natural language that is currently supported by a word processor. A naive implementation might rely on type-fields to indicate the specific language that is currently being used (for example, the interface language in which menus are displayed).

```
class Fonts {/*...*/};
class Internationalization
{
private:
  Lang lg; //type field
  FontResthisce fonts
public:
  enum Lang {English, Hebrew, Danish}
  Internationalization(Lang lang) : lg(lang) {};
  Loadfonts(Lang lang);
};
```

Every modification in `Internationalization` affects all its users, even when they are not supposed to be affected. When adding support for a new language, the users of the already-supported languages have to recompile (or download, which is worse) the

new version of the class. Moreover, as time goes by and support for new languages is
added, the class becomes bigger and more difficult to maintain, and it tends to contain
more bugs. A much better design approach is to use derivation instead of type-fields.
For example

```
class Internationalization //now a base class
{
private:
  FontResthisce fonts
public:
  Internationalization ();
  virtual int Loadfonts();
  virtual void SetDirectionality();
};

class English : public Internationalization
{
public:
  English();
  Loadfonts() { fonts = TimesNewRoman; }
  SetDirectionality(){}//do nothing; default: left to right
};

class Hebrew : public Internationalization
{
public:
  Hebrew();
  Loadfonts() { fonts = David; }
  SetDirectionality() { directionality = right_to_left;}
};
```

Derivation simplifies class structure and localizes the changes that are associated
with a specific language to its corresponding class without affecting others.

Overloading a Member Function Across Class Boundaries

A class is a namespace. The scope for overloading a member function is confined to a
class but not to its derived classes. Sometimes the need arises to overload the same
function in its class as well as in a class that is derived from it. However, using an identical name in a derived class merely hides the base class's function, rather than overloading it. Consider the following:

```
class B
{
public:
  void func();
};
class D : public B
{
public:
  void func(int n); //now hiding B::f, not overloading it
```

```
};

D d;
d.func();//compilation error. B::f is invisible in d;
d.func(1); //OK, D::func takes an argument of type int
```

In order to overload—rather than hide—a function of a base class, the function name of the base class has to be injected explicitly into the namespace of the derived class by a *using declaration*. For example

```
class D : public B
{
using B::func; // inject the name of a base member into the scope of D
public:
   void func(int n); // D now has two overloaded versions of func()
};
D d;
d.func ( ); // OK
d.func ( 10 ); // OK
```

Deciding Between Inheritance and Containment

When designing a class hierarchy, you often face a decision between inheritance, or *is-a*, and containment, or *has-a*, relation. The choice is not always immediately apparent. Assume that you are designing a Radio class, and you already have the following classes implemented for you in some library: Dial and ElectricAppliance. It is obvious that Radio is derived from ElectricAppliance. However, it is not so obvious that Radio is also derived from Dial. In such cases, check whether there is always a 1:1 relationship between the two. Do all radios have one and only one dial? They don't. A radio can have no dials at all—a transmitter/receiver adjusted to a fixed frequency, for example. Furthermore, it might have more than one dial—FM and AM dials. Hence, your Radio class needs to be designed to have Dial(s) rather than being derived from Dial. Note that the relationship between Radio and ElectricAppliance is 1:1 and corroborates the decision to derive Radio from ElectricAppliance.

The Holds-a Relation

Ownership defines the responsibility for the creation and the destruction of an object. An object is an owner of some other resource if and only if it has the responsibility for both constructing and destroying it. In this respect, an object that contains another object also owns it because its constructor is responsible for the invocation of the embedded object's constructor. Likewise, its destructor is responsible for invoking the embedded object's destructor. This is the well-known has-a relationship. A similar relationship is *holds-a*. It is distinguished from has-a by one factor: ownership. A class that indirectly contains—by means of a reference or a pointer—another object that is constructed and destroyed independently is said to hold that object. Here's an example:

```
class Phone {/*...*/};
class Dialer {/*...*/};
class Modem
{
private:
  Phone* pline;
  Dialer& dialer;
public:
  Modem (Phone *pp, Dialer& d) : pline(pp), dialer (d){}
//Phone and Dialer objects are constructed and destroyed
//independently of Modem
};

void f()
{
  Phone phone;
  Dialer dialer;
  Modem modem(&phone, dialer);
  //...use modem
}
```

Modem uses Phone and Dialer. However, it is not responsible for constructing or destroying them.

Empty Classes

A class that contains no data members and no member functions is an *empty class*. For example

```
class PlaceHolder {};
```

An empty class can serve as a placeholder for a yet-to-be defined class. Imagine an interface class that serves as a base for other classes; instead of waiting for its full implementation to be completed, it can be used this way in the interim. Additionally, an empty class can also be used as a means of forcing derivation relationship among classes that are not originally descended from one base class. (This is a bottom-up design). Finally, it can be used as a dummy argument to distinguish between overloaded versions of a function. In fact, one of the standard versions of operator new (see also Chapter 11, "Memory Management") uses this technique:

```
#include <new>
using namespace std;
int main()
{
  try
  {
    int *p = new int[100]; //exception-throwing new
  }
```

```
catch(bad_alloc & new_failure) {/*..*/}

int *p = new (nothrow) int [100]; // exception-free version of operator new
if (p)
{/*..*/}
return 0;
}
```

The nothrow argument is of type nothrow_t, which is an empty class by itself.

Using **structs** as a Shorthand for Public Classes

Traditionally, structs serve as data aggregates. However, in C++ a struct can have constructors, a destructor, and member functions—just like a class. The only difference between the two is the default access type: By default, a class has private access type to its members and derived objects, whereas a struct has public access. Consequently, structs are sometimes used as shorthand for classes, whose members are all public. Abstract classes are a good example of classes that have all public members.

Friendship

A class can grant access to its members on a selective basis by declaring external classes and functions as friends. A friend has full access to all the grantor's members, including private and protected ones. Friendship is sometimes unjustly criticized for exposing implementation details. However, this is radically different from declaring data members as public because friendship enables the class to declare explicitly which clients can access its members; in contrast, a public declaration provides indiscriminate access to a member. Here's an example:

```
bool operator ==( const Date & d1, const Date& d2);
{
  return (d1.day == d2.day) &&
           (d1.month == d2.month) &&
           (d1.year == d2.year);
}
class Date
{
  private:
    int day, month, year;
  public:
    friend bool operator ==( const Date & d1, const Date& d2);
};
```

Remember that friendship is not inherited, so nonpublic members of any class that is derived from Date are not accessible to operator ==.

Nonpublic Inheritance

When a derived class inherits from a nonpublic base, the is-a relationship between a derived object and its nonpublic base does not exist. For example:

```
class Mem_Manager {/*..*/};
class List: private Mem_Manager {/*..*/};

void OS_Register( Mem_Manager& mm);

int main()
{
  List li;
  OS_Register( li ); //compile time error; conversion from
                     //List & to Mem_Manager& is inaccessible
  return 0;
}
```

Class List has a private base, Mem_Manager, which is responsible for its necessary memory bookkeeping. However, List is not a memory manager by itself. Therefore, private inheritance is used to block its misuse. Private inheritance is similar to containment. As a matter of fact, the same effect might have been achieved by making Mem_Manager a member of class List. Protected inheritance is used in class hierarchies for similar purposes.

Common Root Class

In many frameworks and software projects, all classes are forced to be descendants of one common root class, which is usually named Object. This design policy prevails in other OO languages such as Smalltalk and Java, whose classes are derived from class Object implicitly. However, imitating this in C++ incurs many compromises and potential bugs. It creates artificial kinship among classes that have absolutely nothing in common. Bjarne Stroustrup addresses the issue: "Now what is the common relationship between a smile, the driver of my CD-ROM reader, a recording of Richard Strauss's Don Juan, a line of text, my medical records, and a real-time clock? Placing them all in a single hierarchy when their only shared property is that they are programming artifacts (they are all "objects") is of little fundamental value and can cause confusion." (*The C++ Programming Language*, 3rd ed., page 732).

If you are looking for genericity, that is, if you need an algorithm/container/function that works for every data type, you might find that templates serve you better. Moreover, a common root design policy also forces you to refrain from multiple inheritance entirely because any class that is derived simultaneously from two or more base classes faces the *dreadful derivation diamond* problem: It embeds more than one base subobject. Finally, the common root class usually serves as a means of implementing exception handling and RTTI, both of which are integral parts of C++ anyway.

Forward Declarations

Consider the following common situation in which classes refer to one another:

```
//file: bank.h
class Report
{
public:
  void Output(const Account& account); // compile time error;
                                       // Account is not declared yet
};
class Account
{
public:
  void Show() {Rep.Output(*this);}
};
```

An attempt to compile this header file causes compilation errors because the compiler does not recognize the identifier Account as a class name when class Report is compiled. Even if you relocate the declaration of class Account and place it before class Report, you encounter the same problem: Report is referred to from Account. For that purpose, a *forward declaration* is required. A forward declaration instructs the compiler to hold off reporting such errors until the entire source file has been scanned. For example

```
//file: bank.h
class Acount; //forward declaration
class Report
{
public:
  void Output(const Account& account); //fine
};

class Account
{
private:
  Report rep;
public:
  void Show() {Report::Output(*this);}
};
```

The forward declaration in the beginning of the source file enables class Report to refer to class Account even though its definition has not yet been seen. Note that only references and pointers can refer to a forward declared class.

Local Classes

A class can be declared inside a function or a block. In such cases, it is not visible from anywhere else, and instances thereof can only be created within the scope in which it is declared. This can be useful if you need to hide an ancillary object that is not to be accessible or used anywhere else. For example

```
void f(const char *text)
{
  class Display  //local helper class; visible only in f()
  {
    const char *ps;
  public:
    Display(const char *t) : ps(t) {}
    ~Display() { cout<<ps; }
  };
Display ucd(text);  //local object of type Display
}
```

A local class has no linkage.

Multiple Inheritance

Multiple inheritance was introduced to C++ in 1989. It isn't an exaggeration to say that it has been the most controversial feature ever added to C++. The opponents of multiple inheritance maintain that it adds an unnecessary complexity to the language, that every design model that uses multiple inheritance can be modeled with single inheritance, and that it complicates compiler writing. Of the three arguments, only the third one is true. Multiple inheritance is optional. Designers who feel that they can make do without it are never forced to use it. The added level of complexity that is ascribed to multiple inheritance is not a compelling argument either because the same criticism is applicable to other language features such as templates, operator overloading, exception handling, and so on.

Multiple inheritance enables the designer to create objects that are closer to their reality. A fax modem card is essentially a modem and a fax combined in one. Similarly, a `fax_modem` class that is publicly derived from both `fax` and `modem` represents the concept of a fax/modem better than a single inheritance model does. But the most compelling argument in favor of multiple inheritance is that some designs cannot be realized without it. For example, implementing the `Observer` pattern in Java is nearly impossible because Java lacks multiple inheritance ("Java vs. C++—A Critical Comparison," *C++ Report*, January 1997). `Observer` is not the only pattern that relies on multiple inheritance—`Adapter` and `Bridge` also do (ibid.).

Using Multiple Inheritance to Conjoin Features

Derived classes can combine the functionality of several base classes simultaneously, by means of multiple inheritance. Trying to achieve the same effect using single inheritance can be very difficult, to say the least. For example

```
class Persistent //abstract base class used by
{
                    //all persistence-supporting objects
```

```
public:
  virtual void WriteObject(void *pobj, size_t sz) = 0;
  virtual void* ReadObject(Archive & ar) = 0;
};

class Date {/*...*/};

class PersistentDate: public Date, public Persistent
{ /*..*/} //can be stored and retrieved
```

Virtual Inheritance

Multiple inheritance can lead to a problem known as the *DDD* (or *dreadful diamond of derivation*), as shown in the following case:

```
class ElectricAppliance
{
private:
  int voltage,
  int Hertz ;
public:
  //...constructor and other useful methods
  int getVoltage () const { return voltage; }
  int getHertz() const {return Hertz; }
};
class Radio : public ElectricAppliance {/*...*/};
class Tape : public ElectricAppliance {/*...*/};
class RadioTape: public Radio, public Tape { /*...*/};

int main()
{
  RadioTape rt;
  //the following statement is a compilation Error - ambiguous call.
  //Two copies getVoltage() exist in rt: one from Radio and one
  //from Tape. Furthermore, which voltage value should be returned?
  int voltage = rt.getVoltage();
  return 0;
}
```

The problem is obvious: rt is derived simultaneously from two base classes, each of which has its own copy of the methods and data members of ElectricAppliance. Consequently, rt has two copies of ElectricAppliance. This is the DDD. However, giving up multiple inheritance leads to a design compromise. In such cases, where reduplication of data and methods from a common base class is undesirable, use virtual inheritance:

```
class Radio : virtual public ElectricAppliance {/*...*/};
class Tape : virtual public ElectricAppliance {/*...*/};

class RadioTape: public Radio, public Tape
{/*...*/};
```

Now class `RadioTape` contains a single instance of `ElectricAppliance` that is shared by `Radio` and `Tape`; therefore, there are no ambiguities and no need to give up the powerful tool of multiple inheritance.

```cpp
int main()
{
  RadioTape rt;
  int voltage = rt.getVoltage(); //now OK
  return 0;
}
```

How does C++ ensure that only a single instance of a virtual member exists, regardless of the number of classes derived from it? This is implementation-dependent. However, all implementations currently use an additional level of indirection to access a virtual base class, usually by means of a pointer.

```cpp
//Note: this is a simplified description of iostream classes

class  ostream: virtual public ios { /*..*/ }
class  istream: virtual public ios { /*..*/ }

class iostream : public istream, public ostream { /*..*/ }
```

In the preceding example, each object in the `iostream` hierarchy has a pointer to the shared instance of the `ios` subobject. The additional level of indirection has a slight performance overhead. It also implies that the location of virtual subobjects is not known at compile time; therefore, RTTI might be needed to access virtual subobjects in some circumstances (this is discussed further in Chapter 7, "Runtime Type Information").

When multiple inheritance is used, the memory layout of such an object is implementation-dependent. The compiler can rearrange the order of the inherited subobjects to improve memory alignment. In addition, a virtual base can be moved to a different memory location. Therefore, when you are using multiple inheritance, do not assume anything about the underlying memory layout of an object.

Non-virtual Multiple Inheritance

Virtual inheritance is used to avoid multiple copies of a base class in a multiply-inherited object, as you just saw. However, there are cases in which multiple copies of a base are needed in a derived class. In such cases, virtual inheritance is intentionally avoided. For example, suppose you have a scrollbar class that serves as a base for two other subclasses:

```cpp
class Scrollbar
{
private:
  int x;
  int y;
public:
  void Scroll(units n);
  //...
  };
class HorizontalScrollbar : public Scrollbar {/*..*/};
class VerticalScrollbar : public Scrollbar {/*..*/};
```

Now imagine a window that has both a vertical scrollbar and a horizontal one. It can be implemented and used in the following way:

```
class MultiScrollWindow: public VerticalScrollbar,
                         public HorizontalScrollbar {/*..*/};

MultiScrollWindow msw;
msw.HorizontalScrollbar::Scroll(5);    // scroll left
msw.VerticalScrollbar::Scroll(12);    //...and up
```

The user can scroll such a window up and down as well as left and right. For this purpose, the window object has to have two distinct Scrollbar subobjects. Therefore, virtual inheritance is intentionally avoided in this case.

Choosing Distinct Names for Member Functions

When two or more classes serve as base classes in multiple inheritance, you want to choose a distinct name for each member function in order to avoid name ambiguity. Consider the following concrete example:

```
class AudioStreamer //real-time sound player
{
public:
  void Play();
  void Stop();
};
class VideoStreamer //real-time video player
{
public:
  void Play();
  void Stop();
};

class AudioVisual: public AudioStreamer, public VideoStreamer {/*...*/};
AudioVisual player;
player.play(); //error:  AudioStreamer::play() or VideoStreamer::play() ?
```

One way to overcome the ambiguity is specifying the function's fully-qualified name:

```
Player.AudioStreamer::play(); //fine but tedious
```

However, a preferable solution is the use of distinct names for member functions in the base classes:

```
class AudioStreamer
{
public:
  void au_Play(); };
class VideoStreamer
{
public:
  void vd_Play();
};
Player.au_play(); //now distinct
```

Conclusions

C++ is used today in fields as diverse as embedded systems, database engines, Web engines, financial systems, artificial intelligence, and more. This versatility can be attributed to its flexibility of programming styles, backward compatibility with C, and the fact that it is the most efficient object-oriented programming language in existence.

As a procedural programming language, C++ offers a tighter type-checking than C does. It also provides better memory management, inline functions, default arguments, and reference variables, which make it a "better C".

Object-based programming solves some of the noticeable weaknesses of procedural programming by bundling data types and the set of operations that are applied to them in a single entity. The separation of implementation details from an interface localizes changes in the design, thereby yielding more robust and extensible software. However, it does not support class hierarchies.

Object-oriented programming relies on encapsulation, information hiding, polymorphism, inheritance, and dynamic binding. These features enable you to design and implement class hierarchies. The advantages of object-oriented programming over object-based programming are faster development time, easier maintenance, and simpler extensibility.

C++ supports advanced object-oriented programming features such as multiple inheritance, static and dynamic polymorphism, and a clear-cut distinction between a class and an object. Object-oriented design begins with locating the classes and their interrelations: inheritance, containment, and ownership. The symmetry between constructors and destructors is the basis for useful design idioms such as "resource aquisition is initialization" and smart pointers.

An additional programming paradigm that is supported in C++, generic programming, is not directly related to object-oriented programming. In fact, it can be implemented in procedural languages as well. Nonethless, the combination of object-oriented programming and generic programming makes C++ a very powerful language indeed, as you will read in Chapter 10.

Facilities for Extensible and Robust Design

6

Exception Handling

Introduction

Large software applications are built in layers. At the lowest level, you usually find library routines, API functions, and proprietary infrastructure functions. At the highest level, there are user interface components that enable a user to, for instance, fill out a data sheet in a spreadsheet application. Consider an ordinary flight-booking application: Its topmost layer consists of GUI components that display contents on the user's screen. These high-level components interact with data access objects, which in turn encapsulate database API routines. At a lower level, the database API routines interact with the database engine. The database engine itself invokes system services that deal with low-level hardware resources such as physical memory, file system, and security modules. In general, severe runtime errors are detected in these lower code layers, which cannot—or should not—attempt to handle these errors on their own. The handling of severe runtime errors is the responsibility of higher-level components. In order to handle an error, however, higher-level components have to be informed that an error has occurred. Essentially, error handling consists of detecting an error and notifying the software components that are in charge. These components in turn attempt to recover from the error.

Traditional Error Handling Methods

In its earlier stages, C++ did not have a built-in facility for handling runtime errors. Instead, the traditional C methods were used for that purpose. These methods can be grouped into three design policies:

- Return a status code with agreed-upon values to indicate either success or failure.
- Assign an error code to a global variable and have other functions examine it.
- Terminate the program altogether.

Each of these methods has significant drawbacks and limitations in an object-oriented environment. Some of them might be totally unacceptable, particularly in large-scale applications. The following sections examine each of these methods more closely in order to assess their inherent limitations and hazards.

Returning an Error Code

To some extent, this method can be useful in small programs in which an agreed-upon, closed set of error codes exists, and in which a rigorous policy of reporting errors and checking the returned status of a function is applied. However, this method has some noticeable limitations; for example, neither the error types nor their enumerated values are standardized. Thus, in one library the implementer might choose a return value of 0 (meaning *false*, perhaps) to indicate an error, whereas another vendor might choose 0 to indicate success and any nonzero value to indicate an error condition. Usually, the return codes are shared in a common header file in the form of symbolic constants so that some commonality can be maintained throughout an application or a development team. These codes are not standardized, however.

Needless to say, the process of combining noncompatible software libraries from different vendors or programmers becomes very difficult and confusing when conflicting error codes are used. Another disadvantage is that every returned code has to be looked up and interpreted—a tedious and costly operation. This policy requires that the return value of every function be checked every time by every caller; failing to do so might lead to runtime disasters. When an error code is detected, a return statement disrupts the normal execution flow and passes the error code on to the caller. The additional code that wraps every function call (to examine the return status and decide whether to continue normally) can easily double the size of the program and cause serious difficulties in the software's maintenance and readability. Worse yet, returning an error value is sometimes impossible. For instance, constructors do not return values, so they cannot use this method to report the failed construction of an object.

Turning on a Global Flag

An alternative approach for reporting runtime errors is to use global flags, which indicate whether the last operation ended successfully. Unlike the return code policy, this method is standardized. The C <errno.h> header file defines a mechanism for examining and assigning the value of a global integer flag, errno. Note that the inherent drawbacks of this policy are not negligible. In a multithreaded environment, the error code that is assigned to errno by one thread can be inadvertently overwritten by another thread before the caller has had a chance to examine it. In addition, the use of an error code instead of a more readable message is disadvantageous because the codes might not be compatible among different environments. Finally, this method requires a well-disciplined programming style that relies on constant checking of the current value of errno.

The global flag policy is similar to the function return value policy: Both provide a mechanism for reporting an error, but neither guarantees that the error is actually handled. For example, a function that fails to open a file can indicate a failure by assigning an appropriate value to errno. However, it cannot prevent another function from attempting to write into the file or close it. Furthermore, if errno indicates an error and the programmer detects and handles it as is expected, errno still has to be reset explicitly. A programmer might forget to do so, thereby causing other functions, which assume that the error has not been handled, to attempt to rectify the problem—with unpredictable results.

Terminating the Program

The most drastic method of handling a runtime error is simply to terminate the program immediately when a severe error has been detected. This solution averts some of the drawbacks of the previous two methods; for example, there is no need for repetitive examination of the status that is returned from every function call, nor does the programmer have to assign a global flag, test its value, and clear it in a repetitive and error-prone manner. The standard C library has two functions that terminate a program: exit() and abort(). exit() can be called to indicate successful termination of a program (as the final statement in main()), or it can be called in the case of a runtime error. Before returning control to the environment, exit() first flushes open streams and closes open files. abort(), on the other hand, indicates abnormal program termination. It terminates immediately, without flushing streams or closing open files.

Critical applications cannot just halt abruptly on every occurrence of a runtime error. It would be disastrous if a life support machine stopped functioning just because its controller detected a division by zero. Similarly, applications such as the billing system of a telephone company or a banking application cannot break down altogether whenever a runtime exception occurs. Robust, real world applications can—and must—do better than that.

Program termination is problematic even for applications, such as an operating system, that are expected to abort in the case of serious runtime errors. A function that detects the error usually does not have the necessary information to estimate the severity of the error. A memory allocation function, for example, cannot tell whether an allocation request has failed because the user is currently using a debugger, a Web browser, a spreadsheet, and a word processor all at once, or because the system has become unstable due to a severe hardware fault. In the first scenario, the system can simply display a message, requesting that the user close unnecessary applications. In the second scenario, a more drastic measure might be required. Under this policy, however, the allocation function simply aborts the program (the operating system kernel, in this case), regardless of the severity of the error. This is hardly applicable in nontrivial applications. Good system design has to ensure that runtime errors are detected and reported, but it also has to ensure a minimal level of fault tolerance.

Terminating the program might be acceptable under extreme conditions or during debugging phases. However, `abort()` and `exit()` are never to be used in an object-oriented environment, even during debugging, because they are unaware of the C++ object model.

`exit()` and `abort()` Do Not Destroy Objects

An object can hold resources that are acquired by the constructor or a member function: memory allocated on the free store, file handles, communication ports, database transaction locks, I/O devices, and so on. These resources have to be properly released by the object that uses them when it's done. Usually, these resources are released by the destructor. This design idiom is called *resource acquisition is initialization* (this is discussed in greater detail in Chapter 5, "Object-Oriented Programming and Design"). Local objects that are created on the stack are destroyed automatically when their block or function exits. Neither `abort()` nor `exit()`, however, invokes the destructors of local objects. Therefore, an abrupt program termination caused by calling these functions can cause irreversible damage: A database can be corrupted, files can be lost, and valuable data can evaporate. For this reason, do not use either `abort()` or `exit()` in an object-oriented environment.

Enter Exception Handling

As you have observed, none of the traditional error handling methods of C are adequate for C++; one of the goals of C++ was to enable better and safer large-scale software development than is offered by C.

The designers of C++ were aware of the considerable difficulties resulting from the lack of a proper error handling mechanism. They sought a solution that was free from all the ailments of C's traditional error handling. The suggested mechanism was based on the automatic transfer of control to the system when an exception is triggered. The mechanism had to be simple, and it had to free the programmer from the drudgery of constantly examining a global flag or the returned value of a function. Additionally, it had to ensure that the code sections that handle the exception are automatically informed when an exception occurs. Finally, it had to ensure that when an exception is not handled locally, local objects are properly destroyed and their resources are released before the exception is propagated to a higher handler.

In 1989, after several years of research and a plethora of draft proposals, exception handling was added to C++. C++ is not the first language to offer structured runtime error handling support. Back in the 1960s, PL/1 offered a built-in exception handling mechanism; Ada provided its own version of exception handling in the early 1980s, as did several other languages. But none of these exception handling models fit the C++ object model and program structure. Therefore, the proposed exception handling for C++ was unique, and it has served as a model for newer languages that have appeared since.

Implementing an exception handling mechanism turned out to be a real challenge. The first C++ compiler, cfront, ran on UNIX. Like many UNIX compilers, it was a translator that first transformed C++ code into C, and then compiled the resultant C code. Release 4.0 of cfront was supposed to include exception handling. However, the implementation of an exception handling mechanism that met all the requirements got so complicated that the development team of cfront 4.0 decided to abandon the project entirely after spending a whole year designing it. cfront 4.0 was never released; however, exception handling became an integral part of Standard C++. Other compilers that started to appear later supported it. The following section explains why it was it so difficult to implement exception handling under cfront, and under any other compiler in general.

The Challenges of Implementation of Exception Handling

The difficulties in implementing exception handling arise from several factors. First, the implementation must ensure that the proper handler for a specific exception is found.

Secondly, exception objects can be polymorphic; in that case, the implementation also considers handlers of base classes when it cannot locate a matching handler for a derived object. This requirement implies a sort of runtime type checking to recover the dynamic type of the exception object. Yet C++ did not have any runtime type checking facilities whatsoever before exception handling was developed; these facilities had to be created from scratch for that purpose.

As an additional complication, the implementation must invoke the destructors of all local objects that were constructed on the path from a try block to a throw expression before control passes to the appropriate handler. This process is called *stack unwinding* (the stack unwinding process is discussed in further detail later in this chapter). Because early C++ compilers translated the C++ source file into pure C and only then compiled the code into machine code, the implementers of exception handling had to implement runtime type identification and stack unwinding in C. Fortunately, these obstacles have all been overcome.

Applying Exception Handling

Exception handling is a flexible and sophisticated tool. It overcomes the drawbacks of C's traditional error handling methods and it can be used to handle a variety of runtime errors. Still, exception handling, like other language features, can easily be misused. To use this feature effectively, it is important to understand how the underlying runtime machinery works and what the associated performance penalties are. The following sections delve into exception handling internals and demonstrate how to use this tool to create robust, bulletproof applications.

Exception Handling Constituents

Exception handling is a mechanism for transferring control from a point in a program where an exception occurs to a matching handler. Exceptions are variables of built-in data types or class objects. The exception handling mechanism consists of four components: a try *block*, a sequence of one or more *handlers* associated with a try block, a throw *expression*, and the exception itself. The try block contains code that might throw an exception. For example

```
try
{
 int * p = new int[1000000]; //may throw std::bad_alloc
}
```

A try block is followed by a sequence of one or more catch statements, or handlers, each of which handles a different type of exception. For example

```
try
{
 int * p = new int[1000000]; //may throw std::bad_alloc
 //...
}
catch(std::bad_alloc& )
{
}
catch (std::bad_cast&)
{
}
```

A handler is invoked only by a throw expression that is executed in the handler's try block or in functions that are called from the handler's try block. A throw expression consists of the keyword throw and an *assignment expression*. For example

> **Caution**
>
> Some of the code samples in the following sections use new exception handling features such as function try blocks and exception specifications. Several compilers do not support these features yet; therefore, it is recommended that you read the technical documentation of your compiler to check whether it fully supports exception handling.

```
try
{
  throw 5; // 5 is assigned to n in the following catch statement
}
catch(int n)
{
}
```

A `throw` expression is similar to a `return` statement. An *empty throw* is a `throw` statement without an operand. For example

```
throw;
```

An empty throw inside a handler indicates a *rethrow*, which is discussed momentarily. Otherwise, if no exception is presently being handled, executing an empty throw calls `terminate()`.

Stack Unwinding

When an exception is thrown, the runtime mechanism first searches for an appropriate handler in the current scope. If such a handler does not exist, the current scope is exited and the block that is higher in the calling chain is entered into scope. This process is iterative: It continues until an appropriate handler has been found. An exception is considered to be handled upon its entry to a handler. At this point, the stack has been unwound and all the local objects that were constructed on the path from a `try` block to a `throw` expression have been destroyed. In the absence of an appropriate handler, the program terminates. Note, however, that C++ ensures proper destruction of local objects only when the thrown exception is handled. Whether an uncaught exception causes the destruction of local objects during stack unwinding is implementation-dependent. To ensure that destructors of local objects are invoked in the case of an uncaught exception, you can add a `catch all` statement in `main()`. For example

```
int main()
{
  try
  {
    //...
  }
  catch(std::exception& stdexc)    // handle expected exceptions
  {
    //...
  }
  catch(...)    // ensure proper cleanup in the case of an uncaught exception
  {
  }
  return 0;
}
```

The stack unwinding process is very similar to a sequence of `return` statements, each returning the same object to its caller.

Passing Exception Objects to a Handler

An exception can be passed by value or by reference to its handler. The memory for the exception that is being thrown is allocated in an unspecified way (but it is not allocated on the free store). Some implementations use a dedicated exception stack, on which exception objects are created. When an exception is passed by reference, the handler receives a reference to the exception object that is constructed on the exception stack. Passing an exception by reference ensures its polymorphic behavior. Exceptions that are passed by value are constructed on the stack frame of the caller. For example

```
#include  <cstdio>
class ExBase {/*...*/};
class FileEx: public ExBase {/*...*/};

void Write(FILE *pf)
{
  if (pf == NULL) throw FileEx();
  //... process pf normally
}
int main ()
{
  try
  {
    Write(NULL); //will cause a FileEx exception to be thrown
  }
  catch(ExBase& exception) //catch ExBase or any object derived from it
  {
  //diagnostics and remedies
  }
}
```

Repeatedly copying objects that are passed by value is costly because the exception object can be constructed and destroyed several times before a matching handler has been found. However, it occurs only when an exception is thrown, which only happens in abnormal and—hopefully—rare situations. Under these circumstances, performance considerations are secondary (exception handling performance is discussed at the end of this chapter) to maintaining an application's integrity.

Exception Type Match

The type of an exception determines which handler can catch it. The matching rules for exceptions are more restrictive than are the matching rules for function overloading. Consider the following example:

```
try
{
  throw int();
}
```

```
catch (unsigned int) //will not catch the exception from the previous try-block
{
}
```

The thrown exception is of type int, whereas the handler expects an unsigned int. The exception handling mechanism does not consider these to be matching types; as a result, the thrown exception is not caught. The matching rules for exceptions allow only a limited set of conversions: For an exception E and a handler taking T or T&, the match is valid under one of the following conditions:

- T and E are of the same type (const and volatile specifiers are ignored)
- T is an unambiguous public base class of E.

If E and T are pointers, the match is valid if E and T are of the same type or if E points to an object that is publicly and unambiguously derived from the class that is pointed to by T. In addition, a handler of type array of T or function returning T is transformed into pointer to T or pointer to function returning T, respectively.

Exceptions as Objects

As you have probably noticed, the traditional convention of returning an integer as an error flag is problematic and unsatisfactory in Object-Oriented Programming. The C++ exception handling mechanism offers more flexibility, safety, and robustness. An exception can be a fundamental type such as int or a char *. It can be a full-fledged object as well, with data members and member functions. Such an object can provide the exception handler with more options for recovery. A clever exception object, for example, can have a member function that returns a detailed verbal description of the error, instead of letting the handler to look it up in a table or a file. It can have member functions that enable the program to recover from the runtime error after the error has been handled properly. Consider a logger class that appends new records to an existing log file: If it fails to open the log file, it throws an exception. When it is caught by the matching handler, the exception object can have a member function, which creates a dialog box. The operator can choose recovery measures from the dialog box, including creation of a new log file, redirecting the logger to an alternative file, or simply allowing the system to run without a logger.

Exception Specification

A function that might throw an exception can warn its users by specifying a list of the exceptions that it can throw. Exception specifications are particularly useful when users of a function can view its prototype but cannot access its source file. Following is an example of specifying an exception:

```
class Zerodivide{/*..*/};
int divide (int, int) throw(Zerodivide);    // function may throw an exception
                                            // of type Zerodivide, but no other
```

If your function never throws any exceptions, it can be declared as follows:

```
bool equals (int, int) throw(); //no exception is thrown from this function
```

Note that a function that is declared without an exception specification such as

```
bool equals (int, int);
```

guarantees nothing about its exceptions: It might throw any exception, or it might throw no exceptions.

Exception Specifications Are Enforced at Runtime

An exception specification might not be checked at compile time, but rather at runtime. When a function attempts to throw an exception that it is not allowed to throw according to its exception specification, the exception handling mechanism detects the violation and invokes the standard function unexpected(). The default behavior of unexpected() is to call terminate(), which terminates the program. A violation of an exception specification is most likely a bug, and should not occur—this is why the default behavior is program termination. The default behavior can be altered, nonetheless, by using the function set_unexpected().

Because exception specifications are enforced only at runtime, the compiler might deliberately ignore code that seemingly violates exception specifications. Consider the following:

```
int f();    // no exception specification, f can throw any type of exception
void g(int j) throw()    // g promises not to throw any exception at all
{
  int result = f(); // if f throws an exception, g will violate its guarantee
                    //not to throw an exception. still, this code is legal
}
```

In this example, the function g(), which is not allowed to throw any exception, invokes the function f(). f(), however, is free to throw any exception because it has no exception specification. If f() throws an exception, it propagates through g(), thereby violating g()'s guarantee not to throw any exception. It might seem surprising that exception specifications are enforced only at runtime because at least some of the violations can be caught at compile time and flagged as errors. This is not the case, however. There are several compelling reasons for the runtime checking policy. In the preceding example, f() can be a legacy C function. It is impossible to enforce every C function to have an exception specification. Forcing the programmer to write unnecessary try and catch(...) blocks in g() "just in case" is impractical as well—what if the programmer knows that f() doesn't throw any exception at all and the code is therefore safe? By enforcing exception specifications at runtime, C++ applies the "trust the programmer" policy instead of forcing an unnecessary burden on both the programmer and the implementation.

Concordance of Exception Specification

C++ requires exception specification concordance in derived classes. This means that an overriding virtual function in a derived class has to have an exception specification that is at least as restrictive as the exception specification of the overridden function in the base class. For example

```
// various exception classes
class BaseEx{};
class DerivedEx: public BaseEx{};
class OtherEx {};

class A
{
public:
  virtual void f() throw (BaseEx);
  virtual void g() throw (BaseEx);
  virtual void h() throw (DerivedEx);
  virtual void i() throw (DerivedEx);
  virtual void j() throw(BaseEx);
};

class D: public A
{
public:
  void f() throw (DerivedEx); //OK, DerivedEx is derived from BaseEx
class D: public A
{
public:
  void f() throw (DerivedEx); //OK, DerivedEx is derived from BaseEx
  void g() throw (OtherEx);  //error; exception specification is
                            //incompatible with A's
  void h() throw (DerivedEx); //OK, identical to the exception
                            //specification in base
  void i() throw (BaseEx); //error, BaseEx is not a DerivedEx nor is it
                          //derived from DerivedEx
  void j()  throw (BaseEx,OtherEx); //error, less restrictive than the
                                   //specification of A::j
};

};
```

The same concordance restrictions apply to pointers to functions. A pointer to a function that has an exception specification can be assigned only to a function that has an identical or a more restrictive exception specification. This implies that a pointer to function that has no exception specification cannot be assigned to a function that has one. Note, however, that an exception specification is not considered part of the function type. Therefore, you cannot declare two distinct functions that differ only in their exception specification. For example

```
void f(int) throw (Y);
void f(int) throw (Z); //error; redefinition of 'void f(int)'
```

For the same reason, declaring a `typedef` that contains an exception specification is also an error:

```
typedef void (*PF) (int) throw(Exception); // error
```

Exceptions During Object's Construction and Destruction

Constructors and destructors are invoked automatically; in addition, they cannot return values to indicate a runtime error. Seemingly, the most plausible way of reporting run-time errors during object construction and destruction is by throwing an exception. However, there are additional factors that you have to consider before throwing an exception in these cases. You should be particularly cautious about throwing an exception from a destructor.

Throwing Exceptions from a Destructor Is Dangerous

Throwing an exception from a destructor is not recommended. The problem is that a destructor might be invoked due to another exception as part of the stack unwinding. If a destructor that was invoked due to another exception also throws an exception of its own, the exception handling mechanism invokes `terminate()`. If you really have to throw an exception from a destructor, it is advisable to check first whether another uncaught exception is currently being processed.

Checking for an Uncaught Exception

A thrown exception is considered caught when its corresponding handler has been entered (or, if such a handler cannot be found, when the function `unexpected()` has been invoked). In order to check whether a thrown exception is currently being processed, you can use the standard function `uncaught_exception()` (which is defined in the standard header `<stdexcept>`). For example

```
class FileException{};
File::~File() throw (FileException)
{
  if ( close(file_handle) != success) // failed to close current file?
  {
    if (uncaught_exception()  == true ) // is there any uncaught exception
                                        //being processed currently?
       return;  // if so, do not throw an exception
    throw FileException(); // otherwise, it is safe to throw an exception
                        // to signal an error
  }
  return; // success
}
```

Still, a better design choice is to handle exceptions within a destructor rather than let them propagate into the program. For example

```
void cleanup() throw (int);

class C
{
public:
  ~C();
};

C::~C()
{
  try
  {
    cleanup();
  }
  catch(int)
  {
    //handle the exception within the destructor
  }
}
```

If an exception is thrown by `cleanup()`, it is handled inside the destructor. Otherwise, the thrown exception will propagate outside the destructor, and if the destructor has been invoked while unwinding the stack due to another exception, `terminate()` will be called.

Global Objects: Construction and Destruction

Conceptually, the construction of global objects takes place before program outset. Therefore, any exception that is thrown from a constructor of a global object can never be caught. This is also true for a global object's destructor—the destruction of a global object executes after a program's termination. Hence, an exception that is thrown from a global object's destructor cannot be handled either.

Advanced Exception Handling Techniques

The simple `try-throw-catch` model can be extended even further to handle more complicated runtime errors. This section discusses some of the more advanced uses of exception handling, including exception hierarchies, rethrowing exceptions, function `try` blocks and the `auto_ptr` class.

Standard Exceptions

C++ defines a hierarchy of standard exceptions that are thrown at runtime when abnormal conditions arise. The standard exception classes are derived from std::exception (defined in the <stdexcept> header). This hierarchy enables the application to catch these exceptions in a single catch statement:

```
catch (std::exception& exc)
{
  // handle exception of type std::exception as well as
  //any exception derived from it
}
```

The standard exceptions that are thrown by built-in operators of the language are

```
std::bad_alloc      //by operator new
std::bad_cast       //by operator dynamic_cast < >
std::bad_typeid     //by operator typeid
std::bad_exception  //thrown when an exception specification of
                    //a function is violated
```

All standard exceptions have provided the member function what(), which returns a const char * with an implementation-dependent verbal description of the exception. Note, however, that the standard library has an additional set of exceptions that are thrown by its components.

Exception Handlers Hierarchy

Exceptions are caught in a bottom-down hierarchy: Specific (most derived classes) exceptions are handled first, followed by groups of exceptions (base classes), and, finally, a catch all handler. For example

```
#include <stdexcept>
#include <iostream>
using namespace std;

int main()
{
  try
  {
      char * buff = new char[100000000];
      //...use buff
  }
  catch(bad_alloc& alloc_failure)    // bad_alloc is
                                     //derived from exception
  {
    cout<<"memory allocation failure";
    //... handle exception thrown by operator new
  }
  catch(exception& std_ex)
  {
    cout<< std_ex.what() <<endl;
  }
  catch(...)  // exceptions that are not handled elsewhere are caught here
  {
    cout<<"unrecognized exception"<<endl;
```

```
    }
    return 0;
}
```

Handlers of the most derived objects must appear before the handlers of base classes. This is because handlers are tried in order of appearance. It is therefore possible to write handlers that are never executed, for example, by placing a handler for a derived class after a handler for a corresponding base class. For example

```
catch(std::exception& std_ex) //bad_alloc exception is always handled here
{
  //...handle the exception
}
catch(std::bad_alloc& alloc_failure)    //unreachable
{
  cout<<"memory allocation failure";
}
```

Rethrowing an Exception

An exception is thrown to indicate an abnormal state. The first handler to catch the exception can try to fix the problem. If it fails to do so, or if it only manages to perform a partial recovery, it can still rethrow the exception, thereby letting a higher try block handle it. For that purpose, try blocks can be nested in a hierarchical order, enabling a rethrown exception from a lower catch statement to be caught again. A rethrow is indicated by a throw statement without an operand. For example

```
#include <iostream>
#include <string>

using namespace std;
enum {SUCCESS, FAILURE};

class File
{
  public: File (const char *) {}
  public: bool IsValid() const {return false; }
  public: int OpenNew() const {return FAILURE; }
};
class Exception {/*..*/}; //general base class for exceptions

class FileException: public Exception
{
  public: FileException(const char *p) : s(p) {}
  public: const char * Error() const { return s.c_str(); }
  private: string s;
};

void func(File& );
```

```
int main()
{

  try //outer try
  {
    File f ("db.dat");
    func(f);     // 1
  }
catch(...) // 7
  //this handler will catch the re-thrown exception;
  //note: the same exception type is required
  {

    cout<<"re-thrown exception caught";
  }
  return 0;
}

void func(File & f)
{
  try //inner try
  {

    if (f.IsValid() == false )
    throw FileException("db.dat");   // 2
  }
  catch(FileException &fe) // 3
//first chance to cope with the exception
  {
    cout<<"invalid file specification" <<fe.Error()<<endl;
    if (f.OpenNew() != SUCCESS) (5)
    //re-throw the original exception and let a higher handler deal with it
    throw; // 6
  }
}
```

In the preceding example, the function func() is called from the try block inside
main() (1). The second try block inside func() throws an exception of type
FileException (2). This exception is caught by the catch block inside func() (3). The
catch block attempts to remedy the situation by opening a new file. This attempt fails
(5), and the FileException is rethrown (6). Finally, the rethrown exception is caught—
this time, by the catch(...) block inside main() (7).

Function try Blocks

A *function* try *block* is a function whose body consists of a try block and its associated
handlers. A function try block enables a handler to catch an exception that is thrown
during the execution of the *initializer expressions* in the constructor's member initialization list or during the execution of the constructor's body. Note, however, that unlike

handlers of ordinary exceptions, the handler of a function `try` block merely catches the exception—it cannot continue the object's construction normally. This is because the partially constructed object is destroyed as a result of the stack unwinding. In addition, the handler of a function `try` block cannot execute a `return` statement (eventually, the handler must exit by a `throw`). What is the use of a function `try` block then? The handler enables you to throw a different exception than the one that it just caught, thereby preventing a violation of the exception specification. For example

```
class X{};
C::C(const std::string& s) throw (X) //  allowed to throw X only
try
: str(s) // str's constructor might throw a bad_alloc exception,
         // might violate C's exception specification
{
  // constructor function body
}
catch (...) //handle any exception thrown from ctor initializer or ctor body
{
  //...
  throw X(); //replace bad_alloc exception with an exception of type X
}
```

In this example, a `string` object is first constructed as a member of class `C`. `string` might throw a `bad_alloc` exception during its construction. The function try block catches the `bad_alloc` exception and throws instead an exception of type `X`, which satisfies the exception specification of `C`'s constructor.

Use `auto_ptr<>` to Avoid Memory Leaks

The Standard Library supplies the class template `auto_ptr<>` (discussed in Chapter 10, "STL and Generic Programming"), which automatically deallocates memory that is allocated on the free store in much the same manner as local objects are reclaimed in case of exiting their scope. When an `auto_ptr<>` is instantiated, it can be initialized with a pointer to an object that is allocated on the free store. When the current scope is exited, the destructor of the `auto_ptr<>` object automatically deletes the object that is bound to it. By using `auto_ptr<>`, you can avoid memory leakage in the case of an exception. Furthermore, `auto_ptr<>` can simplify programming by sparing the bother of explicitly deleting objects that were allocated on the free store. `auto_ptr<>` is defined in the standard <memory> header file.

For example

```
#include <memory>
#include <iostream>
using namespace std;

class Date{ public: const char * DateString(); };

void DisplayDate()
{
```

```
                //create a local object of type auto_ptr<Date>
        auto_ptr<Date> pd (new Date); //now pd is owned by the template object
        cout<< pd-> DateString();
        //pd is automatically deleted by the destructor of auto_ptr;
    }
```

In the preceding example, the auto_ptr<> instance, pd, can be used like an ordinary pointer to Date. The overloaded operators *, ->, and & of auto_ptr<> provide the pointer-like syntax.

pd's bound object is automatically destroyed when DisplayDate() exits.

Exception Handling Performance Overhead

By nature, exception handling relies heavily on runtime type checking. When an exception is thrown, the implementation has to determine whether the exception was thrown from a try block (an exception can be thrown from a program section that is not enclosed within a try block—by operator new, for example). If indeed the exception was thrown from a try block, the implementation compares the type of the exception and attempts to find a matching handler in the current scope. If a match is found, control is transferred to the handler's body. This is the optimistic scenario. What if the implementation cannot find a matching handler for the exception, though, or what if the exception was not thrown from a try block? In such a case, the current function is unwound from the stack and the next active function in the stack is entered. The same process is reiterated until a matching handler has been found (at that point, all the automatic objects that were created on the path from a try block to a throw expression have been destroyed). When no matching handler can be found in the program, terminate() is invoked and the program terminates.

Additional Runtime Type Information

The exception handling mechanism has to store additional data about the type of every exception object and every catch statement in order to perform the runtime matching between an exception and its matching handler. Because an exception can be of any type, and because it can be polymorphic as well, its dynamic type must be queried at runtime, using *runtime type information (RTTI)*. RTTI, imposes an additional overhead in terms of both execution speed and program size (see Chapter 7, "Runtime Type Information"). Yet RTTI alone is not enough. The implementation also requires runtime *code* information, that is, information about the structure of each function. This information is needed to determine whether an exception was thrown from a try block. This information is generated by the compiler in the following way: The compiler divides each function body into three parts: one that is outside a try block with no active objects, a second part that is also outside a try block but that has active objects that have to be destroyed during stack unwinding, and a third part that is within a try block.

Toggling Exception Handling Support

The technicalities of exception handling implementation vary among compilers and platforms. In all of them, however, exception handling imposes additional overhead even when no exception is ever thrown. The overhead lies in both execution speed and program size. Some compilers enable you to toggle exception handling support. When it is turned off, the additional data structures, lookup tables, and auxiliary code are not generated. However, turning off exception handling is rarely an option. Even if you do not use exceptions directly, you are probably using them implicitly: Operator new, for example, might throw a `std::bad_alloc` exception when it fails—and so do other built-in operators; STL containers might throw their own exceptions, and so might other functions of the Standard Library. Code libraries that are supplied by third party vendors might use exceptions as well. Therefore, you can safely turn off exception handling support only when you are porting pure C code into a C++ compiler. As long as pure C code is used, the additional exception handling overhead is unnecessary and can be avoided.

Misuses of Exception Handling

Exception handling is not confined to errors. Some programmers might use it simply as an alternative control structure to for loops or while and do blocks. For example, a simple application that prompts the user to enter data until a certain condition has been fulfilled can be (rather naively) implemented as follows:

```cpp
#include <iostream>
using namespace std;

class Exit{}; //used as exception object

int main()
{
 int num;
 cout<< "enter a number; 99 to exit" <<endl;

 try
 {
   while (true) //infinitely
   {
     cin>>num;
     if (num == 99)
         throw Exit(); //exit the loop
     cout<< "you entered: " << num << "enter another number " <<endl;
   }
 }
 catch (Exit& )
 {
   cout<< "game over" <<endl;
 }

 return 0;
}
```

In the preceding example, the programmer locates an infinite loop within a try block. The `throw` statement breaks the loop and transfers control to the following `catch` statement. This style of programming is not recommended, however. It is very inefficient due to the excess overhead of exception handling. Furthermore, it is rather verbose and might have been much simpler and shorter had it been written with a `break` statement. In demo apps such as this one, the difference is mostly a stylistic one. In large-scale applications, the use of exception handling as an alternative control structure imposes a significant performance overhead.

Simple runtime errors that can be handled safely and effectively without the heavy machinery of exception handling need to also be treated by traditional methods. For example, a password entry dialog box should not throw an exception if the user mistyped his or her password. It is much simpler to redisplay the password entry dialog again with an appropriate error message. On the other hand, if the user enters wrong passwords dozens of times in a row, this can indicate a malicious break-in attempt. In this case, an exception should be thrown. The appropriate handler can page the system administrator and security officer.

Conclusions

The exception handling mechanism of C++ overcomes the problems associated with the traditional methods. It frees the programmer from writing tedious code that checks the success status of every function call. Exception handling also eliminates human mistakes. Another important advantage of exception handling is the automatic unwinding of the stack, which ensures that local active objects are properly destroyed and their resources are released.

Implementing an exception handling mechanism was not a trivial task. The need to query the dynamic type of exception led to the introduction of RTTI into C++. The additional overhead of exception handling derives from the RTTI data structures, the "scaffolding" code that is generated by the compiler, and other implementation-dependent factors. Exceptions can be grouped into categories; the standard exception classes are a good example of this. In recent years, a few loopholes in the exception handling mechanism have been fixed. The first was the addition of exception specifications to functions' prototypes. The second was the introduction of a function `try` block, which enables the program to handle an exception that is thrown during the execution of the initializer expressions in the constructor's member initialization list or during the execution of the constructor's body.

Exception handling is a very powerful and flexible tool for handling runtime errors effectively. However, use it judiciously.

7

Runtime Type Information

Introduction

Originally, C++ did not provide standardized support for runtime type information (RTTI). Furthermore, its creators balked at the idea of adding RTTI support for at least two reasons. First, they wanted to preserve backward compatibility with C. Secondly, they were concerned about efficiency. Other RTTI-enabled languages, such as Smalltalk and Lisp, were characterized by their notoriously sluggish performance. The performance penalty of dynamic type checking results from the relatively slow process of retrieving the object's type at runtime as well as from the additional information that the system needs to store for every type. C++ designers wanted to preserve the efficiency of C.

Another claim against the addition of RTTI to the language was that, in many cases, the use of virtual member functions could serve as an alternative to explicit runtime type checking. However, the addition of multiple inheritance (and consequently, of virtual inheritance) to C++ gave overwhelming ammunition to the proponents of RTTI (multiple inheritance is discussed in Chapter 5, "Object-Oriented Programming and Design"); it became apparent that under some circumstances, static type checking and virtual functions were insufficient.

Eventually, the C++ standardization committee approved the addition of RTTI to the language. Two new operators, `dynamic_cast<>` and `typeid`, were introduced. In addition, the class `std::type_info` was added to the Standard Library.

Structure of This Chapter

This chapter consists of three major parts. The limitations of virtual functions are presented first. Then, the standard RTTI constituents are explained and exemplified. Finally, RTTI performance and design issues are discussed.

Making Do Without RTTI

Virtual member functions can provide a reasonable level of dynamic typing without the need for additional RTTI support. A well-designed class hierarchy can define a meaningful operation for every virtual member function that is declared in the base class. The virtual dispatch mechanism ensures that every object in the hierarchy does the right thing even when its dynamic type differs from its static type.

Virtual Functions

Suppose you have to develop a file manager application as a component of a GUI-based operating system. The files in this system are represented as icons that respond to the right-click of a mouse, displaying a menu with options such as open, close, read, and so on. The underlying implementation of the file system relies on a class hierarchy that represents files of various types. In a well-designed class hierarchy, there is usually an abstract class serving as an interface:

```
class File //abstract,  all members are pure virtual
{
  public: virtual void open() =0;
  public: virtual void read() =0;
  public: virtual void write() =0;
  public: virtual ~File () =0;
};
File::~File ()   //pure virtual destructor must be defined
{}
```

At a lower level in the hierarchy, you have a set of derived classes that implement the common interface that they inherit from File. Each of these subclasses represents a different family of files. To simplify the discussion, assume that there are only two file types in this system: binary .exe files and text files.

```
class BinaryFile : public File
{
public:
  void open () { OS_execute(this); }  //implement the pure virtual function
  //...other member functions
};
class TextFile : public File
{
public:
  void open () { Activate_word_processor (this); }
  //...other member functions of File are implemented here
```

```
  void virtual print();  // an additional member function
};
```

The pure virtual function open() is implemented in every derived class, according to the type of the file. Thus, in a TextFile object, open() activates a word processor, whereas a BinaryFile object invokes the operating system's API function OS_execute(), which in turn executes the program that is stored in the binary file.

There are several differences between a binary file and a text file. For example, a text file can be printed directly on a screen or a printer because it consists of a sequence of printable characters. Conversely, a binary file with an .exe extension contains a stream of bits; it cannot be printed or displayed directly on a screen. It must be converted to a text file first, usually by a utility that translates the binary data into their symbolic representations. (For instance, the sequence 0110010 in an executable file can be replaced by a corresponding *move esp, ebp* assembly directive.) In other words, an executable file must be converted to a text file in order to be viewed or printed. Therefore, the member function print() appears only in class TextFile.

In this file manager, right-clicking the mouse on a file icon opens a menu of messages (options) to which the object can respond. For that purpose, the operating system has a function that takes a reference to a File:

```
OnRightClick (File & file); //operating system's API function
```

Obviously, no object of class File can be instantiated because File is an abstract class (see Chapter 5). However, the function OnRightClick() can accept any object that is derived from File. When the user right-clicks on a file icon and chooses the option Open, for instance, OnRightClick invokes the virtual member function open of its argument, and the appropriate member function is called. For example

```
OnRightClick (File & file)
{
  switch (message)
  {
  //...
  case m_open:
    file.open();
  break;
  }
}
```

So far, so good. You have implemented a polymorphic class hierarchy and a function that does not depend on the dynamic type of its argument. In this case, the language support for virtual functions was sufficient for your purposes; you did not need any explicit runtime type information (RTTI). Well, not exactly....You might have noticed the lack of file printing support. Look at the definition of class TextFile again:

```
class TextFile : public File
{
public:
  void open () { Activate_word_processor (this); }
  void virtual print();
};
```

The member function `print()` is not a part of the common interface that is implemented by all files in your system. It would be a design error to move `print()` to the abstract class `File` because binary files are nonprintable and cannot define a meaningful operation for it. Then again, `OnRightClick()` has to support file printing when it handles a text file. In this case, ordinary polymorphism in the form of virtual member functions will not do. `OnRightClick()` only knows that its argument is derived from `File`. However, this information is not sufficient to tell whether the actual object is printable. Clearly, `OnRightClick()` needs more information about the dynamic type of its argument in order to properly handle file printing. This is where the need for runtime type information arises. Before delving into the implementation of `OnRightClick()`, an overview of RTTI constituents and their role is necessary.

RTTI Constituents

The operators `typeid` and `dynamic_cast<>` offer two complementary forms of accessing the runtime type information of their operand. The operand's runtime type information itself is stored in a `type_info` object. This section exemplifies how these three constituents are used.

RTTI Is Applicable to Polymorphic Objects Exclusively

It is important to realize that RTTI is applicable solely to polymorphic objects. A class must have at least one virtual member function in order to have RTTI support for its objects. C++ does not offer RTTI support for non-polymorphic classes and primitive types. This restriction is just common sense—a fundamental type such as `double` or a concrete class such as `string` cannot change its type at runtime. Therefore, there is no need to detect their dynamic types because they are identical to their static types. But there is also a practical reason for confining RTTI support to polymorphic classes exclusively, as you will see momentarily.

As you probably know, every object that has at least one virtual member function also contains a special data member that is added by the compiler (more on this in Chapter 13, "C Language Compatibility Issues"). This member is a pointer to the virtual function table. The runtime type information is stored in this table, as is a pointer to a `std::type_info` object.

Class `type_info`

For every distinct type, C++ instantiates a corresponding RTTI object that contains the necessary runtime type information. The RTTI object is an instance of the standard class `std::type_info` or an implementation-defined class derived from it. (`std::type_info` is defined in the standard header `<typeinfo>`). This object is owned by the implementation and cannot be altered in any way by the programmer. The interface of `type_info` looks similar to the following (namespaces will be covered in Chapter 8, "Namespaces"):

```
namespace std { //class type_info is declared in namespace std
  class type_info
  {
  public:
    virtual ~type_info(); //type_info can serve as a base class
    bool operator==(const type_info&  rhs ) const; // enable comparison
    bool operator!=(const type_info&  rhs ) const; // return !( *this == rhs)
    bool before(const type_info&  rhs ) const; // ordering
    const char* name() const; //return a C-string containing the type's name
  private:
    //objects of this type cannot be copied
        type_info(const type_info&  rhs );
        type_info& operator=(const type_info&  rhs);
  }; //type_info
}
```

In general, all instances of the same type share a single `type_info` object. The most widely used member functions of `type_info` are `name()` and `operator==`. But before you can invoke these member functions, you have to access the `type_info` object itself. How is it done?

Operator `typeid`

Operator `typeid` takes either an object or a type name as its argument and returns a matching `const` `type_info` object. The dynamic type of an object can be examined as follows:

```
OnRightClick (File & file)
{
  if ( typeid( file)  == typeid( TextFile ) )
  {
    //received a TextFile object; printing should be enabled
  }
  else
  {
    //not a TextFile object, printing disabled
  }
}
```

To understand how it works, look at the highlighted source line:

```
if ( typeid( file)  == typeid( TextFile ) ).
```

The `if` statement tests whether the dynamic type of the argument `file` is `TextFile` (the static type of `file` is `File`, of course). The leftmost expression, `typeid(file)`, returns a `type_info` object that holds the necessary runtime type information that is associated with the object `file`. The rightmost expression, `typeid(TextFile)`, returns the type information that is associated with class `TextFile`. When `typeid` is applied to a class name rather than an object, it always returns a type_info object that corresponds to that class name. As you saw earlier, type_info overloads the operator ==. Therefore, the type_info object that is returned by the leftmost typeid expression is compared to the type_info object that is returned by the rightmost typeid expression. If indeed file is an instance of TextFile, the if statement evaluates to true. In this case, OnRightClick displays an additional option in the menu—print(). If, on the other hand, file is not a TextFile, the if statement evaluates to false, and the print() option is disabled. This is all well and good, but a typeid-based solution has a drawback. Suppose that you want to add support for a new type of files, for example HTML files. What happens when the file manager application has to be extended? HTML files are essentially text files. They can be read and printed. However, they differ from plain text files in some respects. An open message applied to an HTML file launches a browser rather than a word processor. In addition, HTML files have to be converted to a printable format before they can be printed. The need to extend a system's functionality at a minimal cost is a challenge that is faced by software developers every day. Object-oriented programming and design can facilitate the task. By subclassing TextFile, you can reuse its existing behavior and implement only the additional functionality that is required for HTML files:

```
class HTMLFile : public TextFile
{
  void open () { Launch_Browser (); }
  void virtual print();  // perform the necessary conversions to a
                         //printable format and then print file
};
```

This is, however, only half of the story. OnRightClick() fails badly when it receives an object of type HTMLFile. Look at it again to see why:

```
OnRightClick (File & file) //operating system's API function
{
  if ( typeid( file)  == typeid( TextFile ) )
  {
    //we received a TextFile object; printing should be enabled
  }
  else //OOPS! we get here when file is of type HTMLFile
  {
  }
}
```

typeid returns the exact type information of its argument. Therefore, the if statement in OnRightClick() evaluates to false when the argument is an HTMLFile. But a false value implies a binary file! Consequently, printing is disabled. This onerous bug is likely to occur every time you add support for a new file type. Of course, you can modify OnRightClick() so that it performs another test:

```
OnRightClick (File & file) //operating system's API function
{
  if ( (typeid( file)  == typeid( TextFile ))
    |¦ (typeid( file)  == typeid( HTMLFile)) ) //check for HTMLFile as well
  {
    //we received either a TextFile or an HTMLFile; printing should be enabled
  }
  else //it's a binary file, no print option
  {
  }
}
```

However, this solution is cumbersome and error prone. Furthermore, it imposes an unacceptable burden on the programmers who maintain this function. Not only are they required to clutter up OnRightClick() with additional code every time a new class is derived from File, but they also have to be on guard to detect any new class that has been derived from File lately. Fortunately, C++ offers a much better way to handle this situation.

Note

You can use typeid to retrieve the type information of non-polymorphic objects and fundamental types. However, the result refers to a type_info object that represents the static type of the operand. For example

```
#include<typeinfo>
#include <iostream>
#include <string>
using namespace std;

typedef int I;
void fundamental()
{
  cout<<typeid(I).name()<<endl; //display 'int'
}
void non_polymorphic()
{
  cout<<typeid(string).name()<<endl;
}
```

Note, however, that applying dynamic_cast to fundamental types or non-polymorphic classes is a compile time error.

Operator `dynamic_cast<>`

It is a mistake to allow `OnRightClick()` to take care of every conceivable class type. In doing so, you are forced to modify `OnRightClick()` any time you add a new file class or modify an existing class. In software design, and in object-oriented design in particular, you want to minimize such dependencies. If you examine `OnRightClick()` closely, you can see that it doesn't really need to know whether its argument is an instance of class `TextFile` (or of any other class, for that matter). Rather, all it needs to know is whether its argument is a `TextFile`. There is a big difference between the two—an object *is-a* `TextFile` if it is an instance of class `TextFile` or if it is an instance of any class derived from `TextFile`. However, `typeid` is incapable of examining the derivation hierarchy of an object. For this purpose, you have to use the operator `dynamic_cast<>`. `dynamic_cast<>` takes two arguments: The first is a type name, and the second argument is an object, which `dynamic_cast<>` attempts to cast at runtime to the desired type. For example

```
dynamic_cast <TextFile &> (file); //attempt to cast file to a reference to
                                  //an object of type TextFile
```

The preceding dynamic_cast<> expression succeeds if file *is-a* TextFile. This is exactly the information needed by OnRightClick to operate properly. But how do you know whether dynamic_cast<> was successful?

Pointer Cast and Reference Cast

There are two flavors of `dynamic_cast<>`. One uses pointers and the other uses references. Accordingly, `dynamic_cast<>` returns a pointer or a reference of the desired type when it succeeds. When `dynamic_cast<>` cannot perform the cast, it returns a `NULL` pointer or, in the case of a reference, it throws an exception of type `std::bad_cast`. Look at the following pointer cast example:

```
TextFile * pTest = dynamic_cast < TextFile *> (&file); //attempt to cast
                                  //file address to a pointer to TextFile

if (pTest) //dynamic_cast succeeded, file is-a TextFile
{
  //use pTest
}
else // file is not a TextFile;  pTest has a NULL value
{
}
```

C++ does not have `NULL` references. Therefore, when a reference `dynamic_cast<>` fails, it throws an exception of type `std::bad_cast`. That is why you always need to place a reference `dynamic_cast<>` expression within a `try`-block and include a suitable `catch`-statement to handle `std::bad_cast` exceptions (see also Chapter 6, "Exception Handling"). For example

```
try
{
  TextFile  tf = dynamic_cast < TextFile &> (file);
  //use tf safely,
}
catch (std::bad_cast)
{
  //dynamic_cast<> failed
}
```

Now you can revise OnRightClick() to handle HTMLFile objects properly:

```
OnRightClick (File & file)
{
  try
  {
    TextFile temp = dynamic_cast<TextFile&> (file);
    //display options, including "print"
    switch (message)
    {
    case m_open:
      temp.open();   //either TextFile::open or HTMLFile::open
    break;
    case m_print:
      temp.print();//either TextFile::print or HTMLFile::print
    break;
    }//switch
  }//try
  catch (std::bad_cast& noTextFile)
  {
    // treat file as a BinaryFile; exclude"print"
  }
}// OnRightClick
```

The revised version of OnRightClick() handles an object of type HTMLFile appro-priately because an object of type HTMLFile *is-a* TextFile. When the user clicks on the open message in the file manager application, the function OnRightClick() invokes the member function open() of its argument, which behaves as expected because it was overridden in class HTMLFile. Likewise, when OnRightClick() detects that its argu-ment is a TextFile, it displays a print option. If the user clicks on this option, OnRightClick() sends the message print to its argument, which reacts as expected.

Other Uses of dynamic_cast<>

Dynamic type casts are required in cases in which the dynamic type of an object—rather than its static type—is necessary to perform the cast properly. Note that any attempt to use a static cast in these cases is either flagged as an error by the compiler, or—even worse—it might result in undefined behavior at runtime.

Cross Casts

A *cross cast* converts a multiply-inherited object to one of its secondary base classes. To demonstrate what a cross cast does, consider the following class hierarchy:

```
struct A
{
  int i;
  virtual ~A () {} //enforce polymorphism; needed for dynamic_cast
};
struct B
{
  bool b;
};

struct D: public A, public B
{
  int k;
  D() { b = true; i = k = 0; }
};

A *pa = new D;
B *pb = dynamic_cast<B*> pa;  //cross cast; access the second base
                             //of a multiply-derived object
```

The static type of pa is "pointer to A", whereas its dynamic type is "pointer to D". A simple static_cast<> cannot convert a pointer to A into a pointer to B because A and B are unrelated (your compiler issues an error message in this case). A brute force cast, (for example reinterpret_cast<> or C-style cast), has disastrous results at runtime because the compiler simply assigns pa to pb. However, the B subobject is located at a different address within D than the A subobject. To perform the cross cast properly, the value of pb has to be calculated at runtime. After all, the cross cast can be done in a translation unit that doesn't even know that class D exists! The following program demonstrates how the results of applying dynamic cast and a static cast differ:

```
int main()
{
  A *pa = new D;
  B *pb = (B*) pa;  // disastrous; pb points to the subobject A within d
  bool bb = pb->b;  // bb has an undefined value
  cout<< "pa: " << pa << " pb: "<<pb <<endl;  // pb was not properly
                                      //adjusted; pa and pb are identical
  pb = dynamic_cast<B*> (pa); //cross cast; adjust pb correctly
  bb= pb->b; //OK, bb is true
  cout<< "pa: "<< pa << " pb: " << pb <<endl; // OK, pb was properly adjusted;
                                     // pa and pb have distinct values
  return 0;
}
```

The program displays two lines of output; the first shows that the memory addresses of pa and pb are identical. The second line shows that the memory addresses of pa and pb are different after performing a dynamic cast as required.

Downcasting from a Virtual Base

A *downcast* is a cast from a base to a derived object. Before the introduction of RTTI to the language, downcasts were regarded as a bad programming practice. They were unsafe, and some even viewed the reliance on the dynamic type of an object a violation of object-oriented principles (see also Chapter 2, "Standard Briefing: The Latest Addenda to ANSI/ISO C++"). dynamic_cast<> enables you to use safe, standardized, and simple downcasts from a virtual base to its derived object. Look at the following example:

```
struct V
{
  virtual ~V (){} //ensure polymorphism
};
struct A: virtual V {};
struct B: virtual V {};
struct D: A, B {};

#include <iostream>
using namespace std;
int main()
{
 V *pv = new D;
 A* pa = dynamic_cast<A*> (pv); // downcast
 cout<< "pv: "<< pv << " pa: " << pa <<endl; // OK, pv and pa have
                                            //different addresses

 return 0;
}
```

V is a virtual base for classes A and B. D is multiply-inherited from A and B. Inside main(), pv is declared as a "pointer to V" and its dynamic type is "pointer to D". Here again, as in the cross cast example, the dynamic type of pv is needed in order to properly downcast it to a pointer to A. A static_cast<> would be rejected by the compiler. As you read in Chapter 5, the memory layout of a virtual subobject might be different from that of a nonvirtual subobject. Consequently, it is impossible to calculate at compile time the address of the subobject A within the object pointed to by pv. As the output of the program shows, pv and pa indeed point to different memory addresses.

The Cost of Runtime Type Information

Runtime type information is not free. To estimate how expensive it is in terms of performance, it is important to understand how it is implemented behind the scenes. Some of the technical details are platform-dependent. Still, the basic model that is presented here can give you a fair idea of the performance penalties of RTTI in terms of memory overhead and execution speed.

Memory Overhead

Additional memory is needed to store the `type_info` object of every fundamental and user-defined type. Ideally, the implementation associates a single `type_info` object with every distinct type. However, this is not a requirement, and under some circumstances—for example, dynamically linked libraries—it is impossible to guarantee that only one `type_info` object per class exists. Therefore, an implementation can create more than one `type_info` object per type.

As was previously noted, there is a practical reason that `dynamic_cast<>` is applicable only to polymorphic objects: An object does not store its runtime type information directly (as a data member, for example).

Runtime Type Information of Polymorphic Objects

Every polymorphic object has a pointer to its virtual functions table. This pointer, traditionally named `vptr`, holds the address of a dispatch table that contains the memory addresses of every virtual function in this class. The trick is to add another entry to this table. This entry points at the class's `type_info` object. In other words, the `vptr` data member of a polymorphic object points at a table of pointers, in which the address of `type_info` is kept at a fixed position. This model is very economical in terms of memory usage; it requires a single `type_info` object and a pointer for every polymorphic class. Note that this is a fixed cost, regardless of how many instances of the class actually exist in the program. The cost of retrieving an object's runtime type information is therefore a single pointer indirection, which might be less efficient than direct access to a data member; still, though, it is equivalent to a virtual function invocation.

Additional Overhead

A pointer indirection, a `type_info` object, and a pointer per class sound like a reasonable price to pay for RTTI support. This is not the full picture, however. The `type_info` objects, just like any other object, have to be constructed. Large programs that contain hundreds of distinct polymorphic classes have to construct an equivalent number of `type_info` objects as well.

RTTI Support Can Usually Be Toggled

This overhead is imposed even if you never use RTTI in your programs. For this reason, most compilers enable you to switch off their RTTI support (check the user's manual to see the default RTTI setting of your compiler and how it can be modified). If you never use RTTI in your programs, you can turn off your compiler's RTTI support. The results are smaller executables and a slightly faster code.

typeid Versus dynamic_cast<>

Until now, this chapter has discussed the indirect cost of RTTI support. It is now time to explore the cost of its direct usage—that is, applying typeid and dynamic_cast<>.

A typeid invocation is a constant time operation. It takes the same length of time to retrieve the runtime type information of every polymorphic object, regardless of its derivational complexity. In essence, calling typeid is similar to invoking a virtual member function. For instance, the expression typeid(obj) is evaluated into something similar to the following:

```
return *(obj->__vptr[0]); //return the type_info object whose address
                          // is stored at offset 0 in the virtual table of obj
```

Note that the pointer to a class's type_info object is stored at a fixed offset in the virtual table (usually 0, but this is implementation-dependent).

Unlike typeid, dynamic_cast<> is not a constant time operation. In the expression dynamic_cast<T&> (obj), where T is the target type and obj is the operand, the time that is needed to cast the operand to the target type depends on the complexity of the class hierarchy of obj. dynamic_cast<> has to traverse the derivation tree of the obj until it has located the target object in it. When the target is a virtual base, the dynamic cast becomes even more complicated (albeit unavoidable, as you have seen); consequently, it takes longer to execute. The worst case scenario is when the operand is a deeply derived object and the target is a nonrelated class type. In this case, dynamic_cast<> has to traverse the entire derivation tree of obj before it can confidently decide that obj cannot be cast to a T. In other words, a failed dynamic_cast<> is an $O(n)$ operation, where n is the number of base classes of the operand.

You might recall the conclusion that from a design point of view, dynamic_cast<> is preferable to typeid because the former enables more flexibility and extensibility. Notwithstanding that, the runtime overhead of typeid can be less expensive than dynamic_cast<>, depending on the derivational complexity of the entities involved.

Conclusions

The RTTI mechanism of C++ consists of three components: operator typeid, operator dynamic_cast<>, and class std::type_info. RTTI is relatively new in C++. Some existing compilers do not support it yet. Furthermore, compilers that support it can usually be configured to disable RTTI support. Even when there is no explicit usage of RTTI in a program, the compiler automatically adds the necessary "scaffolding" to the resultant executable. To avert this, you can usually switch off your compiler's RTTI support.

From the object-oriented design point of view, operator dynamic_cast<> is preferable to typeid because it enables more flexibility and robustness, as you have seen. However, dynamic_cast<> can be slower than typeid because its performance depends on the proximity of its target and operand, as well as on the derivational complexity of the latter. When complex derivational hierarchies are used, the incurred performance penalty might be noticeable. It is recommended, therefore, that you use RTTI judiciously. In many cases, a virtual member function is sufficient to achieve the necessary polymorphic behavior. Only when virtual member functions are insufficient should RTTI be considered.

Following are a few additional notes to keep in mind when using RTTI:

- In order to enable RTTI support, an object must have at least one virtual member function. In addition, switch on your compiler's RTTI support (please consult your user's manual for further information) if it isn't already on.

- Make sure that your program has a `catch`-statement to handle `std::bad_cast` exceptions whenever you are using `dynamic_cast<>` with a reference. Note also that an attempt to dereference a null pointer in a `typeid` expression, as in `typeid(*p)` where `p` is `NULL`, results in a `std::bad_typeid` exception being thrown.

- When you are using `dynamic_cast<>` with a pointer, always check the returned value.

8

Namespaces

Introduction

Namespaces were introduced to the C++ Standard in 1995. This chapter explains what namespaces are and why they were added to the language. You will see how namespaces can avoid name conflicts and how they facilitate configuration management and version control in large-scale projects. Finally, you will learn how namespaces interact with other language features.

The Rationale Behind Namespaces

In order to understand why namespaces were added to the language in the first place, here's an analogy: Imagine that the file system on your computer did not have directories and subdirectories at all. All files would be stored in a flat repository, visible all the time to every user and application. Consequently, extreme difficulties would arise: Filenames would clash (with some systems limiting a filename to eight characters, plus three for the extension, this is even more likely to happen), and simple actions such as listing, copying, or searching files would be much more difficult. In addition, security and authorization restrictions would be severely compromised.

Namespaces in C++ are equivalent to directories. They can be nested easily, they protect your code from name conflicts, they enable you to hide declarations, and they do not incur any runtime or memory overhead. Most of the components of the C++ Standard Library are grouped under namespace std.

A Brief Historical Background

In the early 1990s, when C++ was gaining popularity as a general purpose programming language, many vendors were shipping proprietary implementations of various component classes. Class libraries for string manipulations, mathematical functions, and data containers were integral parts of frameworks such as MFC, STL, OWL, and others. The proliferation of reusable components caused a name-clashing problem. A class named `vector`, for instance, might appear in a mathematical library and in another container library that were both used at the same time; or a class named `string` might be found in almost every framework and class library. It was impossible for the compiler to distinguish between different classes that had identical names. Similarly, linkers could not cope with identical names of member functions of classes with indistinguishable names. For example, a member function

```
vector::operator==(const vector&);
```

might be defined in two different classes—the first might be a class of a mathematical library, whereas the other might belong to some container library.

Large-Scale Projects Are More Susceptible to Name Clashes

Name-clashes are not confined to third-party software libraries. In large-scale software projects, short and elegant names for classes, functions, and constants can also cause name conflicts because it is likely that the same name might be used more than once to indicate different entities by different developers. In the pre-namespace era, the only workaround was to use various affixes in identifiers' names. This practice, however, is tedious and error prone. Consider the following:

```
class string  // short but dangerous. someone else may have picked
              //this name already...
{
    //...
};

class excelSoftCompany_string  // a long name is safer but tedious.
                               //A nightmare if company changes its name...
{
    //...
};
```

Namespaces enable you to use convenient, short, and intelligible names safely. Instead of repeating the unwieldy affixes time after time, you can group your declarations in a namespace and factor out the recurring affix as follows:

```
//file excelSoftCompany.h
namespace excelSoftCompany { // a namespace definition

    class string {/*..*/};
    class vector {/*..*/};
}
```

Namespace members, like class members, can be defined separately from their declarations. For example

```
#include <iostream>
using namespace std;
namespace A
{
  void f(); //declaration
}

void A::f()    //definition in a separate file
{
  cout<<"in f"<<endl;
}

int main()
{
  A::f();
  return 0;
}
```

Properties of Namespaces

The following sections discuss the syntactic constructs of namespaces. These include fully qualified names, a using declaration, a using directive, and other namespace properties.

Fully Qualified Names

A namespace is a scope in which declarations and definitions are grouped together. In order to refer to any of these from another scope, a *fully qualified name* is required. A fully qualified name of an identifier consists of its namespaces, followed by a scope resolution operator (::), its class name, and, finally, the identifier itself. Because both namespaces and classes can be nested, the resulting name can be rather long—but it ensures unique identification:

```
unsigned int  maxPossibleLength =
   std::string::npos;  //a fully qualified name. npos is a member of string;
                       //string  belongs to namespace std
   int *p = ::new int; //distinguish global new from overloaded new
```

However, repeating the fully qualified name is tedious and less readable. Instead, you can use a *using declaration* or a *using directive*.

A using Declaration and a using Directive

A using declaration consists of the keyword using, followed by a *namespace::member*. It instructs the compiler to locate every occurrence of a certain identifier (type, operator, function, constant, and so on) in the specified namespace, as if the fully qualified name were supplied. For example

```
#include <vector>  //STL vector;  defined in namespace std
int main()
{
   using std::vector;  //using declaration; every occurrence of vector
                       //is looked up in std
   vector <int> vi;
   return 0;
}
```

A using directive, on the other hand, renders all the names of a specified namespace accessible in the scope of the directive. It consists of the following sequence: using namespace, followed by a namespace name. For example

```
#include <vector>    // belongs to namespace std
#include <iostream> //iostream classes and operators are also in namespace std
int main()
{
   using namespace std; // a using-directive; all <iostream> and <vector>
                        //declarations  now accessible
   vector  <int> vi;
   vi.push_back(10);
   cout<<vi[0];
   return 0;
}
```

Look back at the string class example (the code is repeated here for convenience):

```
//file excelSoftCompany.h
namespace excelSoftCompany
{
   class string {/*..*/};
   class vector {/*..*/};
}
```

You can now access your own string class as well as the standard string class in the same program as follows:

```
#include <string> //  std::string
#include "excelSoftCompany.h"
int main()
{
   using namespace excelSoftCompany;
   string s; //referring to class excelSoftCompany::string
   std::string standardstr; //now instantiate an ANSI string
   return 0;
}
```

Namespaces Can Be Extended

The C++ standardization committee was well aware of the fact that related declarations can span across several translation units. Therefore, a namespace can be defined in parts. For example

```
//file proj_const.h
namespace MyProj
{
    enum NetProtocols
    {
        TCP_IP,
        HTTP,
        UDP
    };  // enum
}
```

```
//file proj_classes.h
namespace MyProj
{ // extending MyProj namespace
    class RealTimeEncoder{ public: NetProtocols detect();  };
    class NetworkLink {};
    class UserInterface {};
}
```

In a separate file, the same namespace can be extended with additional declarations. The complete namespace `MyProj` can be extracted from both files as follows:

```
//file app.cpp

#include "proj_const.h"
#include "proj_classes.h"

int main()
{
  using namespace MyProj;
  RealTimeEncoder encoder;
  NetProtocols protocol = encoder.detect();
  return 0;
}
```

Namespace Aliases

As you have observed, choosing a short name for a namespace can eventually lead to a name clash. However, very long namespaces are not easy to use. For this purpose, a *namespace alias* can be used. The following example defines the alias `ESC` for the unwieldy `Excel_Software_Company` namespace. Namespace aliases have other useful purposes, as you will see soon.

```
//file decl.h
namespace Excel_Software_Company
{
```

```
  class Date {/*..*/};
  class Time {/*..*/};
}

//file calendar.cpp
#include "decl.h"
int main()
{
  namespace ESC = Excel_Software_Company; //ESC is an alias for
                                          // Excel_Software_Company

  ESC::Date date;
  ESC::Time time;
  return 0;
}
```

Koenig Lookup

Andrew Koenig, one of the creators of C++, devised an algorithm for resolving namespace members' lookup. This algorithm, also called *argument dependent lookup*, is used in all standard-compliant compilers to handle cases such as the following:

```
namespace MINE
{
  class C {};
  void func(C);
}

MINE::C c; // global object of type MINE::C

int main()
{
  func( c ); // OK, MINE::f called
  return 0;
}
```

Caution

Please note that some existing compilers do not yet fully support Koenig lookup. Consequently, the following programs—which rely on Koenig lookup—might not compile under compilers that are not fully compliant to the ANSI/ISO standard in this respect.

Neither a `using` declaration nor a `using` directive exists in the program. Still, the compiler did the right thing—it correctly identified the unqualified name `func` as the function declared in namespace `MINE` by applying Koenig lookup.

Koenig lookup instructs the compiler to look not just at the usual places, such as the local scope, but also at the namespace that contains the argument's type. Therefore, in the following source line, the compiler detects that the object `c`, which is the argument of the function `func()`, belongs to namespace `MINE`. Consequently, the compiler looks at namespace `MINE` to locate the declaration of `func()`, "guessing" the programmer's intent:

```
func( c ); // OK, MINE::f called
```

Without Koenig lookup, namespaces impose an unacceptable tedium on the programmer, who has to either repeatedly specify the fully qualified names or use numerous `using` declarations. To push the argument in favor of Koenig lookup even further, consider the following example:

```
#include<iostream>
using std::cout;

int main()
{
  cout<<"hello";    //OK, operator << is brought into scope by Koenig lookup
  return 0;
}
```

The `using` declaration injects `std::cout` into the scope of `main()`, thereby enabling the programmer to use the nonqualified name `cout`. However, the overloaded `<<` operator, as you might recall, is not a member of `std::cout`. It is a friend function that is defined in namespace `std`, and which takes a `std::ostream` object as its argument. Without Koenig lookup, the programmer has to write something similar to the following:

```
std::operator<<(cout, "hello");
```

Alternatively, the programmer can provide a `using namespace std;` directive. None of these options are desirable, however, because they clutter up code and can become a source of confusion and errors. (`using` directives are the least favorable form for rendering names visible in the current scope because they make all the members of a namespace visible indiscriminately). Fortunately, Koenig lookup "does the right thing" and saves you from this tedium in an elegant way.

Koenig lookup is applied automatically. No special directives or configuration switches are required to activate it, nor is there any way to turn it off. This fact has to be kept in mind because it can have surprising results in some circumstances. For example

```
namespace NS1
{
  class B{};
  void f(B);
```

```
};

void f(NS1::B);

int main()
{
  NS1::B b;
  f(b);  // ambiguous; NS1::f() or f(NS1::B)?
  return 0;
}
```

A Standard-compliant compiler should issue an error on ambiguity between NS1::f(NS1::B) and f(NS1::B). However, noncompliant compilers do not complain about the ambiguous call; they simply pick one of the versions of f(). This, however, might not be the version that the programmer intended. Furthermore, the problem might arise only at a later stage of the development, when additional versions of f() are added to the project—which can stymie the compiler's lookup algorithm. This ambiguity is not confined to global names. It might also appear when two namespaces relate to one another—for instance, if a namespace declares classes that are used as parameters of a class member function that is declared in a different namespace.

Namespaces in Practice

The conclusion that can be drawn from the previous examples is that namespaces, like other language features, must be used judiciously. For small programs that contain only a handful of classes and a few source files, namespaces are not necessary. In most cases, such programs are coded and maintained by a single programmer, and they use a limited number of components. The likelihood of name clashes in this case is rather small. If name clashes still occur, it is always possible to rename the existing classes and functions, or simply to add namespace later.

On the other hand, large-scale projects—as was stated previously—are more susceptible to name clashes; therefore, they need to use namespaces systematically. It is not unusual to find projects on which hundreds of programmers on a dozen or so development teams are working together. The development of Microsoft Visual C++ 6.0, for example, lasted 18 months, and more than 1000 people were involved in the development process. Managing such a huge project requires well documented coding policies—and namespaces are one of the tools in the arsenal.

Namespace Utilization Policy in Large-Scale Projects

To see how namespaces can be used in configuration management, imagine an online transaction processing system of an imaginary international credit card company, Unicard. The project comprises several development teams. One of them, the database administration team, is responsible for the creation and maintenance of the database tables, indexes, and access authorizations. The database team also has to provide the access routines and data objects that retrieve and manipulate the data in the database. A second team is responsible for the graphical user interface. A third team deals with the international online requests that are initiated by the cinemas, restaurants, shops, and so on where tourists pay with their international Unicard. Every purchase of a cinema ticket, piece of jewelry, or art book has to be confirmed by Unicard before the card owner is charged. The confirmation process involves checking for the validity of the card, its expiration date, and the card owner's balance. A similar confirmation procedure is required for domestic purchases. However, international confirmation requests are transmitted via satellite, whereas domestic confirmations are usually done on the telephone.

In software projects, code reuse is paramount. Because the same business logic is used for both domestic and international confirmations, the same database access objects need to be used to retrieve the relevant information and perform the necessary computations. Still, an international confirmation also involves a sophisticated communication stack that receives the request that is transmitted via satellite, decrypts it, and returns an encrypted response to the sender. A typical implementation of satellite-based confirmation application can be achieved by means of combining the database access objects with the necessary communication objects that encapsulate protocols, communication layers, priority management, message queuing, encryption, and decryption. It is not difficult to imagine a name conflict resulting from the simultaneous use of the communication components and the database access objects.

For example, two objects—one encapsulating a database connection and the other referring to a satellite connection—can have an identical name: `Connection`. If, however, communication software components and database access objects are declared in two distinct namespaces, the potential of name clashes is minimized. Therefore, `com::Connection` and `dba::Connection` can be used in the same application simultaneously. A systematic approach can be based on allocating a separate namespace for every team in a project in which all the components are declared. Such a policy can help you avoid name clashes among different teams and third party code used in the project.

Namespaces and Version Control

Successful software projects do not end with the product's rollout. In most projects, new versions that are based on their predecessors are periodically released. Moreover, previous versions have to be supported, patched, and adjusted to operate with new operating systems, locales, and hardware. Web browsers, commercial databases, word processors, and multimedia tools are examples of such products. It is often the case that the same development team has to support several versions of the same software product. A considerable amount of software can be shared among different versions of the same product, but each version also has its specific components. Namespace aliases can be used in these cases to switch swiftly from one version to another.

Continuous projects in general have a pool of infrastructure software components that are used ubiquitously. In addition, every version has its private pool of specialized components. Namespace aliases can provide *dynamic namespaces*; that is, a namespace alias can point at a given time to a namespace of version X and, at another time, it can refer to a different namespace. For example

```
namespace ver_3_11  //16 bit

{
  class Winsock{/*..*/};
  class FileSystem{/*..*/};
};

namespace ver_95 //32 bit
{
  class Winsock{/*..*/};
  class FileSystem{/*..*/};
}


int main()//implementing 16 bit release
{
  namespace current = ver_3_11; // current is an alias of ver_3_11
  using current::Winsock;
  using current::FileSystem;

  FileSystem  fs; // ver_3_11::FileSystem
  //...
  return 0;
}
```

In this example, the alias current is a symbol that can refer to either ver_3_11 or ver_95. To switch to a different version, the programmer only has to assign a different namespace to it.

Namespaces Do Not Incur Additional Overhead

Namespace resolution, including Koenig lookup, are statically resolved. The underlying implementation of namespaces occurs by means of *name mangling,* whereby the compiler incorporates the function name with its list of arguments, its class name, and its namespace in order to create a unique name for it (see Chapter 13, "C Language Compatibility Issues," for a detailed account of name mangling). Therefore, namespaces do not incur any runtime or memory overhead.

The Interaction of Namespaces with Other Language Features

Namespaces interact with other features of the language and affect programming techniques. Namespaces also made some features in C++ superfluous or undesirable. The following sections discuss the interaction of namespaces with other language features and programming conventions.

Scope Resolution Operator Should Not Be Used to Designate Global Names

In some frameworks (MFC, for instance), it is customary to add the scope resolution operator, ::, before a global function's name to mark it explicitly as a function that is not a class member (as in the following example):

```
void String::operator = (const String& other)
{
  ::strcpy (this->buffer, other.getBuff());
}
```

This practice is not recommended. Many of the standard functions that were once global are now grouped inside namespaces. For example, strcpy now belongs to namespace std, as do most of the Standard Library's functions. Preceding these functions with the scope resolution operator might confuse the lookup algorithm of the compiler; furthermore, doing so undermines the very idea of partitioning the global namespace. Therefore, it is recommended that you leave the scope resolution operator off the function's name.

Turning an External Function into a File-Local Function

In standard C, a nonlocal identifier that is declared to be static has *internal linkage*, which means that it accessible only from within the translation unit in which it is declared (see also Chapter 2, "Standard Briefing: The Latest Addenda to ANSI/ISO C++"). This technique is used to support information hiding (as in the following example):

```
//File hidden.c

static void decipher(FILE *f); // accessible only from within this file

    // now use this function in the current source file
decipher ("passwords.bin");

    //end of file
```

Although it is still supported in C++, this convention is now considered a *deprecated feature*. Future releases of your compiler might issue a warning message when they find a static identifier that is not a member of a class. In order to make a function accessible only from within its translation unit, use an *unnamed namespace* instead. The following example demonstrates the process:

```
//File hidden.cpp

namespace          //unnamed
{
  void decipher(FILE *f);  // accessible only from within this file
}
```

```
//now use the function in the current source file.
//No using declarations or directives are needed
decipher ("passwords.bin");
```

Although names in an unnamed namespace might have external linkage, they can never be seen from any other translation unit; the net effect of this is that the names of an unnamed namespace appear to have static linkage. If you declare another function with the same name in an unnamed namespace of another file, the two functions are hidden from one another, and their names do not clash.

Standard Headers Names

All Standard C++ header files now have to be included as follows:

```
#include <iostream> //note: no ".h" extension
```

That is, the .h extension is omitted. Standard C header files also obey this convention, with the addition of the letter *c* to their name. Therefore, a C standard header that was formerly named <xxx.h> is now <cxxx>. For example

```
#include <cassert> //formerly: <assert.h>
```

The older convention for C headers, <xxx.h>, is still supported; however, it is now considered deprecated and, therefore, is not to not be used in new C++ code. The reason for this is that C <xxx.h> headers inject their declarations into the global namespace. In C++, however, most standard declarations are grouped under namespace std, as are the <cxxx> Standard C headers. No inference is to be drawn from the actual name convention that is used on the physical location of a header file or its underlying name. In fact, most implementations share a single physical file for the <xxx.h> and its corresponding <cxxx> notation. This is feasible due to some under-the-hood pre-processor tricks. Recall that you need to have a using declaration, a using directive, or a fully qualified name in order to access the declarations in the new style standard headers. For example

```
#include <cstdio>
using namespace std;

void f()
{
    printf ("Hello World\n");
}
```

Restrictions on Namespaces

The C++ Standard defines several restrictions on the use of namespaces. These restrictions are meant to avert anomalies or ambiguities that can create havoc in the language.

Namespace `std` Cannot Be Modified

Generally, namespaces are open, so it is perfectly legal to expand existing namespaces with additional declarations and definitions across several files. The only exception to the rule is namespace `std`. According to the Standard, the result of modifying namespace `std` with additional declarations—let alone the removal of existing ones—yields undefined behavior, and is to be avoided. This restriction might seem arbitrary, but it's just common sense—any attempt to tamper with namespace `std` undermines the very concept of a namespace dedicated exclusively to standard declarations.

User-Defined `new` and `delete` Cannot Be Declared in a Namespace

The Standard prohibits declarations of `new` and `delete` operators in a namespace. To see why, consider the following example:

```
char *pc; //global
namespace A
{
  void* operator new ( std::size_t );
  void operator delete ( void * );

  void func ()
  {
    pc = new char ( 'a'); //using A::new
  }
} //A

void f() { delete pc; } // call A::delete or
```

Some programmers might expect the operator `A::delete` to be selected because it matches the operator `new` that was used to allocate the storage; others might expect the standard operator `delete` to be called because `A::delete` is not visible in function `f()`. By prohibiting declarations of `new` and `delete` in a namespace altogether, C++ avoids any such ambiguities.

Conclusions

Namespaces were the latest addition to the C++ Standard. Therefore, some compilers do not yet support this feature. However, all compiler vendors will incorporate namespace support in the near future. The importance of namespaces cannot be overemphasized. As you have seen, any nontrivial C++ program utilizes components of the Standard Template Library, the iostream library, and other standard header files—all of which are now namespace members.

Large-scale software projects can use namespaces cleverly to avoid common pitfalls and to facilitate version control, as you have seen.

C++ offers three methods for injecting a namespace constituent into the current scope. The first is a `using` directive, which renders all the members of a namespace visible in the current scope. The second is a `using` declaration, which is more selective and enables the injection of a single component from a namespace. Finally, a fully qualified name uniquely identifies a namespace member. In addition, the argument-dependent lookup, or Koenig lookup, captures the programmer's intention without forcing him or her to use wearying references to a namespace.

IV

Templates and Generic Programming

9

Templates

Introduction

A *template* is a mold from which the compiler generates a family of classes or functions. C++ programming styles and concepts have changed considerably since the first implementation of templates back in 1991 (in cfront 2.0). Initially, templates were viewed as a support for generic container classes such as Array and List. In recent years, the experience of using templates has shown that this feature is most useful in designing and implementing general-purpose libraries such as the Standard Template Library. Templatized libraries and frameworks are both efficient and portable. With the widespread usage of templates, C++ has added more sophisticated constructs to control their behavior and performance, including partial specializations, explicit specializations, member templates, exported templates, default type arguments, and more.

This chapter discusses various aspects of designing and implementing templates. First, class templates are explained. Function templates come next. Finally, template issues of special concern—such as pointers to members, virtual member functions within a template class, inheritance relations, and explicit instantiations—are discussed.

Class Templates

Many algorithms and data structures can be defined independently of the concrete data type that they manipulate. Often, the reliance on a hardwired data type is merely a programming artifact. The concept of a complex number, for instance, is not exclusively limited to the fundamental type `double`. Rather, it is applicable to every floating-point type. Designing a type-independent class that abstracts the concept of a complex number has many advantages because it enables users to choose the desired level of precision for a specific application without having to reduplicate code manually. In addition, type-independent classes are more portable among different platforms and locales.

Declaration of a Class Template

A class template is declared using the keyword `template`, followed by a *template parameter list* that is enclosed in angular brackets and a declaration or a definition of the class. For example

```
template <class T> class Vector; //declaration

template <class T> class Vector  //definition
{
private:
  size_t sz;
  T * buff;
public:
  explicit Vector<T>(size_t s = 100);
  Vector<T> (const Vector <T> & v); //copy constructor
  Vector<T>& operator= (const Vector<T>& v); //assignment operator
  ~Vector<T>(); //destrcutor
  //other member functions
  T& operator [] (unsigned int index);
  const T& operator [] (unsigned int index) const;
  size_t size() const;
};
```

Member functions of a class template can be defined outside the class body. In this case, they have to be explicitly declared as member functions of their class template. For example

```
//definitions of Vector's member functions
//follow the class declaration

template <class T> Vector<T>::Vector<T> (size_t s) //constructor definition
: sz(s),
buff (new T[s])
{}
template <class T> Vector<T>::Vector<T> (const Vector <T> & v) //copy ctor
{
  sz = 0;
  buff = 0;
  *this = v; //use overloaded assignment operator
}
```

```
template <class T> Vector<T>& Vector<T>::operator=   // assignment operator
(const Vector <T> & v)
{
  if (this == &v)
    return *this;
  this->Vector<T>::~Vector<T>(); //call destructor
  buff = new T[v.size()]; //allocate sufficient storage
  for (size_t i =0; i < v.size(); i++)
    buff[i] = v[i]; //memberwise copy
  sz = v.size();
  return *this;
}
template <class T> Vector<T>::~Vector<T> () //destructor
{
  delete [] buff;
}

template <class T> inline T& Vector<T>::operator [] (unsigned int i)
{
  return buff[i];
}

template <class T> inline const T& Vector<T>::operator [] //const version
(unsigned int i) const
{
  return buff[i];
}

template <class T> inline size_t Vector<T>::size () const
{
  return sz;
}
//Vector.hpp
```

The prefix `template <class T>` indicates that `T` is a *template parameter*, which is a placeholder for a yet unspecified type. The keyword `class` is of particular interest because the corresponding argument for the parameter `T` is not necessarily a user-defined type; it can also be a fundamental type, such as `char` or `int`. If you prefer a more neutral term, you can use the `typename` keyword instead (`typename` also has other uses, though, as you will see next):

```
template <typename T> class Vector //typename instead of class
                                   //no semantic difference between the two forms
{
  //...
};
template <typename T> Vector<T>::Vector<T> (size_t s)
: sz(s), buff (new T[s]) {}
```

Within the scope of Vector, qualification with the parameter T is redundant, so the member functions can be declared and defined without it. The constructor, for example, can be declared as follows:

```
template <class T> class Vector
{
public:
 Vector (size_t s = 100);  // equivalent to Vector <T>(size_t s = 100);
};
```

Similarly, the constructor's definition can omit the redundant parameter:

```
// equivalent to template <class T> Vector<T>::Vector<T>(size_t s)
template <class T> Vector<T>::Vector (size_t s) :
buff (new T[s]), sz(s)
{}
```

Instantiation and Specialization

A class template is not a class. The process of instantiating a class from a class template and a type argument is called *template instantiation*. A *template id*, that is, a template name followed by a list of arguments in angular brackets (for example, Vector<int>), is called a *specialization*. A specialization of a class template can be used exactly like any other class. Consider the following examples:

```
void func (Vector <float> &); //function parameter
size_t n = sizeof( Vector <char>); //sizeof expression
class myStringVector: private Vector<std::string> //base class
{/*...*/};
#include <iostream>
#include <typeinfo>
#include <string>
using namespace std;
cout<<typeid(Vector< string>).name(); //typeid expression
Vector<int> vi; // creating an object
```

The compiler instantiates only the necessary member functions of a given specialization. In the following example, points of member instantiation are numbered:

```
#include <iostream>
#include "Vector.hpp"
using namespace std;

int main()
{
  Vector<int> vi(5);  // 1
  for (int i = 0; i<5; i++)
  {
    vi[i] = i; //fill vi    // 2
    cout<<vi[i]<<endl;
  }
  return 0;  // 3
}
```

The compiler generates code only for the following `Vector` member functions, which are used either explicitly or implicitly in the program:

```
Vector<int>::Vector<int> (size_t s) //1: constructor
: sz(s), buff (new int[s]) {}

inline int& Vector<int>::operator [] (unsigned int idx) //2: operator []
{
  return buff[idx];
}

Vector<int>::~Vector<int> () //3: destructor
{
  delete [] buff;
}
```

In contrast, code for the member function `size_t Vector<int>::size() const` is not generated by the compiler because it is not required. For some compilers, it might be simpler to instantiate all the class members at once whether they are needed or not. However, the "generate on demand" policy is a Standard requirement, and has two functions:

- **Efficiency**—It is not uncommon for certain class templates to define hundreds of member functions (STL containers, for example); normally, however, fewer than a dozen of these are actually used in a program. Generating the code for unused member functions times the number of specializations used in the program can easily bloat the size of the executable—and it might unnecessarily increase compilation and linkage time.

- **Flexibility**—In some cases, not every type supports all the operations that are defined in a class template. For example, a container class can use `ostream`'s operator << to display members of fundamental types such as `char` and `int` and user-defined types for which an overloaded version of << is defined. However, a POD (plain old data) struct for which no overloaded version of << exists can still be stored in such a container as long as the << is not invoked.

Template Arguments

A template can take type parameters, that is, symbols that represent an as yet unspecified type. For example

```
template <class T > class Vector {/*...*/};
```

A template can also take ordinary types such as `int` and `long` as parameters:

```
template <class T, int n> class Array
{
private:
  T a[n];
  int size;
```

```
public:
  Array() : size (n){}
  T& operator [] (int idx) { return a[idx]; }
};
```

Note, however, that when an ordinary type is used as a parameter, the template argument must be a constant or a constant expression of an integral type. For example

```
void  array_user()
{
  const int cn = 5;
  int num = 10;

  Array<char, 5> ac;  // OK, 5 is a const
  Array<float, cn> af;  // OK, cn is const
  Array<unsigned char, sizeof(float)> auc;  // OK, constant expression used
  Array<bool,  num> ab;  // error, num is not a constant
}
```

Besides constant expressions, other arguments that are allowed are a non-overloaded pointer to member and the address of an object or a function with external linkage. This also implies that a string literal cannot be used as a template argument because it has internal linkage. For example:

```
template <class T, const char *> class A
{/*...*/};

void  array_user()
{
  const char * p ="illegal";
  A<int, "invalid"> aa;  // error, string literal used as a template argument
  A<int, p> ab; // also an error, p doesn't have external linkage
}
```

A template can take a template as an argument. For example

```
int send(const Vector<char*>& );
int main()
{

  Vector <Vector<char*> > msg_que(10); //a template used as an argument
  //...fill msg_que

  for (int i =0; i < 10; i++) //transmit messages
    send(msg_que[i]);
  return 0;
}
```

Note that when a template is used as an argument, the space between the left two angular brackets is mandatory:

```
Vector <Vector<char*> > msg_que(10);
```

Otherwise, the >> sequence is parsed as the right shift operator.

A `typedef` can be used to avert this mishap and improve readability, both for the compiler and for the human reader:

```
typedef  Vector<char *> msg;
Vector<msg> msg_que;
```

Default Type Arguments

Class templates can have default type arguments.

As with default argument values of a function, the default type of a template gives the programmer more flexibility in choosing the optimal type for a particular application. For instance, the `Vector` template can be optimized for special memory management tasks. Instead of using the hard-coded `size_t` type for storing the size of a `Vector`, it can have a size type as a parameter. For most purposes, the default type `size_t` is used. However, for managing extremely large memory buffers on the one hand—or very small ones on the other hand—the programmer is free to choose other suitable data types instead. For example

```
template <class T, class S = size_t > class Vector
{
private:
  S sz;
  T * buff;
public:
  explicit Vector(S s = 100): sz(s), buff(new T[s]){}
  ~Vector();
  //other member functions
  S size() const;
};

template <class T, class S> Vector<T,S>::~Vector<T,S>()//destructor definition
{
  delete [] buff;
}

template <class T, class S> S Vector<T,S>::size() const
{
  return sz;
}

int  main()
{
  Vector <int> ordinary;
  Vector <int, unsigned char> tiny(5);
  return 0;
}
```

An additional advantage of a default size type is the capability to support implementation-dependent types. On a machine that supports 64-bit integers, for instance, programmers can use `Vector` to easily manipulate very large memory buffers:

```
Vector <int, unsigned __int64> very_huge;
```

The fact that the programmer does not have to make any changes to the definition of Vector to get the appropriate specialization cannot be overemphasized. Without templates, such a high level of automation is very difficult to achieve.

Static Data Members

Templates can have static data members. For example

```
template<class T> class C
{
public:
  static T stat;
};
template<class T> T C<T>::stat = 5; //definition
```

A static data member can be accessed as follows:

```
void f()
{
  int n = C<int>::stat;
}
```

Friendship

A friend of a class template can be a function template or class template, a specialization of a function template or class template, or an ordinary (nontemplate) function or class. The following sections discuss the various types of friendship that a class template can have.

Nontemplate Friends

Nontemplate friend declarations of a class template look quite similar to friend declarations of a nontemplate class. In the following example, the class template Vector declares the ordinary function f() and class Thing as its friends:

```
class Thing;
template <class T> class Vector
{
public:
  //...
  friend void f ();
  friend class Thing;
};
```

Each specialization of Vector has the function f() and class Thing as friends.

Specializations

You can declare a specialization as a friend of a class template. In the following example, the class template Vector declares the specialization C<void*> as its friend:

```
template <class T> class C{/*...*/};
template <class T> class Vector
```

```
{
public:
  //...
  friend class C<void*>; //other specializations are not friends of Vector
};
```

Template Friends

A friend of a class template can be a template by itself. For instance, you can declare a class template as a friend of another class template:

```
template <class U> class D{/*...*/};
template <class T> class Vector
{
public:
  //...
  template <class U> friend class D;
};
```

Every specialization of D is a friend of every specialization of Vector. You can also declare a function template as a friend (function templates will be discussed in further detail shortly). For instance, you might add an overloaded operator == function template to test the equality of two Vector objects. Consequently, for every specialization of Vector, the implementation will generate a corresponding specialization of the overloaded operator ==. In order to declare a friend template function, you first have to forward declare the class template and the friend function template as follows:

```
template <class T> class Vector; // class template forward declaration
  // forward declaration of the function template to be used as a friend
template <class T> bool operator== (const Vector<T>& v1, const Vector<T>& v2);
```

Next, the friend function template is declared inside the class body:

```
template <class T> class Vector
{
public:
  //...
  friend bool operator==<T> (const Vector<T>& v1, const Vector<T>& v2);
};
```

Finally, the friend function template is defined as follows:

```
template <class T> bool operator== (const Vector<T>& v1, const Vector<T>& v2)
{
// two Vectors are equal if and only if:
// 1) they have the same number of elements;
// 2) every element in one Vector is identical to the
// corresponding element in the second one

  if (v1.size() != v2.size())
    return false;
  for (size_t i = 0; i<v1.size(); i++)
  {
```

```
    if(v1[i] != v2[i])
    return false;
  }
  return true;
}
```

Partial Specialization

It is possible to define a *partial specialization* of a class template. A partial specialization provides an alternative definition of the *primary template*. It is used instead of the primary definition when the arguments in any specialization match those that are given in the partial specialization. For instance, a partial specialization of Vector can handle pointer types exclusively. Thus, for specializations of fundamental types and user-defined types, the primary Vector class is used. For pointers, the partial specialization is used instead of the primary class template. A pointer partial specialization can optimize the manipulation of pointers in several ways. In addition, some operations that manipulate pointers involve dereferencing and the use of operator ->, neither of which is used with non-pointer types.

A partial specialization is defined as follows:

```
//filename: Vector.hpp

template <class T> class Vector <T*> //partial specialization of Vector <T>
{
private:
  size_t size;
  void * p;
public:
  Vector();
  ~Vector();
  //...member functions
  size_t size()  const;
};
```

```
//Vector.hpp
```

A partial specialization is indicated by the parameter list that immediately follows the class template name (remember that the primary template is declared without the list after its name). Compare these two forms:

```
 template <class T> class Vector //primary template
{};
template <class T> class Vector <T*> //partial specialization
{};
```

Partial specializations of a class template that has several parameters are declared as follows:

```
template<class T, class U, int i> class A { };    // primary
template<class T, int i>  class A<T, T*, i>  { };   // partial specialization
template<class T> class A<int, T*, 8> { };   // another partial specialization
```

Partial specializations must appear after the primary declaration of a class template, and its parameter cannot contain default types.

Explicit Specialization of a Class Template

An *explicit specialization* of a class template provides an alternative definition of the primary template. It is used instead of the primary definition if the arguments in a particular specialization match those that are given in the explicit specialization. When is it useful? Consider the Vector template: The code that is generated by the compiler for the specialization Vector<bool> is very inefficient. Instead of storing every Boolean value in a single bit, it occupies at least an entire byte. When you are manipulating large amounts of bits, for example in logical operations or digital signal processing, this is unacceptable. In addition, bit-oriented operations can be performed more efficiently using the bitwise operators. Obviously, there are significant advantages to defining a Vector template that is specifically adjusted to manipulate bits. Following is an example of an explicit specialization Vector<bool> that manipulates bits rather than bytes:

```
template <> class Vector <bool> //explicit specialization
{
private:
  size_t sz;
  unsigned char * buff;
public:
  explicit Vector(size_t s = 1) : sz(s),
    buff (new unsigned char [(sz+7U)/8U] ) {}

  Vector<bool> (const Vector <bool> & v);
  Vector<bool>& operator= (const Vector<bool>& v);
  ~Vector<bool>();
  //other member functions
  bool& operator [] (unsigned int index);
  const bool& operator [] (unsigned int index) const;
  size_t size() const;
};
void bitmanip()
{
 Vector< bool> bits(8);
 bits[0] = true; //assign
 bool seventh = bits[6]; //retrieve
}
```

The template<> prefix indicates an explicit specialization of a primary template. The template arguments for a specialization are specified in the angular brackets that immediately follow the class name. The specialization hierarchy of Vector that has been defined thus far is as follows:

```
template <class T> class Vector //primary template
{};
template <class T> class Vector <T*> //partial specialization
```

```
{};
template <> class Vector <bool> //explicit specialization
{};
```

Fortunately, the Standard Template Library already defines a specialization of
`std::vector<bool>` for manipulating bits optimally, as you will read in the next chapter, "STL and Generic Programming."

Specializations of Class Template Functions

The overloaded operator == of class `Vector` performs a plausible comparison between
two `Vector` objects when their elements are either fundamental types or objects that
overload operator ==. However, a comparison of two objects that store C strings is
likely to yield the wrong result. For example

```
#include "Vector.hpp"
extern const char msg1[] = "hello";
extern const char msg2[] = "hello";
int main()
{
  Vector<const char *> v1(1), v2(1); //the same number of elements
  v1[0] = msg1;
  v2[0] = msg2;
  bool equal = (v1 == v2); //false, strings are equal but pointers aren't
  return 0;
}
```

Although v1 and v2 have the same number of elements and their elements hold the
same string value, operator == returns `false` because it compares the addresses of the
strings rather than the strings themselves. You can alter this behavior by defining a specialized version of operator == for type `const char *` exclusively, which compares the
strings rather than their addresses. The compiler picks the specialized version only
when objects of type Vector<const char *> are compared. Otherwise, it uses the primary version of operator ==. It is not necessary to add the declaration of the specialized friend operator == in the declaration of the template class `Vector`. However, it is
still recommended that you do so in order to document the existence of a specialized
operator ==. For example

> **Note**
> Whether identical string literals are treated as distinct objects is implementation-dependent. Some
> implementations might store the constants msg1 and msg2 at the same memory address (on such imple-
> mentations, the expression bool equal = (v1 == v2); yields true). However, the discussion here
> assumes that msg1 and msg2 are stored in two distinct memory addresses.

```
template <class T> class Vector;
template <class T> bool operator== (const Vector<T>& v1, const Vector<T>& v2);
template <class T> class Vector
{
//...
public:
  friend bool operator==<T> (const Vector<T>& v1,
                             const Vector<T>& v2); // primary
  friend bool operator== ( //specialized version
                           const Vector<const char *>& v1,
                           const Vector<const char *>& v2);

};
```

The definition of the specialized function must appear after the generic version.
Therefore, you place it at the same header file, right after the generic version.
Following is the specialized version:

```
//appended to vector.hpp
#include <cstring> //needed for strcmp
using namespace std;
template <> bool operator== (
                                      const Vector<const char *>& v1,
                                      const Vector<const char *>& v2 )
{
  if (v1.size() != v2.size())  //as before
    return false;
  for (size_t i = 0; i<v1.size(); i++)
  {
    if (strcmp(v1[i], v2[i])  != 0) //compare string values
      return false;
  }
  return true;
}
```

Here again, the empty angular brackets that follow the keyword `template` indicate a
specialized version that overrides a previously defined generic version. The compiler
now uses the specialized form of operator == to compare v1 and v2; as expected, the
result is now `true`.

Specialized functions operate in a way that resembles the behavior of virtual member functions in a derived class. In both cases, the actual function that is being called
depends on the type. However, the virtual dispatch mechanism relies on the dynamic
type of the object, whereas template function specializations are resolved statically.

Function Templates

Many algorithms perform a sequence of identical operations, regardless of the data
type they manipulate. min and max, array sort, and swap are examples of such type-
independent algorithms. In the pre-template era, programmers had to use alternative

techniques to implement generic algorithms—macros, void pointers, and a common root base—all of which incurred significant drawbacks. This section exemplifies the drawbacks of these techniques and then demonstrates how function templates are used in implementing generic algorithms.

Function-Like Macros

Function-like macros were the predominant form of implementing generic algorithms in C. For example

```
#define min(x,y)  ((x)<(y))?(x):(y)

void f()
{
  double dlower = min(5.5, 5.4);
  int ilower = min(sizeof(double), sizeof(int));
  char clower = min('a', 'b');
}
```

The C Standard library defines various function-like macros. To some extent, they can be used effectively because they avoid the overhead that is associated with a full-blown function call. However, macros have significant drawbacks as well. The pre-processor macro expansion is a simple text substitution, with very limited awareness of scope rules and type-checking. Furthermore, macros are notoriously hard to debug because the compiler scans a source file that might look very different from the original file. For this reason, compiler diagnostics can refer to code that the original source file does not contain. Macros can easily bloat the size of a program because every macro call is expanded inline. When large macros are called repeatedly, the result can be a dramatic increase in the size of the program. In spite of the syntactic similarity, macros are semantically very different from functions—they have no linkage, address, or storage type. For these reasons, use macros sparingly—if at all.

void Pointers

An alternative approach to macros is the use of a generic pointer, void *, which can hold the address of any data type. The C standard library defined two generic functions that rely on this feature: qsort and bsearch. qsort is declared in the header <stdlib.h> as follows:

```
void qsort( void *,
            size_t,
            size_t,
            int (*) (const void *, const void *)
          );
```

The type-unawareness of these generic functions is achieved by using void pointers and an abstract, user-defined comparison function. Still, there are noticeable limitations to this technique. void pointers are not type-safe, and the repeated function callbacks impose runtime overhead that, in most cases, cannot be avoided by inlining.

A Common Root Base

In some other object-oriented languages, every object is ultimately derived from a common base class (this design approach and its deficiencies in C++ are described in further detail in Chapter 5, "Object-Oriented Programming and Design"). Generic algorithms can rely on this feature. For example

```cpp
// pseudo C++ code
class Object // a common root class
{
public:
  virtual bool operator < (const Object&) const; //polymorphic behavior
  //..other members
};

const Object& min(const Object &x, const Object& y)
{
  return  x.operator<(y) ? x : y; //x and y can be objects of any class type
}
```

Imitating this approach in C++ is not as useful as it is in other languages, though. C++ does not force a common root class. Therefore, it is the programmer's—not the implementation's—responsibility to ensure that every class is derived from a common base. Worse yet, the common root class is not standardized. Thus, such algorithms are not portable. In addition, these algorithms cannot handle fundamental types because they are limited to class objects exclusively. Finally, the extensive use of runtime type checking imposes an unacceptable performance on general-purpose algorithms.

Function templates are free from all these drawbacks. They are type-safe, they can be inlined by the compiler to boost performance, and—most importantly—they are applicable to fundamental types and user-defined types alike.

A function template declaration contains the keyword `template`, followed by a list of template parameters and a function declaration. As opposed to ordinary functions, which are usually declared in one translation unit and defined in another, the definition of a function template follows its declaration. For example

```cpp
template <class T> T max( T t1, T t2)
{
  return (t1 > t2) ? t1 : t2;
}
```

Unlike class templates, function template parameters are implicitly deduced from the type of their arguments.

In the following example, the compiler instantiates three distinct specializations of `max`, according to the type of arguments used in each invocation:

```cpp
#include <string>
using namespace std;

int main()
{
  int i = 0, j = 8;
```

```
      char c = 'a', d = 'z';
      string s1 = "first", s2 = "second";

      int nmax = max(i, j);    // int max (int, int);
      char cmax = max(c, d);   // char max (char, char);
      string smax = max(s1, s2);   // string max (string, string);
      return 0;
}
```

It is possible to define several function templates with the same name (that is, to overload it) or to combine ordinary functions with function templates that have the same name. For example

```
template <class T> T max( T t1, T t2)
{
  return (t1 > t2) ? t1 : t2;
}

int max (int i, int j)
{
  return (i > j) ? i : j;
}
```

The compiler does not generate an `int` specialization of `max()`. Instead, it invokes the function `int max (int, int)` when `max()` is called with arguments of type `int`.

Performance Considerations

C++ provides several facilities for controlling the instantiation of templates, including explicit instantiation of templates and exported templates. The following sections demonstrate how to use these features, as well as other techniques to enhance performance.

Type Equivalence

Two templates are equivalent (that is, they refer to the same template id) when all the following conditions hold:

- **Name equivalence**—The names of the templates are identical and they refer to the same template.
- **Argument Equivalence**—The type arguments of the templates are the same.
- **Identical Non-Type Arguments**—The non-type arguments of integral or enumeration type of both templates have identical values, and their non-type arguments of pointer or reference type refer to the same external object or function.
- **Template-template Arguments**—The template-template arguments of both templates refer to the same template.

Following are some examples:

```
template<class T, long size> class Array
{ /* ... */ };

void func()
{
Array<char, 2*512> a;
Array<char, 1024> b;
}
```

The compiler evaluates constant expressions such as 2*512, so templates a and b are of the same type. Following is another example:

```
template<class T, int(*error_code_fct)()> class Buffer
{ /* ... */ };
int error_handler();
int another_error_handler();
void func()
{
  Buffer<int, &error_handler> b1;
  Buffer<int, &another_error_handler> b2;
  Buffer<int, &another_error_handler> b3;
  Buffer<unsigned int, &another_error_handler> b4;
}
```

b2 and b3 are of the same type because they are instances of the same template and they take the same type and non-type arguments. Conversely, b1 and b4 are of distinct types.

The function func() instantiated three distinct specializations from the same class template: one for b1, a second for b2 and b3, and a third for b4. Unlike ordinary function overloading, the compiler generates a distinct class from the template for every unique type. On machines that have the same underlying representation for long and int types, the following code still results in the instantiation of two distinct templates:

```
void too_prolific()
{
  Buffer<int, &error_handler> buff1;
  Buffer<long, &error_handler> buff2;
}
```

Similarly, char and unsigned char are distinct types, even on machines that treat char as unsigned by default. Programmers who are accustomed to the lenient matching rules of ordinary function overloading are not always aware of the potential code bloat that can result from using templates with very similar yet distinct types.

Avoiding Unnecessary Instantiations

In the following example, three distinct copies of the template min are generated—one for each type that is used:

```
template < class T > T min(T f, T s)
{
```

```
    return f < s? f: s;
}
void use_min()
{
  int n = 5, m= 10;
  int j = min(n,m);        //min<int> instantiated
  char c = 'a', d = 'b';
  char k = min(c,d);     //min<char> instantiated
  short int u = 5, v = 10;
  short int w = min(u,v);   // min<short int> instantiated
}
```

On the other hand, an ordinary function avoids the automatic generation of redundant specializations:

```
int min(int f, int s)
{
  return f < s? f: s;
}
void use_min()
{
// all three invocation of min
// use int min (int, int);
  int n = 5, m= 10;
  int j = min(n,m);
  char c = 'a', d = 'b';
  char k = min(c,d);
  short int u = 5, v = 10;
  short int w = min(u,v);
}
```

Still, the template version of min has a clear advantage over the function: It can handle pointers and any other user-defined types. You want the benefits of a template while avoiding the unnecessary generation of specializations. How can these be avoided? A simple solution is to safely cast the arguments into one common type before invoking the function template. For example:

```
void no_proliferation()
{
  short n = 5, m= 10;
  int j = min( static_cast<int> (n),
             static_cast<int> (m) ); //min<int> instantiated
  char c = 'a', d = 'b';
  char k = static_cast<char> (min( static_cast<int> ,
                             static_cast<int> (d) ) ); //min<int> used
}
```

This technique can also be applied to pointers: First, they have to be cast to void *, and then they must be cast back to their original type. When you are using pointers to polymorphic objects, pointers to derived objects are cast to pointers to a base class.

For very small templates such as min, casting the arguments into a common denominator type is not worth the trouble. Nonetheless, when nontrivial templates that contain hundreds of code lines are used, you might consider doing so.

Explicit Template Instantiation

As was previously noted, templates are instantiated only if they are used in the program. Generally, compilers generate the necessary code for a specialization when they encounter its use in the source file. When large applications that consist of hundreds of source files have to be compiled, this can cause a significant increase in compilation time because the compiler's processing is repeatedly interrupted when it has to generate code for sporadic specializations. The recurrent interruption can occur in almost every source file because they use—almost without exception—template classes of the Standard Library. Consider a simple project that consists of only three source files:

```
//filename func1.cpp
#include <string>
#include <iostream>
using namespace std;

void func1()
{
  string s;  //generate default constructor and destructor
  s = "hello";  //generate assignment operator for const char *
  string s2;
  s2 = s;  // generate operator = const string&, string&
  cout<<s2.size(); // generate string::size, ostream& operator <<(int)
}
//func1.cpp

//filename func2.cpp
#include <string>
#include <iostream>
using namespace std;

void func2()
{
 string s;  //generate default constructor and destructor
cout<<"enter a string: "<<endl; //generate ostream& operator<<(const char *)
 cin>>s //generate istream& operator>>(string&)
}
//func2.cpp

//filename main.cpp
int main()
{
  func1();
  func2();
  retrun 0;
}
// main.cpp
```

The compilation time can be reduced if all the necessary template code is instantiated all at once, thereby avoiding the repeated interruption of the compiler's processing. For this purpose, you can use an *explicit instantiation*. An explicit instantiation is indicated by the keyword `template` (without the <>), followed by a template declaration. Here are a few examples of explicit template instantiations:

```
template <class T> class A{/*..*/};
template<class T> void func(T&) { }
  //filename instantiations.hpp
template class Vector<short>;  //explicit instantiation of a class template
template A<int>::A<int>(); //explicit instantiation of a member function
template class
  std::basic_string<char>; //explicit instantiation of a namespace member
template void func<int>(int&); //explicit instantiation of a function template
```

Examples of Explicit Instantiations in the Standard Library

The Standard Library defines several specializations of class templates. One example is the class template `basic_string<>`. Two specialized versions of this class are `std::string` and `std::wstring`, which are `typedefs` of the specializations `basic_string<char>` and `basic_string<wchar_t>`, respectively. Usually, there is no need to instantiate any of these explicitly because the header <string> already instantiates these specializations:

```
#include <string> //definitions of std::string and std::wstring
using namespace std;

bool TranslateToKorean(const string& origin,
                       wstring& target ); //English / Korean dictionary
  int main()
  {
    string EnglishMsg = "This program has performed an illegal operation";
    wstring KoreanMsg;
    TranslateToKorean(EnglishMsg, KoreanMsg);
  }
```

Exported Templates

A template definition can be `#included` in several translation units; consequently, it can be compiled several times. As you have observed, this can considerably increase compilation and linkage time. Instead of `#including` a complete definition of the template, it is possible to compile the template definition only once, and use only the template's declaration in other translation units. This is very similar to the compilation of external functions and classes, in which the definition is compiled only once and then only the declarations are required.

> **Note**
>
> Exported templates are relatively new in C++; therefore, not all compilers support this feature yet. Please consult your user's manual to check whether your compiler supports it.

To compile a template separately and then use its declaration, the template has to be *exported*. This is done by preceding the template's definition with the keyword export:

```
//filename min.cpp
export template < class T > T min (const T& a, const T& b)
{
  return a > b ? b : a;
}
```

Now only the declaration of the template is required when it is used in other translation units. For example

```
//file min.c
template < class T > T min (const T & a, const T & b); //declaration only
int main()
{
  int j=0, k=1;
  in smaller = min(j,k);
  return 0;
}
```

Inline function templates cannot be exported. If an inline template function is declared both export and inline, the export declaration has no effect and the template is only inline. Declaring a class template exported is equivalent to declaring all its non-inline member functions, static data members, and member classes exported. Templates in an unnamed namespace are not to be exported.

Interaction with Other Language Features

The interaction of templates with other language features can sometimes yield surprising results. The following sections discuss various aspects of interaction between templates and other language features, including ambiguous interpretation of qualified template names, inheritance, and virtual member functions.

The typename Keyword

Using qualified names in a template can cause ambiguity between a type and a non-type. For example

```
int N;
template < class T > T func()
{
  T::A * N;  // ambiguous: multiplication  or a pointer declaration?
  //
}
```

If T::A is a typename, the definition of N inside func() creates a pointer. If, on the other hand, T::A is a non-type (for example, if A is data member of type int), T::A * N is an expression statement that consists of the multiplication of the qualified member T::A by a global int N. By default, the compiler assumes that an expression such as

T::A refers to a non-type. The `typename` keyword instructs the compiler to supersede this default interpretation and resolve the ambiguity in favor of a type name rather than a non-type. In other words, the preceding (seemingly ambiguous) statement is actually resolved as a multiplication expression, the result of which is discarded. In order to declare a pointer, the `typename` keyword is required:

```
int N;
template < class T > T func()
{
  typename T::A * N; // N is a now pointer since T::A is a typename
//...
};
```

Inheritance Relationship of Templates

A common mistake is to assume that a container of pointers or references to objects of a derived class is a container of pointers or references to a base class. For example

```
#include<vector>
using namespace std;

class Base
{
public: virtual void f() {}
};
class Derived : public Base
{
public: void f() {}
};

void func( vector<Base*>& vb);
int main()
{
  Derived d;
  vector<Derived*> vd;
  vd.push_back(&d);
  func(vd); //error, vector<Derived*>& is not a vector<Base*>
}
```

Although the is-a relationship exists between the classes `Derived` and `Base`, there is no such relationship between specializations of the same class template that contain pointers or references to related objects.

Virtual Member Functions

A member function template should not be virtual. However, ordinary member functions in a class template *can* be virtual. For example

```
template <class T> class A
{
public:
```

```
template <class S> virtual void f(S);    //error
virtual int g(); // OK
};
```

A specialization of a member function template does not override a virtual function that is defined in a base class. For example

```
class Base
{
public:
  virtual void f(char);
};

class Derived : public Base
{
public:
  template <class T> void f(T);    //does not override  B::f(int)
};
```

Pointers to Members of a Class Template

Pointers to class members can take the address of a specialized member function of a class template. As with ordinary classes, pointers to members cannot take the address of a static member function. In the following example, the specialization `std::vector<int>` is used:

```
#include<vector>
using namespace std;
  // a typedef is used to hide the unwieldy syntax
typedef void (vector< int >::*pmv) (size_t);

void func()
{
  pmv  reserve_ptr = &vector< int >::reserve;
  //...use reserve_ptr
}
```

Conclusions

Templates simplify and streamline the implementation of generic containers and functions. The benefits of templates have allured software vendors, who are now migrating from plain object-oriented frameworks to object-oriented generic frameworks. However, parameterized types are not unique to C++. Back in 1983, Ada introduced generic packages, which were roughly equivalent to class templates. Other languages implemented similar mechanisms of automated code generation from a skeletal user-written code.

The two main template categories in C++ are class templates and function templates. A class template encapsulates parameterized data members and function members. Function templates are a means of implementing generic algorithms. The traditional methods of implementing generic algorithms in pre-template C++ were rather limited, unsafe, and inefficient compared to templates. An important aspect of templates is the support of object semantics.

C++ enables programmers to control the instantiation of templates by explicitly instantiating them. It is possible to instantiate an entire class, a certain member function of a class, or a particular specialization of a function template. An explicit instantiation of a template is indicated by the keyword `template`, without angular brackets that are followed by the template declaration. Explicit specializations of a class template are always required. For function templates, the compiler usually deduces the specialization from the type of the arguments. It is possible to define partial specialization of a class template that overrides the primary class template for a set of types. This feature is most useful for modifying the behavior of a class template that manipulates pointers. A partial specialization is indicated by a secondary list of parameters following the name of the template. An explicit specialization enables the programmer to override the automatic instantiation of a class template for a certain type. An explicit specialization is indicated by the keyword `template`, followed by empty angular brackets and a list of type arguments after the template's name.

Templates and operator overloading are the building blocks of generic programming. The Standard Template Library is an exemplary framework of generic programming, as you will see in the next chapter.

10

STL and Generic Programming

Introduction

Object-oriented design offers A limited form of code reuse—inheritance and poly-morphism. The generic programming paradigm is designed to enable a higher level of reusability. Instead of data hiding, it relies on data independence. C++ has two features that support data independence: templates and operator overloading. A combination of these features allows a generic algorithm to assume very little about the actual object to which it is applied, whether it is a fundamental type or a user-defined type. Consequently, such an algorithm is not confined to a specific data type, and it has a higher reusability potential than does a type-dependent algorithm.

The *Standard Template Library (STL)* is an exemplary framework that is built on the foundations of generic programming. STL is a collection of generic algorithms and containers that communicate through iterators. This chapter explores the principles of generic programming, focusing on STL. A complete account of every STL container and algorithm can fill a book of its own, so this chapter only discusses the basic con-cepts of generic programming. It starts with an overview of STL header files. STL components are discussed next: containers, iterators, algorithms, function objects, adap-tors, and allocators. This discussion presents some of the most widely used containers and algorithms of STL. Finally, class `string` is described in detail.

Generic Programming

Generic software is primarily reusable software. Reusability is characterized by two key features: adaptability and efficiency. It is not difficult to imagine highly adaptive software components that are too inefficient to become widely used (these are usually implemented by complex inheritance hierarchies, virtual functions, and extensive use of runtime type information). Conversely, efficient components are generally written in low-level, platform-dependent code that is both nonportable and hard to maintain. Templates overcome these difficulties because they are checked at compile time rather than at runtime, because they do not require any inheritance relation among objects, and because they are applicable to fundamental types. The most useful generic components are containers and algorithms. For years, programmers were implementing their own lists, queues, sets, and other container types to make up for the lack of language support; however, homemade containers suffer from significant drawbacks. They are not portable, they are sometimes less than 100% bug free, their interfaces vary from one implementation to another, and they can be less than optimal in terms of runtime performance and memory usage.

In the latest phases of the standardization of C++, Alex Stepanov suggested adding a generic library of containers and algorithms to C++. He based his proposal on a similar generic library that he had previously designed for Ada. At that time (November 1993), the committee was under pressure to complete the ongoing standardization process as fast as possible. Consequently, suggestions for language extensions were rejected one after another. However, Stepanov's proposal was too good to be forsaken—the committee adopted it unanimously.

The proposed generic library was a collection of containers based on mathematical data models such as vector, queue, list, and stack. It also contained a set of generic algorithms such as sort, merge, find, replace, and so on. These library constituents were implemented with templates. Still, templates alone are insufficient because fundamental types, pointers, user-defined types, and single bits are manipulated by different language constructs and operators. Operator overloading provides the necessary uniform interface that abstracts the actual data type of a container or an algorithm. The following section examines these components in greater detail.

Organization of STL Header Files

STL components are grouped under namespace std. They are defined in the following header files. Note that prestandardized implementations of STL might use different header names, as indicated below.

Containers

Container classes are defined in the following header files (see Table 10.1). The associative containers multimap and multiset are defined in <map> and <set>, respectively. Similarly, priority_queue and deque are defined in <queue>. (On some prestandardized implementations, the container adaptors stack, queue, and priority_queue are in <stack.h>).

Table 10.1 **STL Containers**

Header	Contents
<vector>	An array of T
<list>	A doubly-linked list of T
<deque>	A double-ended queue of T
<queue>	A queue of T
<stack>	A stack of T
<map>	An associative array of T
<set>	A set of T
<bitset>	A set of Boolean values

Algorithms

STL generic algorithms can be applied to a sequence of elements. They are defined in the following header file (see Table 10.2). (On prestandardized implementations, generic algorithms are defined in <algo.h>.)

Iterators

Iterators are used to navigate sequences. They are defined in the following header file (see Table 10.3).

Numeric Library

STL provides several classes and algorithms that are specifically designed for numeric computations (see Table 10.4).

Table 10.2 **STL Algorithms**

Header	Contents
<algorithm>	A collection of generic algorithms

Table 10.3 **STL Iterators**

Header	Contents
<iterator>	Various types of iterators and iterator support

Table 10.4 **Numeric Containers and Algorithms**

Header	Contents
<complex>	Complex numbers and their associated operations
<valarray>	Mathematical vectors and their associated operations
<numerics>	Generalized numeric operations

Table 10.5 **General Utilities**

Header	Contents
<utility>	Operators and pairs
<functional>	Function objects
<memory>	Allocators and auto_ptr

Utilities

The following headers define auxiliary components that are used in STL containers and algorithms (see Table 10.5). These include function adaptors, pairs, and class auto_ptr (discussed later).

Containers

A container is an object that can hold other objects as its elements. A generic container is not confined to a specific type—it can store objects of any kind. C supports one container type in the form of built-in arrays. Other languages support other data models. Pascal, for example, has a built-in set type, and Lisp supports lists (hence its name). C++ inherited from C its support for arrays. Arrays have several properties that more or less correspond to the mathematical notion of a vector: They can store any data type and they provide random access—that is, the time needed to access any element is identical, regardless of the element's position.

Still, under some circumstances, arrays are less convenient than other data models; it is impossible to insert a new element in the middle of an array. Also, you cannot append new elements to the end of an array. With other data models, (a list, for example), it is possible to insert new elements in the middle of the container or to append elements to its end. A special type of list, a *heterogenic list*, can hold elements of different types at the same time.

Sequence Containers

A sequence container organizes a collection of objects of the same type T into a strictly linear arrangement. Following are examples of sequence containers:

- **T v[n]**—A built-in array that stores a fixed number of *n* elements and provides random access to them.

- **std::vector<T>**—An array-like container that stores a varying number of *n* elements and provides random access to them. Insertions and deletions at the end of a vector are constant time operations.

- **std::deque<T>**—A double-ended queue that provides random access to a sequence of varying length, with constant time insertions and deletions at the beginning and the end.

- **std::list<T>**—A list that provides linear time access to a sequence of varying length, with constant time insertions and deletions at any position.

Interestingly, built-in arrays are considered sequence containers because STL algorithms are designed to work with them as they work with other sequence types.

Requirements for STL Containment

Elements of STL containers must be *copy-constructible* and *assignable*. Essentially, copy-constructible means that an object and a copy of that object must be identical (although the formal definition in the Standard is somewhat more complicated than that). Likewise, assignable means that assigning one object to another results in two identical objects. These definitions might sound trivial because objects in general are copy-constructible and assignable; later, however (when class auto_ptr is discussed), you will see an example of an object that does not meet these requirements and is, therefore, not to be stored in STL containers.

An additional requirement is that container elements must have their copy constructor, default constructor, assignment operator, and destructor publicly declared (either explicitly or implicitly).

The vector Container Class

The standard containers share a common interface, but each container also defines particular operations. Following is the interface of class vector<T>:

```
namespace std {
      template <class T, class Allocator = allocator<T> >
      class vector {
      public:
        // implementation-defined types
        typedef implementation defined              iterator;
        typedef implementation defined              const_iterator;
        typedef implementation defined              size_type;
        typedef implementation defined              difference_type;
        // additional types
        typedef typename Allocator::reference       reference;
        typedef typename Allocator::const_reference const_reference;
        typedef T value_type;
```

```
typedef Allocator                            allocator_type;
typedef typename Allocator::pointer          pointer;
typedef typename Allocator::const_pointer    const_pointer
typedef std::reverse_iterator<iterator>      reverse_iterator;
typedef std::reverse_iterator<const_iterator> const_reverse_iterator;

// construction, copying destruction and assignment operations
explicit vector(const Allocator& = Allocator());
explicit vector(size_type n, const T& value = T(),
                    const Allocator& = Allocator());
template <class InputIterator>
  vector(InputIterator first, InputIterator last,
    const Allocator& = Allocator());
vector(const vector<T,Allocator>& x);
~vector();
vector<T,Allocator>& operator=(const vector<T,Allocator>& x);
template <class InputIterator>
  void assign(InputIterator first, InputIterator last);
void assign(size_type n, const T& u);
allocator_type get_allocator() const;
//iterators
iterator              begin();
const_iterator        begin() const;
iterator              end();
const_iterator        end() const;
reverse_iterator      rbegin();
const_reverse_iterator rbegin() const;
reverse_iterator      rend();
const_reverse_iterator rend() const;
//capacity operations
size_type size() const;
size_type max_size() const;
void      resize(size_type sz, T c = T());
size_type capacity() const;
bool      empty() const;
void      reserve(size_type n);

//element access operations
reference       operator[](size_type n);
const_reference operator[](size_type n) const;
const_reference at(size_type n) const;
reference       at(size_type n);
reference       front();
const_reference front() const;
reference       back();
const_reference back() const;
// modifiers
void push_back(const T& x);
void pop_back();
iterator insert(iterator position, const T& x);
void     insert(iterator position, size_type n, const T& x);
```

```
         template <class InputIterator>
             void insert(iterator position,
                         InputIterator first, InputIterator last);
         iterator erase(iterator position);
         iterator erase(iterator first, iterator last);
         void    swap(vector<T,Allocator>&);
         void    clear();
     }; //class vector
     //non-member overloaded operators
     template <class T, class Allocator>
       bool operator==(const vector<T,Allocator>& x,
                       const vector<T,Allocator>& y);
     template <class T, class Allocator>
       bool operator< (const vector<T,Allocator>& x,
                       const vector<T,Allocator>& y);
     template <class T, class Allocator>
       bool operator!=(const vector<T,Allocator>& x,
                       const vector<T,Allocator>& y);
     template <class T, class Allocator>
       bool operator> (const vector<T,Allocator>& x,
                       const vector<T,Allocator>& y);
     template <class T, class Allocator>
       bool operator>=(const vector<T,Allocator>& x,
                       const vector<T,Allocator>& y);
     template <class T, class Allocator>
       bool operator<=(const vector<T,Allocator>& x,
                       const vector<T,Allocator>& y);

     //specialized algorithms
     template <class T, class Allocator>
       void swap(vector<T,Allocator>& x, vector<T,Allocator>& y);
   }//namespace std
```

On most implementations, the parameterized types `size_type` and `difference_type` have the default values `size_t` and `ptrdiff_t`, respectively. However, they can be replaced by other types for particular specializations.

The storage of STL containers automatically grows as necessary, freeing the programmer from this tedious and error-prone task. For example, a `vector` can be used to read an unknown number of elements from the keyboard:

```
#include <vector>
#include <iostream>
using namespace std;
int main()
{
  vector <int> vi;
  for (;;) //read numbers from a user's console until 0 is input
  {
    int temp;
    cout<<"enter a number; press 0 to terminate" <<endl;
    cin>>temp;
```

```
       if (temp == 0 ) break; //exit from loop?
       vi.push_back(temp); //insert int into the buffer
    }
    cout<< "you entered "<< vi.size() <<" elements" <<endl;
    return 0;
}//end main
```

Container Reallocation

The memory allocation scheme of STL containers must address two conflicting demands. On the one hand, a container should not preallocate large amounts of memory because it can impair the system's performance. On the other hand, it is inefficient to allow a container to reallocate memory whenever it stores a few more elements. The allocation strategy has to walk a thin line. On many implementations, a container initially allocates a small memory buffer, which grows exponentially with every reallocation. Sometimes, however, it is possible to estimate in advance how many elements the container will have to store. In this case, the user can preallocate a sufficient amount of memory in advance so that the recurrent reallocation process can be avoided. Imagine a mail server of some Internet service provider: The server is almost idle at 4 a.m. At 9 a.m., however, it has to transfer thousands of emails every minute. The incoming emails are first stored in a vector before they are routed to other mail servers across the Web. Allowing the container to reallocate itself little by little with every few dozen emails can degrade performance.

What Happens During Reallocation?

The reallocation process consists of four steps. First, a new memory buffer that is large enough to store the container is allocated. Second, the existing elements are copied to the new memory location. Third, the destructors of the elements in their previous location are successively invoked. Finally, the original memory buffer is released. Obviously, reallocation is a costly operation. You can avert reallocation by calling the member function reserve(). reserve(n) ensures that the container reserves sufficient memory for at least n elements in advance, as in the following example:

```
class Message { /*...*/};
#include <vector>
using namespace std;
int FillWithMessages(vector<Message>& msg_que); //severe time constraints
int main()
{
  vector <Message> msgs;
  // before entering a time-critical section, make room for 1000 Messages
  msgs.reserve(1000);
//no re-allocation should occur before 1000 objects have been stored in vector
  FillWithMessages(msgs);
  return 0;
}
```

capacity() and size()

capacity() returns the total number of elements that the container can hold without requiring reallocation. size() returns the number of elements that are currently stored in the container. In other words, capacity() - size() is the number of available "free slots" that can be filled with additional elements without reallocating. The capacity of a container can be resized explicitly by calling either reserve() or resize(). These member functions differ in two respects. resize(*n*) allocates memory for *n* objects and default-initializes them (you can provide a different initializer value as the second optional argument).

reserve() allocates raw memory without initializing it. In addition, reserve() does not change the value that is returned from size()—it only changes the value that is returned from capacity(). resize() changes both these values. For example

```
#include <iostream>
#include <vector>
#include <string>
using namespace std;
int main()
{
  vector <string> vs;
  vs.reserve(10); //make room for at least 10 more strings
  vs.push_back(string()); //insert an element
  cout<<"size: "<< vs.size()<<endl; //output: 1
  cout<<"capacity: "<<vs.capacity()<<endl; //output: 10
  cout<<"there's room for "<<vs.capacity() - vs.size()
      <<" elements before reallocation"<<endl;
  //allocate 10 more elements, initialized each with string::string()
  vs.resize(20);
  cout<<"size: "<< vs.size()<<endl; //output 20
  cout<<"capacity: "<<vs.capacity()<<endl; //output 20;
  return 0;
}
```

Specifying the Container's Capacity During Construction

Up until now, the examples in this chapter have used explicit operations to preallocate storage by calling either reserve() or resize(). However, it is possible to specify the requested storage size during construction. For example

```
#include <vector>
using namespace std;

int main()
{
  vector<int>  vi(1000); //initial storage for 1000 int's
  //vi contains 1000 elements initialized by int::int()
  return 0;
}
```

Remember that reserve() allocates raw memory without initializing it. The constructor, on the other hand, initializes the allocated elements by invoking their default constructor. It is possible to specify a different initializer value, though:

```
vector<int>  vi(1000, 4); //initial  all 1000 int's with 4
```

Accessing a Single Element

The overloaded operator [] and the member function at() enable direct access to a vector's element. Both have a const and a non-const version, so they can be used to access an element of a const and a non-const vector, respectively.

The overloaded [] operator was designed to be as efficient as its built-in counterpart. Therefore, [] does not check to see if its argument actually refers to a valid element. The lack of runtime checks ensures the fastest access time (an operator [] call is usually inlined). However, using operator [] with an illegal subscript yields undefined behavior. When performance is paramount, and when the code is written carefully so that only legal subscripts are accessed, use the [] operator. The [] notation is also more readable and intuitive. Nonetheless, runtime checks are unavoidable in some circumstances—for instance, when the subscript value is received from an external source such as a function, a database record, or a human operator. In such cases you should use the member function at() instead of operator []. at() performs range checking and, in case of an attempt to access an out of range member, it throws an exception of type std::out_of_range. Here is an example:

```
#include <vector>
#include <iostream>
#include <string>
#include <stdexcept>
using namespace std;
int main()
{
  vector<string> vs; // vs has no elements currently
  vs.push_back("string"); //add first element
  vs[0] = "overriding string"; //override it using []
  try
  {
    cout<< vs.at(10) <<endl; //out of range element, exception thrown
  }
  catch(std::out_of_range & except)
  {
    // handle out-of-range subscript
  }
}//end main
```

Front and Back Operations

Front and back operations refer to the beginning and the end of a container, respectively. The member function push_back() appends a single element to the end of the container. When the container has exhausted its free storage, it reallocates additional storage, and then appends the element. The member function `pop_back()` removes the last element from the container. The member functions `front()` and `back()` access a single element at the container's beginning and end, respectively. `front()` and `back()` both have a `const` and a non-`const` version. For example

```cpp
#include <iostream>
#include <vector>
using namespace std;

int main()
{
  vector <short> v;
  v.push_back(5);
  v.push_back(10);
  cout<<"front: " << v.front() << endl; //5
  cout<<"back: " << v.back() << endl; //10
  v.pop_back(); //remove v[1]
  cout<<"back: " << v.back() << endl; //now 5
  return 0;
}
```

Container Assignment

STL containers overload the assignment operator, thereby allowing containers of the same type to be assigned easily. For example

```cpp
#include <iostream>
#include<vector>
using namespace std;
int main()
{
  vector <int> vi;
  vi.push_back(1);
  vi.push_back(2);
  vector <int> new_vector;
  //copy the contents of vi to new_vector, which automatically grows as needed
  new_vector = vi;
  cout << new_vector[0] << new_vector[1] << endl;   // display 1 and 2
  return 0;
}
```

Contiguity of Vectors

Built-in arrays in C++ reside in contiguous chunks of memory. The Standard, however, does not require that vector elements occupy contiguous memory. When STL was added to the Standard, it seemed intuitive that vectors should store their elements contiguously, so contiguity never became an explicit requirement. Indeed, all current STL implementations follow this convention. The current specification, however, permits implementations that do not use contiguous memory. This loophole will probably be fixed by the Standardization committee in the future, and vector contiguity will become a Standard requirement.

A `vector<Base>` Should Not Store Derived Objects

Each element in a vector must have the same size. Because a derived object can have additional members, its size might be larger than the size of its base class. Avoid storing a derived object in a `vector<Base>` because it can cause object slicing—with undefined results. You can, however, achieve the desired polymorphic behavior by storing a pointer to a derived object in a `vector<Base*>`.

FIFO Data Models

In a queue data model (a queue is also called FIFO—first in first out), the first element that is inserted is located at the topmost position, and any subsequent elements are located at lower positions. The two basic operations in a queue are `pop()` and `push()`. A `push()` operation inserts an element into the bottom of the queue. A `pop()` operation removes the element at the topmost position, which was the first to be inserted; consequently, the element that is located one position lower becomes the topmost element. The STL `queue` container can be used as follows:

```
#include <iostream>
#include <queue>
using namespace std;

int main()
{
 queue <int> iq;
 iq.push(93); //insert the first element, it is the top-most one
 iq.push(250);
 iq.push(10); //last element inserted is located at the bottom
 cout<<"currently there are "<< iq.size() << " elements" << endl;
 while (!iq.empty() )
 {
   cout <<"the last element is: "<< iq.front() << endl; //front() returns
                                                        //the top-most element
  iq.pop(); //remove the top-most element
 }
 return 0;
}
```

STL also defines a double-ended queue, or *deque* (pronounced "deck") container. A `deque` is a queue that is optimized to support operations at both ends efficiently. Another type of queue is a *priority_queue*. A priority_queue has all its elements internally sorted according to their priority. The element with the highest priority is located at the top. To qualify as an element of `priority_queue`, an object has to define the < operator (priority_queue is discussed in detail later, in the section titled "Function Objects").

Iterators

Iterators can be thought of as generic pointers. They are used to navigate a container without having to know the actual type of its elements. Several member functions—such as `begin()` and `end()`—return iterators that point to the ends of a container.

begin() and end()

All STL containers provide the `begin()` and `end()` pair of member functions. `begin()` returns an iterator that points to the first element of the container. For example

```cpp
#include <iostream>
#include <vector>
#include <string>
using namespace std;
int main()
{
  vector <int> v(1);  //room for a single element
  v[0] = 10;
  vector<int>::iterator p  = v.begin();   // p points to the first element of v
  *p = 11; //assign a new value to v[0] through p
  cout << *p;  //output 11
  return 0;
}
```

The member function `end()`, on the other hand, returns an iterator that points one position *past* the last valid element of the container. This sounds surprising at first, but there's nothing really unusual about it if you consider how C-strings are represented: An additional null character is automatically appended one position past the final element of the `char` array. The additional element in STL has a similar role—it indicates the end of the container. Having `end()` return an iterator that points one position past the container's elements is useful in `for` and `while` loops. For example

```cpp
vector <int> v(10);
int n=0;
for (vector<int>::iterator p = v.begin(); p<v.end(); p++)
  *p = n++;
```

`begin()` and `end()` come in two versions: const and non-const. The non-const version returns a *non-const iterator*, which enables the user to modify the values of the container's element, as you just saw. The const version returns a *const iterator*, which cannot modify its container.

For example

```cpp
const vector <char> v(10);
vector<char>::iterator p  = v.begin(); //error, must use a const_iterator
vector<char>::const_iterator cp  = v.begin(); //OK
*cp = 'a'; //error, attempt to modify a const object
cout << *cp;  //OK
```

The member functions `rbegin()` and `rend()` (reverse `begin()` and reverse `end()`) are similar to `begin()` and `end()`, except that they return *reverse iterators*, which apply to reverse sequences. Essentially, reverse iterators are ordinary iterators, except that they invert the semantics of the overloaded ++ and -- operators. They are useful when the elements of a container are accessed in reverse order.

```
#include <iostream>
#include <vector>
#include <string>
using namespace std;
void ascending_order()
{
  vector <double> v(10);
  double d = 0.1;
  for (vector<double>::iterator p = v.begin(); p<v.end(); p++) //initialize
  {
    *p = d;
    d+= 0.1;
  }
   //display elements of v in ascending order
  for (vector<double>::reverse_iterator rp = v.rbegin(); rp < v.rend(); rp++)
  {
    cout<< *rp<<endl;
  }
}
```

Like `begin()` and `end()`, `rbegin()` and `rend()` have a `const` and a non-`const` version.

The Underlying Representation of Iterators

Most implementations of STL use pointers as the underlying representation of iterators. However, an iterator need not be a pointer, and there's a good reason for that. Consider a huge vector of scanned images that are stored on a 6GB disk; the built-in pointer on most machines has only 32 bits, which is not large enough to iterate through this large vector. Instead of a bare pointer, an implementation can use a 64-bit integer as the underlying iterator in this case. Likewise, a container that holds elements such as bits and nibbles (to which built-in pointers cannot refer) can be implemented with a different underlying type for iterators and still provide the same interface. However, bare pointers can sometimes be used to iterate through the elements of a container on certain implementations; for example

```
#include <vector>
#include <iostream>
using namespace std;

void hack()
{
  vector<int> vi;
  vi.push_back(5);
```

```
    int *p = vi.begin();//bad programming practice, although it may work
    *p = 6; //assign vi[0]
    cout<<vi[0]; //output 6 (maybe)
}
```

Using bare pointers instead of iterators is a bad programming practice—avoid it.

"const Correctness" of Iterators

Use the const iterator of a container when the elements that are accessed through it are not to be modified. As with ordinary pointer types, using a non-const iterator implies that the contents of the container are to be changed. A const iterator enables the compiler to detect simple mistakes, and it is more readable.

Initializing a Vector with the Contents of a Built-in Array

As was previously noted, built-in arrays are valid sequence containers. Thus, the addresses of array ends can be used as iterators to initialize a vector with the contents of a built-in array. For example

```
#include<vector>
#include <iostream>
using namespace std;
int main()
{
  int arr[3];
  arr[0] = 4; arr[1] = 8;  arr[2] = 16;
   vector <int> vi ( &arr[0], //address of  the array's beginning
                    &arr[3] ); // must point one element past the array's end
  cout<< vi[0] << '\t' << vi[1] << '\t' << vi[2] <<endl;  // output: 4  8  16
  return 0;
}
```

Iterator Invalidation

Reallocation can occur when a member function modifies its container. Modifying member functions are reserve() and resize(), push_back() and pop_back(), erase(), clear(), insert(), and others. In addition, assignment operations and modifying algorithms can also cause reallocation. When a container reallocates its elements, their addresses change. Consequently, the values of existing iterators are invalidated.

For example

```
#include <iostream>
#include <list>
using namespace std;

int main()
{
```

```
list <double> payroll;
payroll.push_back(5000.00);
list<double>::const_iterator p = payroll.begin(); //points to first element
for (int i = 0 ; i < 10; i++)
{
    payroll.push_back(4500.00); //insert 10 more elements to payroll;
                                //reallocation may occur
}
    // DANGEROUS
cout << "first element in payroll: "<< *p <<endl; // p may have
                                                  //been invalidated
return 0;
}
```

In the preceding example, `payroll` might have reallocated itself during the insertion of ten additional elements, thereby invalidating the value of p. Using an invalid iterator is similar to using a pointer with the address of a deleted object—both result in undefined behavior. To be on the safe side, it is recommended that you reassign the iterator's value after calling a modifying member function. For example

```
list<double>::const_iterator p = payroll.begin();//points to the first element
for (int i = 0 ; i < 10; i++)
{
  payroll.push_back(4500.00); // reallocation may occur here
}
  p = payroll.begin(); // reassign p
  cout <<"first element in payroll: "<<*p<<endl;  // now safe
}
```

Alternatively, you can prevent reallocation by preallocating sufficient storage before the instantiation of an iterator. For example

```
int main()
{
  list <double> payroll;
  payroll.reserve(11);
  payroll.push_back(5000.00);
  list<double>::const_iterator p = payroll.begin();
  for (int i = 0 ; i < 10; i++)
  {
    payroll.push_back(4500.00); //no reallocation
  }
  cout << "first element in payroll: "<< *p <<endl; // OK
  return 0;
}
```

Algorithms

STL defines a rich collection of generic algorithms that can be applied to containers and other sequences. There are three major categories of algorithms: non-modifying sequence operations, mutating sequence operations, and algorithms for sorting.

Non-Modifying Sequence Operations

Non-modifying sequence operations are algorithms that do not directly modify the sequence on which they operate. They include operations such as search, checking for equality, and counting.

The `find()` Algorithm

The generic algorithm `find()` locates an element within a sequence. `find()` takes three arguments. The first two are iterators that point to the beginning and the end of the sequence, respectively.

The third argument is the sought-after value. `find()` returns an iterator that points to the first element that is identical to the sought-after value. If `find()` cannot locate the requested value, it returns an iterator that points one element past the final element in the sequence. For example

```
#include <algorithm> // definition of find()
#include <list>
#include <iostream>
using namespace std;
int main()
{
  list<char> lc;
  lc.push_back('A');
  lc.push_back('T');
  lc.push_back('L');
  list<char>::iterator p = find(lc.begin(), lc.end(), 'A');   // find 'A'
  if (p != lc.end())      // was 'A' found?
    *p = 'S';     // then replace it with 'S'
  while (p != lc.end())   //display the modified list
    cout<<*p++;
  return 0;
}
```

Mutating Sequence Operations

Mutating sequence algorithms modify the sequence on which they operate. They include operations such as copy, fill, replace, and transform.

The `copy()` Algorithm

The Standard Library provides a generic copy function, which can be used to copy a sequence of objects to a specified target. The first and the second arguments of `copy()` are `const` iterators that mark the sequence's beginning and its end, respectively. The third argument points to a container into which the sequence is copied. The following example demonstrates how to copy the elements of a `list` into a `vector`:

```
#include <algorithm>
#include<list>
#include<vector>
```

```
using namespace std;

int main()
{
  list<int> li; vector <int> vi;
  li.push_back(1);
  li.push_back(2);
  vi.reserve( li.size() );  //must make room for copied elements in advance
  //copy list elements into vector, starting at vector's beginning
  copy (li.begin(), li.end(), vi.begin() );
  return 0;
}
```

Sort Operations

This category contains algorithms for sorting and merging sequences and set-like algorithms that operate on sorted sequences. These include sort(), partial_sort(), binary_search(), lower_bound(), and many others.

The sort() Algorithm

sort() takes two arguments of type const iterator that point to the beginning and the end of the sequence, respectively. An optional third algorithm is a *predicate object*, which alters the computation of sort (predicate objects and adaptors are discussed shortly). For example

```
#include <iostream>
#include <algorithm> //definition of sort()
#include <vector>
using namespace std;
int main()
{
  vector <int> vi;
  vi.push_back(7);
  vi.push_back(1);
  vi.push_back(19);
  sort(vi.begin(), vi.end() );   // sort vi; default is ascending order
  cout<< vi[0]  <<", "<< vi[1] <<", "<< vi[2] <<endl;  // output: 1, 7, 19
  return 0;
}
```

One way to force a descending order is to use reverse iterators:

```
sort(vi.rbegin(), vi.rend() ); // now sort in descending order
cout<< vi[0] <<", "<<vi[1]<<", "<<vi[2]<<endl; // output: 19, 7, 1
```

Requirements for Sorting Containers

When sort() operates on a container, it uses the relational operators == and < of the container's elements. User-defined types that do not support these operators can still be stored in a container, but such a container cannot be sorted.

Function Objects

It is customary to use a function pointer to invoke a callback routine. In an object-oriented environment, nonetheless, a function can be encapsulated in a *function object* (see also Chapter 3, "Operator Overloading"). There are several advantages to using a function object, or *functor*, instead of a pointer. Function objects are more resilient because the object that contains the function can be modified without affecting its users. In addition, compilers can inline a function object, which is nearly impossible when function pointers are used. But perhaps the most compelling argument in favor of function objects is their genericity—a function object can embody a generic algorithm by means of a member template.

Implementation of Function Objects

A function object overloads the function call operator. A generic function object defines the overloaded function call operator as a member function template. Consequently, the object can be used like a function call. Remember that the overloaded operator () can have a varying number of arguments, and any return value. In the following example, a function object implements a generic negation operator:

```
#include <iostream>
#include <vector>
using namespace std;

class negate
{
public : //generic negation operator
  template < class T > T operator()  (T t) const { return -t;}
};
void callback(int n, const negate& neg) //pass a function object rather
                                        //than a function pointer
{
  n = neg(n);  //invoke the overloaded () operator to negate n
  cout << n;
}
int main()
{
  callback(5, negate() ); //output: -5
  return 0;
}
```

Uses of Function Objects

Some container operations use function objects. For example, a priority_queue uses the less function object to sort its elements internally. The following example demonstrates a scheduler that stores tasks with different priorities in a priority_queue. Tasks that have higher priority are located at the top. Tasks with identical priority are located according to the order of their insertion, as in an ordinary queue:

```
#include <functional> // definition of less
#include <queue>  // definition of priority_queue
#include <iostream>
using namespace std;

struct Task
{
  int priority;
  friend bool operator < (const Task& t1, const Task& t2);
  Task(int p=0) : priority(p) {}
};

bool operator < (const Task& t1, const Task& t2)
{
  return t1.priority < t2.priority;
}

int main()
{
  priority_queue<Task> scheduler;
  scheduler.push(Task(3));
  scheduler.push(Task(5));
  scheduler.push(Task(1));
  scheduler.push(Task(1));
  cout<< scheduler.top().priority <<endl;   // output 5
  return 0;
}
```

Predicate Objects

A predicate is an expression that returns a Boolean value. Similarly, a function object that returns a Boolean value is a *predicate object*. STL defines several predicate objects that can be used to alter the computation of a generic algorithm. These predicate objects are defined in the header <functional>. In a previous example, you saw the operation of the algorithm sort(). The third argument of sort() is a predicate that alters the computation of this algorithm. For example, the predicate greater<int> can be used to override the default ascending order. Likewise, the predicate less<int> restores the original ascending order:

```
#include <functional> //definitions of STL predicates
#include <algorithm> //definition of sort
#include <vector>
#include <iostream>
using namespace std;
int main()
{
  vector <int> vi;
  vi.push_back(9);
  vi.push_back(5);
```

```
    vi.push_back(10);
    sort(vi.begin(), vi.end(), greater<int> () );   // descending order
    cout<< vi[0] << '\t' << vi[1] << '\t' << vi[2] <<endl;   // output: 10  9  5
    sort(vi.begin(), vi.end(), less<int> () );   // now in ascending order
    cout<< vi[0] << '\t' << vi[1] << '\t' << vi[2] <<endl;   // output: 5  9  10
    return 0;
}
```

Adaptors

An *adaptor* is a component that modifies the interface of another component. STL uses several types of adaptors: sequence adaptors, iterator adaptors, and function adaptors.

Sequence Adaptors

A *sequence adaptor* is a container that is built on another container and that modifies its interface. For example, the container `stack` is usually implemented as a `deque`, whose non-`stack` operations are hidden. In addition, `stack` uses the operations `back()`, `push_back()`, and `pop_back()` of a deque to implement the operations `top()`, `push()`, and `pop()`, respectively. For example

```
#include <string>
#include <stack>
#include <iostream>
using namespace std;

int main()
{
  stack <string> strstack;
  strstack.push("Bjarne");
  strstack.push("Stroustrup");
  string topmost = strstack.top();
  cout<< "topmost element is: "<< topmost << endl; // "Stroustrup"
  strstack.pop();
  cout<< "topmost element is: "<< strstack.top() << endl; // "Bjarne"
  return 0;
}
```

Calling the member function `pop()` on an empty stack is an error. If you are not sure whether a stack contains any elements, you can use the member function `empty()` to check it first. For example

```
stack<int> stk;
//...many lines of code
if (!stk.empty() ) //test stack before popping it
{
    stk.pop();
}
```

Iterator Adaptors

The interface of an iterator can be altered by an *iterator adaptor*. The member functions rend() and rbegin() return reverse iterators, which are iterators that have the meanings of operators ++ and -- exchanged. Using a reverse iterator is more convenient in some computations.

Function Adaptors

Earlier you saw the use of greater as a function adaptor for changing the computation of sort(). STL also provides *negators*, which are used to reverse the result of certain Boolean operations. *Binders* are another type of adaptors, which convert a binary function object into a unary function object by binding an argument to a specific value.

Allocators

Every STL container uses an allocator that encapsulates the memory model that the program uses. Allocators hide the platform-dependent details such as the size of pointers, memory organization, reallocation model, and memory page size. Because a container can work with different allocator types, it can easily work in different environments simply by plugging a different allocator into it. An implementation provides a suitable allocator for every container. Normally, users should not override the default allocator.

Specialized Containers

Chapter 9, "Templates," discussed the benefits of defining template specializations to optimize and rectify the behavior of a primary template for a particular type. vector has a specialized form that manipulates Boolean values optimally, namely vector<bool>. This specialization is implemented in a way that squeezes each element into a single bit, rather than a bool variable, albeit with the familiar vector interface. For example

```
#include <vector>
#include <iostream>
using namespace std

void transmit(vector <bool> &binarystream)
{
  cout<<binarystream[0]; // subscript operator provided
  vector<bool>::const_iterator bit_iter = binarystream.begin(); //iterators
  if (binarystream[0] == true)
  {/* do something */ }
}
```

Associative Containers

An *associative array* is one for which the index need not be an integer. An associative array is also called *map* or *dictionary*. STL defines several associative containers. A map, for instance, stores pairs of values; one serves as the key, and the other is the associated value. The template `pair<class Key, class Value>` serves as a map element. In the following example, a map is used to translate the string value of an enumerator into its corresponding integral value. The string is the key whose associated value is an `int`:

```
#include <map>
#include <string>
#include <iostream>
using namespace std;
enum directions {up, down};
int main()
{
  pair<string, int> Enumerator(string("down"), down); //create a pair
  map<string, int> mi; //create a map
  mi.insert(Enumerator); //insert the pair
  int n = mi["down"]; //n = 1 //string used as subscript
  return 0;
}
```

A map can store only unique keys. A `multimap` is a map that can store duplicate keys.

`set` is similar to a map except that the associated values are irrelevant in this case. A set is used when only the keys are important: to ensure that a database transaction does not attempt to insert a record with a unique key that already exists in a table, for example. `multiset` is a set that allows duplicate keys.

Class `auto_ptr`

The class template `auto_ptr` implements the "resource acquisition is initialization" idiom (discussed in Chapter 5, "Object-Oriented Programming Design"). It is initialized by a pointer to an object allocated on the free store (`auto_ptr` has a default constructor so you can instantiate an empty `auto_ptr` and assign a pointer to it later). The destructor of `auto_ptr` destroys the object that is bound to the pointer. This technique can avoid memory leakage in the case of exceptions (see also Chapter 6, "Exception Handling"), or it can simplify programming by sparing the hassle of explicitly deleting every object allocated on the free store. Class `auto_ptr` is declared in the standard header <memory>. Following is an example of using `auto_ptr` (points of possible object destruction are numbered):

```
#include <memory>
using namespace std;
void f() { if (condition) throw "err";}
int main()
{
  try
```

```
  {
    auto_ptr<double> dptr(new double(0.0));
    *dptr = 0.5; //overloaded * provides pointer-like syntax
    f();
  } // 1: no exception was thrown, dptr destroyed here
  catch(...)
  { // 2: an exception was thrown, dptr destroyed here
  }
  return 0;
}
```

It is guaranteed that the memory that was allocated from the free store is released: If f() throws an exception, the dptr object is destroyed during stack unwinding (2) and, as a result, the memory that was allocated from the free store is released. Otherwise, dptr is destroyed when the try block exits (1).

STL Containers Should Not Store auto_ptr Elements

Elements of STL containers must be copy-constructible and assignable, as was noted previously. During reallocation, a container copy-constructs its elements in a new memory location and destroys the original elements by invoking their destructors. However, an auto_ptr is not copy-constructible. Rather, it provides *strict ownership* semantics, which means that it owns the object to which it holds a pointer (ownership is also discussed in Chapter 5). Copying an auto_ptr object copies that pointer and transfers ownership to the destination. This stands in contrast to the copy-constructible and assignable requirements: One copy of auto_ptr holds a pointer to the free store object, whereas the other copy doesn't. (If more than one auto_ptr owns the same object at the same time, the results are undefined.) Therefore, auto_ptr objects are not to be stored in STL containers.

Nearly Containers

STL defines three additional components that behave, in many ways, like ordinary containers. They have automatic memory management, they have iterators, and they share a container-like interface with member functions such as begin() and end(). Still, they are not considered "first-class citizens" in the STL catalog because they are not generic. A string is similar to vector but is confined to char data type. valarray resembles vector, albeit with a strong bias toward numerical computations. The third class in this category is bitset, which is a set designed to store and manipulate bits in an efficient way. These *nearly containers* have a limited use for general purposes, except for string.

Class string

std::string is a shorthand for std::basic_string<char>, as you saw in Chapter 9. string provides many of the operations of ordinary STL containers; for example, it conforms to the requirements of a sequence and it defines iterators. However, string is optimized for the use of a character string exclusively.

The consideration in the design of string included utmost efficiency, support for C-strings, and generality (that is, string is not targeted for a particular application use).

Constructors

string has a default constructor and five more constructors:

```
namespace std
{
template<class charT, class traits = char_traits<charT>,
            class Allocator = allocator<charT> >
  class basic_string {
  public:
  //...
    explicit basic_string(const Allocator& a = Allocator());
    basic_string(const basic_string& str, size_type pos = 0,
                size_type n = npos, const Allocator& a = Allocator());
    basic_string(const charT* s,
                size_type n, const Allocator& a = Allocator());
    basic_string(const charT* s, const Allocator& a = Allocator());
    basic_string(size_type n, charT c, const Allocator& a = Allocator());
    template<class InputIterator>
    basic_string(InputIterator begin, InputIterator end,
                const Allocator& a = Allocator());
  //...
  };
}
```

In other words, a string can be initialized by a C-string, by another string object, by part of a C-string, by a sequence of characters, or by part of another string. Following are some examples:

```
#include <string>
using namespace std;
void f()
{
  const char text[] = "hello world";
  string s = text;   //initialization of string object with a C-style string
  string s2(s);   //copy construction
  string s3(&text[0], &text[5]); // part of a C-string; s3 = "hello"
  string s4(10, 0); //a sequence of zero initialized characters
  string s5 ( s2.begin(), s2.find(' ')); //initialized part of another string
                                        //s5 = "hello"
}
```

It is important to note that when the initializer is a pointer to char, string does not check the pointer. It is the programmer's responsibility to ensure that the pointer is valid and that it is not NULL. Otherwise, the results are undefined. For example

```
#include<string>
using std::string;

const char * getDescription(int symbol); // may return a NULL pointer

string& writeToString  (int symbol)
{
  // sloppy: initializer might be NULL; undefined behavior in this case
  string *p = new string(getDescription(symbol));
  return *p;
}
```

string does not check for a NULL pointer to avoid the incurred performance overhead. Remember that standard C functions such as strcpy() avoid this overhead too.
Even if string did check the char pointer, it is unclear what it is to do in the case of
a NULL value. Clearly, a NULL pointer is not a valid C-string, so creating an empty string
is incorrect. Throwing an exception is perhaps a plausible approach, but it incurs additional runtime overhead and is not always desirable.

A safer implementation of the preceding example might check the initializing
pointer to make sure that it is not NULL:

```
string& writeToString (int symbol)
{
  const char *p = getDescription(symbol);
  if (p) // now safe
  {
    string *pstr = new string(p);
    return *pstr;
  }
  return *new string;
}
```

Conversion to a C-string

Class string provides two member functions that return the const char * representation of its object. The following sections discuss these member functions.

The c_str() Member Function

string does not define a char * conversion operator. There are two reasons for this.
First, implicit conversions can cause undesirable surprises when you least expect it
(refer to Chapter 3). Another reason is that C-strings must be null-terminated. The
underlying representation of a string object is implementation-dependent and might
not use a null-terminated sequence. Therefore, an implicit conversion of a string
object in a context that requires a null-terminated array of characters can be disastrous. For these reasons, string does not provide such a conversion operator. Instead,
an explicit call to string::c_str() is required. c_str() returns the const char * representation of its object. For example

```
void f()
{
  string  s = "Hello";
  if( strcmp( s.c_str(), "Hello")== 0)
    cout <<"identical"<<endl;
 else
    cout<<"different"<<endl;
}
```

The pointer that is returned from `c_str ()` is owned by the `string` object. The user should not attempt to delete it or to modify its associated `char` array. The returned pointer is not to be used after a non-`const` member function has been called.

The `data()` Member Function

The member function `data()` also returns a `const char *` representation of its object (but the resultant array might not be null-terminated).

Accessing a Single Element

There are two ways to access a single character from a string object. One is to use the overloaded operator `[ ]`, as in the following example:

```
#include <string>
using namespace std;
void  first()
{
  string s = "hello world";
  char c = s[0];  //assign  'h'
}
```

Another way is to use the member function `at()`. Similar to class `vector`, `string::at()` performs range-checking and throws an exception of type `std::out_of_range` when an attempt is made to access an out-of-range character.

Clearing the Contents of a `string`

To explicitly erase the contents of a `string`, you can use the member function `erase()`. For example

```
#include <iostream>
#include <string>
using namespace std;
void f()
{
  char key;
  string msg = "press any key to continue";
  cout<<msg<<endl;
  cin<<key;
  msg.erase(); //clear msg
}
```

Comparison

string defines three versions of operator ==:

```
bool operator == (const string& left, const string right);
bool operator == (const char* left, const string right);
bool operator == (const string& left, const char* right);
```

This proliferation might seem redundant because string has a constructor that automatically converts a const char * to a string object. Therefore, only the first version of operator == is necessary. However, the overhead of creating a temporary string can be unacceptable under some circumstances: The temporary string has to allocate memory on the free store, copy the C-string, and then release the allocated memory. The Standardization committee's intent was to make comparison of strings as efficient as possible. Therefore, the additional versions of operator == were added to enable efficient comparisons.

Additional Overloaded Operators

As was previously noted, a string can be assigned another string, a C-string, or a single character. Similarly, there are three versions of the overloaded operator += that support concatenation of another string, a C-string, or a single character to an existing string. For example

```
#include <string>
using namespace std;
void f()
{
  string s1 = "ab"
  string s2= "cd";
  s1+=s2;
  s1+= "ef";
  s1+='g';
}
```

string also defines an overloaded + that returns a string that concatenates its operands. Similarly, the operators < and > perform a lexicographical comparison between their operands.

Performance Issues

string is probably the most widely used class in C++ programs. The efficiency of its design and implementation were cardinal. For example, string provides optimized container operations—such as find(), copy(), and replace()—that are specifically designed to manipulate characters efficiently. In some respects, string objects are even more efficient than char * in terms of speed and space. The following sections discuss two aspects of string's performance: size computation and reference counting.

Size

string has a data member that holds its size. Calculating the size of a string object is, therefore, a fast constant time operation. On the other hand, the performance of `strlen()` is proportional to the number of characters that are stored in a C-string. When large strings are used and size computations are frequent, `std::string` is more efficient than a C-string.

Reference Counting

In a nutshell, a reference counted model counts how many instances of a class have an identical state. When two or more instances share the same state, the implementation creates only a single copy and counts the number of existing references to this copy. For example, an array of strings can be represented as a single `string` object that holds the number of elements in the array (reference counting is not confined to arrays). Since initially the array elements share the same state (they all are empty strings), only a single object is needed. When one of the array elements changes its state (if it is assigned a different value, for instance), the existing object creates one more object. This is called "copy on write". As you can see, the reference counting model can enhance performance in terms of both memory usage and speed. The Standard's specification of class `string` is formulated to allow—but does not require—a reference counted implementation.

A reference counted implementation must have the same semantics as a non-reference counted implementation. For example

```
string str1("xyz");
string::iterator i = str1.begin();
string str2 = str1;
*i = 'w';  //must modify only  str1
```

Conclusions

STL was designed to allow maximal reusability without sacrificing efficiency. The Standard specifies performance requirements with which STL containers and algorithms must comply. These performance specifications are the minimum requirements; an implementation might offer better performance.

The plug compatibility of STL components, which enables the user to create other components or to modify the interface of existing components, is remarkable. Other frameworks and libraries impose severe constraints on the use of their components, considerably limiting their plug-compatibility.

STL is regarded by C++ creators as the most important addition to the language in recent years. Mastering STL is a worthwhile investment. It is estimated that other programming languages will follow the role model of STL and provide similar generic frameworks. Three major advantages of preferring STL to homemade containers are

- **Portability**—All standard-compliant C++ implementations supply them.
- **Performance**—STL components were designed and implemented to meet strict efficiency demands.
- **Reliability**—STL containers and algorithms were already debugged and tested.

V

Under The Hood

11

Memory Management

Introduction

C++ added the necessary language constructs to the memory model of C to support object semantics. In addition, it fixed some loopholes in the original model and enhanced it with higher levels of abstraction and automation. This chapter delves into the memory model of C++, starting with the three types of data storage. Next, the various versions of operators `new` and `delete` are discussed; finally, some techniques and guidelines for effective and bug-free usage of the memory management constructs are presented.

Types of Storage

C++ has three fundamental types of data storage: automatic storage, static storage, and free store. Each of these memory types has different semantics of object initialization and lifetime.

Automatic Storage

Local objects that are not explicitly declared `static` or `extern`, local objects that are declared `auto` or `register`, and function arguments have *automatic storage*. This type of storage is also called *stack memory*. Automatic objects are created automatically upon entering a function or a block. They are destroyed when the function or block exits.

Thus, on each entry into a function or a block, a new copy of its automatic objects are created. The default value of automatic variables and nonclass objects is indeterminate.

Static Storage

Global objects, static data members of a class, namespace variables, and static variables in functions reside in static memory. The address of a static object remains the same throughout the program's execution. Every static object is constructed only once during the lifetime of the program. By default, static data are initialized to binary zeros. Static objects with a *nontrivial constructor* (see Chapter 4, "Special Member Functions: Default Constructor, Copy Constructor, Destructor, And Assignment Operator") are subsequently initialized by their constructors. Objects with static storage are included in the following examples:

```
int num; //global variables have static storage

int func()
{
  static int calls; //initialized to 0 by default

  return ++calls;
}

class C
{
private:
  static bool b;
};

namespace NS
{
  std::string str; //str has static storage
}
```

Free Store

Free store memory, also called *heap memory* or *dynamic memory*, contains objects and variables that are created by operator new. Objects and variables that are allocated on the free store persist until they are explicitly released by a subsequent call to operator delete. The memory that is allocated from the free store is not returned to the operating system automatically after the program's termination. Therefore, failing to release memory that was allocated using new generally yields memory leaks. The address of an object that is allocated on the free store is determined at runtime. The initial value of raw storage that is allocated by new is unspecified.

POD (Plain Old Data) and Non-POD Objects

A *POD* (*plain old data*) object has one of the following data types: a fundamental type, pointer, union, struct, array, or class that has a trivial constructor and a trivial destructor, and whose data members are all public. Conversely, a non-POD object is one for which a nontrivial constructor exists. The properties of an object are in effect only during its *lifetime*.

The Lifetime of a POD Object

A POD object begins its lifetime when it obtains storage with the proper alignment and size for its type, and its lifetime ends when the storage for the object is either reused or deallocated.

The Lifetime of a Non-POD Object

A non-POD object begins its lifetime after the constructor call has completed; its lifetime ends when its destructor has started.

Allocation and Deallocation Functions

C++ defines the global *allocation functions* new and new[] as well as the corresponding global *deallocation functions* delete and delete[]. These functions are accessible from each translation unit of a program without including the header <new>. Their implicit declarations are as follows:

```
void* operator new(std::size_t) throw(std::bad_alloc);  // new
void* operator new[](std::size_t) throw(std::bad_alloc);  // new []
void operator delete(void*) throw();  // delete
void operator delete[](void*) throw();  // delete[]
```

The implicit declarations introduce only the function names operator new, operator new[], operator delete, and operator delete[]. However, they do not introduce the names std, std::bad_alloc, and std::size_t. An explicit reference to any of these names requires that the appropriate header file be included. For example

```
#include <new> // declarations of std and size_t
using namespace std;
char * allocate (size_t bytes);
int main
{
 char * buff = allocate(sizeof (char) );
 return 0;
}
```

Semantics of Allocation Functions

The return type of an allocation function is void *, and its first parameter is of type size_t. The value of the first parameter is interpreted as the requested memory size. The allocation function attempts to allocate the requested size of memory from the free store. If the allocation request is successful, it returns the address of the start of a block of storage whose size, in bytes, is at least as large as the requested size.

Semantics of Deallocation Functions

The return type of a deallocation function is void; its first parameter is of type void *. A deallocation function can have more than one parameter. The value of the first argument that is supplied to a deallocation function can be NULL (in this case, the deallocation function call has no effect). Otherwise, the value supplied to a deallocation function must be one of the values returned by a previous invocation of a corresponding allocation function. Allocation and deallocation functions perform the basic operations of allocating memory from the free store and releasing it. Note however, that in general, you do not invoke these functions directly. Rather, you use a *new expression* and a *delete expression*. A new expression implicitly invokes an allocation function and then constructs an object on the allocated memory; likewise, a delete expression destroys an object, and then it invokes a deallocation function to release the storage of the destroyed object.

malloc() and free() Versus new and delete

C++ still supports the standard C library functions malloc() and free(). The backward compatibility with C is useful in three cases: for combining legacy code that was originally written in C in C++ programs, for writing C++ code that is meant to be supported in C environment (more on this in Chapter 13, "C Language Compatibility Issues"), and for making new and delete implementable by calling malloc() and free(). Otherwise, malloc() and free() are not to be used in C++ code because—unlike new and delete—they do not support object semantics. new and delete are also significantly safer and more extensible.

Support for Object Semantics

new and delete automatically construct and destroy objects. malloc() and free(), on the other hand, merely allocate and deallocate raw memory from the heap. In particular, using malloc() to create a non-POD object yields undefined behavior. For example

```
#include <cstdlib>
#include <string>
using namespace std;
string* func() //very bad
{
  string *pstr = static_cast<string*> (malloc (sizeof(string))); //disaster!
  return pstr; //any attempt to use pstr as a pointer to a string is undefined
}
```

Note

In the following sections, new and delete refer to a new expression and a delete expression, respectively, unless stated otherwise.

Safety

Operator new automatically calculates the size of the object that it constructs. Conversely, with malloc(), the programmer has to specify explicitly the number of bytes that have to be allocated. In addition, malloc() returns a pointer to void, which has to be explicitly cast to the desired type. This is both tedious and dangerous. Operator new returns a pointer to the desired type, so no explicit type cast is required. For example

```
#include <cstdlib>
using namespace std;
void func()
{
  int * p = static_cast<int *> malloc(sizeof(int));
  int * p2 = new int;
}
```

Extensibility

Operator new can be overloaded by a class. This feature enables specific classes to use different memory management policies, as you will see next. On the other hand, malloc() cannot be overloaded for a specific class.

The results of calling free() to release a pointer that was allocated by new, or of using delete to release memory that was allocated by malloc(), are undefined. The Standard does not guarantee that the underlying implementation of operator new uses malloc(); furthermore, on some implementations malloc() and new use different heaps.

new and delete

New and delete were extended in recent years to support various types of memory management schemes, including allocation and deallocation of objects at a predetermined memory address, and a tighter support for exception handling. The following sections discuss these extensions in detail.

Allocating and Deallocating Arrays Using new[] and delete[]

new[] allocates an array of objects of the specified type. The value that is returned by new[] is the address of the first element in the allocated array. For example

```
int main()
{
```

```
    int *p = new int[10];
    bool equal = (p == &p[0]); //true
    delete[] p;
    return 0;
}
```

Objects that are allocated using new[] must be released by a call to delete[]. Using plain delete instead of delete[] in this case results in undefined behavior. This is because when new[] is executed, the runtime system stores the number of elements in the allocated array in an implementation-defined way. The corresponding delete[] expression retrieves the number of allocated elements to invoke the same number of destructors. How does new[] store the number of elements in the allocated array? The most widely used technique is to allocate extra sizeof(std::size_t) bytes; that is, for a class C, the expression

```
    C * p = new C[n];
```

allocates a memory buffer that contains sizeof(std::size_t) + n * sizeof(C) bytes. The value n is written to the allocated buffer just before the first C object. When delete[] is invoked, it looks for the value n in a fixed offset before p (which must point to the first element in the array). delete[] then invokes C's destructor n times and, finally, releases the memory block. Plain delete, on the other hand, does not perform such offset adjustments—it simply invokes the destructor of the object to which p points.

An alternative technique is to store n in an associative array in which p serves as the key and n is its associated value. When the statement

```
    delete[] p;
```

is executed, delete[] can look up p in an associative array such as

```
    std::map<void *, std::size_t>
```

and retrieve its associated value n. Other techniques for storing the number of array elements can be used as well, but in any one of them, using plain delete instead of delete[] to release an array of objects allocated by new[] results in undefined behavior and should never happen. Similarly, using delete[] to release a single object that was allocated by plain new is also disastrous: It might cause memory leaks, heap corruption, or a program crash.

Contrary to popular belief, the same rules apply to arrays of fundamental types—not just to arrays of objects. Although delete[] does not invoke destructors in the case of fundamental types, it still has to retrieve the number of elements in the array to calculate the complete size of the memory block. For example

```
    #include<string>
    void f()
    {
    char *pc = new char[100];
    string *ps = new std::string[100];
    //...use pc and ps
```

```
    delete[] pc; //no destructors invoked, still delete[] is required
                 // for arrays allocated by new[]
    delete[] ps //ensures each member's destructor is called
}
```

Exceptions and Operator **new**

In pre-Standard C++, new returned a NULL pointer when it failed to allocate the
requested amount of memory. In this respect, new behaved like malloc() in C.
Programmers had to check the value that was returned from new before they used it to
make sure that it was not NULL. For example

```
    void f(int size) //anachronistic usage of new
    {
      char *p = new char [size];
      if (p == 0)    //this was fine until 1994
      {
        //...use p safely
        delete [] p;
      }
      return;
    }

    const int BUF_SIZE = 1048576L;

    int main()
    {
      f(BUF_SIZE);
      return 0;
    }
```

Returning a NULL pointer upon failure, however, was problematic. (Note that the
NULL pointer policy was applicable to both plain new and new[]. Similarly, the modified
behavior applies to new as well as new[].) It forced programmers to test the value that
was returned by every invocation of operator new, which is a tedious and error-prone
process. In addition, the recurrent testing of the returned pointer can increase the size
of the programs and add a runtime performance overhead (you might recall that these
are the drawbacks associated with the return value policy, discussed in Chapter 6,
"Exception Handling"). Failures in dynamic memory allocation are rather rare and
generally indicate an unstable system state. This is exactly the kind of runtime errors
that exception handling was designed to cope with. For these reasons, the C++ standardization committee changed the specification of new a few years ago. The Standard
now states that operator new throws an exception of type std::bad_alloc when it
fails, rather than returning a NULL pointer.

Caution

Although compiler vendors have been sluggish in adopting this change, most C++ compilers now conform to the standard in this respect, and throw an exception of type std::bad_alloc when new fails.
Please consult your compiler's documentation for more details.

A program that calls new either directly or indirectly (for example, if it uses STL containers, which allocate memory from the free store) must contain an appropriate handler that catches a `std::bad_alloc` exception. Otherwise, whenever new fails, the program terminates due to an uncaught exception. The exception-throwing policy also implies that testing the pointer that is returned from new is completely useless. If new is successful, the redundant test wastes system resources. On the other hand, in the case of an allocation failure, the thrown exception aborts the current thread of execution from where it was thrown—so the test is not executed anyway. The revised, standard-conforming form of the previously presented program looks similar to the following:

```
void f(int size) //standard-conforming usage of new
{
  char *p = new char [size];
  //...use p safely
  delete [] p;
  return;
}
#include <stdexcept>
#include <iostream>
using namespace std;

const int BUF_SIZE = 1048576L;

int main()
{
  try
  {
    f(BUF_SIZE);
  }
  catch(bad_alloc& ex)   //handle exception thrown from f()
  {
    cout<<ex.what()<<endl;
    //...other diagnostics and remedies
  }
  return -1;
}
```

Exception-Free Version of Operator new

Still, under some circumstances, throwing an exception is undesirable. For example, exception handling might have been turned off to enhance performance; on some platforms, it might not be supported at all. The Standardization committee was aware of this and added an exception-free version of new to the Standard. The exception-free version of new returns a NULL pointer in the event of a failure, rather than throwing a `std::bad_alloc` exception. This version of new takes an additional argument of type `const std::nothrow_t&` (defined in the header `<new>`). It comes in two flavors, one for plain new and another for new[].

```
//exception-free versions of new and new[] defined in the header <new>

void* operator new(std::size_t size, const std::nothrow_t&) throw();
void* operator new[](std::size_t size, const std::nothrow_t&) throw();
```

The exception-free new is also called *nothrow new*. It is used as follows:
```
#include <new>
#include <string>
using namespace std;

void f(int size) // demonstrating nothrow new
{
  char *p = new (nothrow) char [size]; //array nothrow new
  if (p == 0)
  {
    //...use p
    delete [] p;
  }
  string *pstr = new (nothrow) string; //plain nothrow new
  if (pstr == 0)
  {
    //...use pstr
    delete [] pstr;
  }
  return;
}

const int BUF_SIZE = 1048576L;

int main()
{
  f(BUF_SIZE);
  return 0;
}
```

The argument nothrow is defined and created in header <new> as follows:
```
extern const nothrow_t nothrow;
```

Class nothrow_t is defined as follows:
```
struct nothrow_t {}; //an empty class
```

In other words, the type nothrow_t is an empty class (the empty class idiom is discussed in Chapter 5, "Object-Oriented Program and Design") whose sole purpose is to overload global new.

Placement new

An additional version of operator new enables you to construct an object (or an array of objects) at a predetermined memory position. This version is called *placement new* and has many useful applications, including building a custom-made memory pool or a garbage collector. Additionally, it can be used in mission-critical applications because there is no danger of allocation failure (the memory that is used by placement new has already been allocated). Placement new is also faster because the construction of an object on a preallocated buffer takes less time. Following is an example of using placement new:

```
#include <new>
#include <iostream>
using namespace std;

void placement()
{
  int   *pi = new int;      //plain new
  float *pf = new float[2]; //new []
  int   *p  = new (pi) int (5);  //placement new
  float *p2 = new (pf) float;  //placement new[]
  p2[0] = 0.33f;
  cout<< *p << p2[0] << endl;
  //...
  delete pi;
  delete [] pf;
}
```

Explicit Destructor Invocation Is Required for an Object Created by Placement new

Destructors of objects that were constructed using placement new have to be invoked explicitly. To see why, consider the following example:

```
#include <new>
#include <iostream>
using namespace std;

class C
{
public:
  C() { cout<< "constructed" <<endl; }
  ~C(){ cout<< "destroyed" <<endl; }
};

int main()
{
  char * p = new char [sizeof(C)];  // pre-allocate a buffer
   C *pc = new (p) C;  // placement new
   //... used pc
  pc->C::~C(); // 1:explicit destructor invocation is required
  delete [] p; //2
  return 0;
}
```

Without an explicit destructor invocation in (1), the object that is pointed to by p will never be destroyed, but the memory block on which it was created will be released by the delete[] statement in (2).

Exceptions During Object Construction

As was previously noted, new performs two operations: It allocates memory from the free store by calling an allocation function, and it constructs an object on the allocated memory. The question is, does the allocated memory leak when an exception is thrown during the construction process? The answer is no, it doesn't. The allocated memory is returned to the free store by the system before the exception propagates to the program. Thus, an invocation of operator new can be construed as two consecutive operations. The first operation merely allocates a sufficient memory block from the free store with the appropriate alignment requirements. In the event of failure, the system throws an exception of type std::bad_alloc. If the first operation was successful, the second one begins. The second operation consists of invoking the object's constructor with the pointer that is retained from the previous step. Put differently, the statement

```
C* p = new C;
```

is transformed by the compiler into something similar to the following:

```
#include <new>
using namespace std;

class C{/*...*/};

void __new() throw (bad_alloc)
{
  C * p = reinterpret_cast<C*> (new char [sizeof(C)]); //step 1: allocate
                                                       // raw memory
  try
  {
    new (p) C;  //step 2: construct the objects on previously allocated buffer
  }
  catch(...)   //catch any exception thrown from C's constructor
  {
    delete[] p;  //free the allocated buffer
    throw;  //re-throw the exception of C's constructor
  }
}
```

Alignment Considerations

The pointer that is returned by new has the suitable alignment properties so that it can be converted to a pointer of any object type and then used to access that object or array. Consequently, you are permitted to allocate character arrays into which objects of other types will later be placed. For example

```
#include <new>
#include <iostream>
#include <string>
using namespace std;
```

```
class Employee
{
private:
  string name;
  int age;
public:
  Employee();
  ~Employee();
};

void func() //use a pre allocated char array to construct
          //an object of a different type
{
  char * pc = new char[sizeof(Employee)];
  Employee *pemp = new (pc) Employee;  //construct on char array
  //...use pemp
  pemp->Employee::~Employee(); //explicit destruction
  delete [] pc;
}
```

It might be tempting to use a buffer that is allocated on the stack to avoid the hassle of deleting it later:

```
char pbuff [sizeof(Employee)];
Employee *p = new (pbuff ) Employee;  //undefined behavior
```

However, char arrays of automatic storage type are not guaranteed to meet the necessary alignment requirements of objects of other types. Therefore, constructing an object of a preallocated buffer of automatic storage type can result in undefined behavior. Furthermore, creating a new object at a storage location that was previously occupied by a const object with static or automatic storage type also results in undefined behavior. For example

```
const Employee emp;
void bad_placement() //attempting to construct a new object
                     //at the storage location of a const object
{
  emp.Employee::~Employee();
  new (&emp) const Employee; //  undefined behavior
}
```

Member Alignment

The size of a class or a struct might be larger than the result of adding the size of each data member in it. This is because the compiler is allowed to add additional *padding bytes* between members whose size does not fit exactly into a machine word (see also Chapter 13). For example

```
#include <cstring>
using namespace std;
```

```
struct Person
{
  char firstName[5];
  int age; // int occupies 4 bytes
  char lastName[8];
}; //the actual size of Person is most likely larger than 17 bytes

void func()
{
  Person person = {{"john"}, 30, {"lippman"}};
  memset(&person,  0,  5+4+8  );  //may not erase the contents of
                                  //person properly
}
```

On a 32-bit architecture, three additional bytes can be inserted between the first and the second members of Person, increasing the size of Person from 17 bytes to 20. On some implementations, the memset() call does not clear the last three bytes of the member lastName. Therefore, use the sizeof operator to calculate the correct size:

```
memset(&p, 0, sizeof(Person));
```

The Size of a Complete Object Can Never Be Zero

An empty class doesn't have any data members or member functions. Therefore, the size of an instance is seemingly zero. However, C++ guarantees that the size of a complete object is never zero. Consider the following example:

```
class Empty {};
Empty  e; // e occupies at least 1 byte of memory
```

If an object is allowed to occupy zero bytes of storage, its address can overlap with the address of a different object. The most obvious case is an array of empty objects whose elements all have an identical address. To guarantee that a complete object always has a distinct memory address, a complete object occupies at least one byte of memory. Non-complete objects—for example, base class subobjects in a derived class—can occupy zero bytes of memory.

Overloading **new** and **delete** in a Class

It is possible to override new and delete and define a specialized form for them for a given class. Thus, for a class C that defines these operators, the following statements

```
C* p = new C;
delete p;
```

invoke the class's versions of new and delete, respectively. Defining class-specific versions of new and delete is useful when the default memory management scheme is unsuitable. This technique is also used in applications that have a custom memory pool. In the following example, operator new for class C is redefined to alter the default behavior in case of an allocation failure; instead of throwing `std::bad_alloc`, this specific version throws a `const char *`. A matching operator `delete` is redefined accordingly:

```cpp
#include <cstdlib> // malloc() and free()
#include <iostream>
using namespace std;
class C
{
private:
  int j;
public:
  C() : j(0) { cout<< "constructed"<<endl; }
  ~C() { cout<<"destroyed";}
  void* operator new (size_t size); //implicitly declared static
  void operator delete (void *p); //implicitly declared static
};

void* C::operator new (size_t  size) throw (const char *)
{
  void * p = malloc(size);
  if (p == 0)
    throw "allocation failure";  //instead of std::bad_alloc
  return p;
}

void C::operator delete (void *p)
{
  free(p);
}

int main()
{
  try
  {
    C *p = new C;
    delete p;
  }
  catch (const char * err)
  {
    cout<<err<<endl;
  }
  return 0;
}
```

Remember that overloaded `new` and `delete` are implicitly declared as static members of their class if they are not explicitly declared static. Note also that a user-defined `new` implicitly invokes the objects's constructor; likewise, a user-defined `delete` implicitly invokes the object's destructor.

Guidelines for Effective Memory Usage

Choosing the correct type of storage for an object is a critical implementation decision because each type of storage has different implications for the program's performance, reliability, and maintenance. This section tells you how to choose the correct type of storage for an object and thus avoid common pitfalls and performance penalties. This section also discusses general topics that are associated with the memory model of C++, and it compares C++ to other languages.

Prefer Automatic Storage to Free Store Whenever Possible

Creating objects on the free store, when compared to automatic storage, is more expensive in terms of performance for several reasons:

- **Runtime overhead**—Allocating memory from the free store involves negotiations with the operating system. When the free store is fragmented, finding a contiguous block of memory can take even longer. In addition, the exception handling support in the case of allocation failures adds additional runtime overhead.

- **Maintenance**—Dynamic allocation might fail; additional code is required to handle such exceptions.

- **Safety**—An object might be accidentally deleted more than once, or it might not be deleted at all. Both of these are a fertile source of bugs and runtime crashes in many applications.

The following code sample demonstrates two common bugs that are associated with allocating objects on the free store:

```
#include <string>
using namespace std;
void f()
{
  string *p = new string;
  //...use p
  if (p->empty()!= false)
  {
    //...do something
    return;    //OOPS! memory leak: p was not deleted
  }
  else //string is empty
  {
    delete p;
    //..do other stuff
  }
  delete p; //OOPS! p is deleted twice if isEmpty == false
}
```

Such bugs are quite common in large programs that frequently allocate objects on the free store. Often, it is possible to create objects on the stack, thereby simplifying the structure of the program and eliminating the potential for such bugs. Consider how the use of a local `string` object simplifies the preceding code sample:

```
#include <string>
using namespace std;
void f()
{
  string s;
  //...use s
  if (s.empty()!= false)
  {
    //...do something
    return;
  }
  else
  {
    //..do other stuff
  }
}
```

As a rule, automatic and static storage types are always preferable to free store.

Correct Syntax for Local Object Instantiation

The correct syntax for instantiating a local object by invoking its default constructor is

```
string str;     //no parentheses
```

Although empty parentheses can be used after the class name, as in

```
string str(); //entirely different meaning
```

the statement has an entirely different meaning. It is parsed as a declaration of a function named `str`, which takes no arguments and returns a `string` by value.

Zero as a Universal Initializer

The literal `0` is an `int`. However, it can be used as a universal initializer for every fundamental data type. Zero is a special case in this respect because the compiler examines its context to determine its type. For example:

```
void *p = 0;  //zero is implicitly converted to void *
float salary = 0;   // 0 is cast to a float
char name[10] = {0};   // 0 cast to a '\0'
bool b = 0; // 0 cast to false
void (*pf)(int) = 0;   // pointer to a function
int (C::*pm) ()  = 0; //pointer to a class member
```

Always Initialize Pointers

An uninitialized pointer has an indeterminate value. Such a pointer is often called a *wild pointer*. It is almost impossible to test whether a wild pointer is valid, especially if it is passed as an argument to a function (which in turn can only verify that it is not NULL). For example

```
void func(char *p );
```

```
int main()
{
  char * p; //dangerous: uninitialized
      //...many lines of code; p left uninitialized by mistake
  if (p)//erroneously assuming that a non-null value indicates a valid address
  {
    func(p);    // func has no way of knowing whether p has a valid address
  }
  return 0;
}
```

Even if your compiler does initialize pointers automatically, it is best to initialize them explicitly to ensure code readability and portability.

Explicit Initializations of POD Object

As was previously noted, POD objects with automatic storage have an indeterminate value by default in order to avoid the performance penalty incurred by initialization. However, you can initialize automatic POD objects explicitly when necessary. The following sections explain how this is done.

Initializing Local Automatic Structs and Arrays

One way to initialize automatic POD objects is by calling `memset()` or a similar initialization function. However, there is a much simpler way to do it—without calling a function, as you can see in the following example:

```
struct  Person
{
  long ID;
  int bankAccount;
  bool retired;
};

int main()
{

  Person person ={0}; //ensures that all members of
                      //person are initialized to binary zeros
  return 0;
}
```

This technique is applicable to every POD struct. It relies on the fact that the first member is a fundamental data type. The initializer zero is automatically cast to the appropriate fundamental type. It is guaranteed that whenever the initialization list contains fewer initializers than the number of members, the rest of the members are initialized to binary zeros as well. Note that even if the definition of Person changes—additional members are added to it or the members' ordering is swapped—all its members are still initialized. The same initialization technique is also applicable to local automatic arrays of fundamental types as well as to arrays of POD objects :

```
void f()
{
```

```
    char  name[100] = {0}; //all array elements are initialized to '\0'
    float farr[100] = {0}; //all array elements are initialized to 0.0
    int  iarr[100] = {0};  //all array elements are initialized to 0
    void *pvarr[100] = {0};//array of void * all elements are initialized to NULL
    //...use the arrays
}
```

This technique works for any combination of structs and arrays:

```
struct A
{
  char name[20];
  int age;
  long ID;
};

void f()
{
  A a[100] = {0};
}
```

Union Initialization

You can initialize a union. However, unlike struct initialization, the initialization list of a union must contain only a single initializer, which must refer to the first member in the union. For example

```
union Key
{
  int num_key;
  void *ptr_key;
  char  name_key[10];
};
void func()
{
  Key key = {5};   // first member of Key is of type int
                   // any additional bytes initialized to binary zeros
}
```

Detecting a Machine's Endian-ness

The term *endian* refers to the way in which a computer architecture stores the bytes of a multibyte number in memory. When bytes at lower addresses have lower significance (as is the case with Intel microprocessors, for instance), it is called *little endian ordering*. Conversely, *big endian ordering* describes a computer architecture in which the most significant byte has the lowest memory address. The following program detects the endian-ness of the machine on which it is executed:

```
int main()
{
  union probe
  {
    unsigned int num;
    unsigned char bytes[sizeof(unsigned int)];
  };
```

```
   probe p = { 1U }; //initialize first member of p with unsigned 1
   bool little_endian = (p.bytes[0] == 1U); //in a big endian architecture,
                                            //p.bytes[0] equals 0
   return 0;
}
```

The Lifetime of a Bound Temporary Object

You can safely bind a reference to a temporary object. The temporary object to which the reference is bound persists for the lifetime of the reference. For example

```
class C
{
private:
  int j;
public:
  C(int i) : j(i) {}
  int getVal() const {return j;}
};

int main()
{
  const C& cr = C(2); //bind a reference to a temp; temp's destruction
                      //deferred to the end of the program
  C c2 = cr;   //use the bound reference safely
  int val = cr.getVal();
  return 0;
}//temporary destroyed here along with its bound reference
```

Deleting a Pointer More Than Once

The result of applying `delete` to the same pointer after it has been deleted is undefined. Clearly, this bug should never happen. However, it can be prevented by assigning a NULL value to a pointer right after it has been deleted. It is guaranteed that a NULL pointer deletion is harmless. For example

```
#include <string>
using namespace std;
void func
{
  string * ps = new string;
  //...use ps
  if ( ps->empty() )
  {
    delete ps;
    ps = NULL; //safety-guard: further deletions of ps will be harmless
  }
  //...many lines of code
  delete ps; // ps is deleted for the second time. Harmless however
}
```

Data Pointers Versus Function Pointers

Both C and C++ make a clear-cut distinction between two types of pointers—data pointers and function pointers. A function pointer embodies several constituents, such as the function's signature and return value. A data pointer, on the other hand, merely holds the address of the first memory byte of a variable. The substantial difference between the two led the C standardization committee to prohibit the use of `void*` to represent function pointers, and vice versa. In C++, this restriction was relaxed, but the results of coercing a function pointer to a `void*` are implementation-defined. The opposite—that is, converting data pointers to function pointers—is illegal.

Pointer Equality

Pointers to objects or functions of the same type are considered equal in three cases:

- If both pointers are `NULL`. For example
  ```
  int *p1 = NULL, p2 = NULL;
  bool equal = (p1==p2); //true
  ```

- If they point to the same object. For example
  ```
  char c;
  char * pc1 = &c;
  char * pc2 = &c;
  bool equal = (pc1 == pc2); // true
  ```

- If they point one position past the end of the same array. For example

  ```
  int num[2];
  int * p1 = num+2, *p2 = num+2;
  bool equal = ( p1 == p2); //true
  ```

Storage Reallocation

In addition to `malloc()` and `free()`, C also provides the function `realloc()` for changing the size of an existing buffer. C++ does not have a corresponding reallocation operator. Adding operator `renew` to C++ was one of the suggestions for language extension that was most frequently sent to the standardization committee. Instead, there are two ways to readjust the size of memory that is allocated on the free store. The first is very inelegant and error prone. It consists of allocating a new buffer with an appropriate size, copying the contents of the original buffer to it and, finally, deleting the original buffer. For example

```
void reallocate
{
  char * p new char [100];
  //...fill p
  char p2 = new char [200]; //allocate a larger buffer
  for (int i = 0; i<100; i++) p2[i] = p[i]; //copy
  delete [] p; //release original buffer
}
```

Obviously, this technique is inefficient and tedious. For objects that change their size frequently, this is unacceptable. The preferable method is to use the container classes of the Standard Template Library (STL). STL containers are discussed in Chapter 10, "STL and Generic Programming."

Local Static Variables

By default, local static variables (not to be confused with static class members) are initialized to binary zeros. Conceptually, they are created before the program's outset and destroyed after the program's termination. However, like local variables, they are accessible only from within the scope in which they are declared. These properties make static variables useful for storing a function's state on recurrent invocations because they retain their values from the previous call. For example

```
void MoveTo(int OffsetFromCurrentX, int OffsetFromCurrentY)
{
  static int currX, currY;  //zero initialized
  currX += OffsetFromCurrentX;
  currY += OffsetFromCurrentY;
  PutPixel(currX, currY);
}
void DrawLine(int x, int y, int length)
{
  for (int i=0; i<length; i++)
     MoveTo(x++, y—);
}
```

However, when the need arises for storing a function's state, a better design choice is to use a class. Class data members replace the static variables and a member function replaces the global function. Local static variables in a member function are of special concern: Every derived object that inherits such a member function also refers to the same instance of the local static variables of its base class. For example

```
class Base
{
public:
  int countCalls()
  {
    static int cnt = 0;
    return ++cnt;
  }
};

class Derived1 : public Base { /*..*/};
class Derived2 : public Base { /*..*/};

// Base::countCalls(), Derived1::countCalls() and Derived2::countCalls
// hold a shared copy of cnt
int main()
{
  Derived1 d1;
  int d1Calls = d1.countCalls(); //d1Calls = 1
```

```
      Derived2 d2;
      int d2Calls = d2.countCalls(); //d2Calls = 2, not 1
      return 0;
    }
```

Static local variables in the member function `countCalls` can be used to measure
load balancing by counting the total number of invocations of that member function,
regardless of the actual object from which it was called. However, it is obvious that the
programmer's intention was to count the number of invocations through `Derived2`
exclusively. In order to achieve that, a static class member can be used instead:

```
class Base
{
private:
  static int i;
public:
  virtual int countCalls() {  return ++i; }
};
int Base::i;

class Derived1 : public Base
{
private:
  static int i; //hides Base::i
public:
  int countCalls() {  return ++i; } //overrides Base:: countCalls()
};
int Derived1::i;

class Derived2 : public Base
{
private:
  static int i; //hides Base::i and distinct from Derived1::i
public:
  virtual int countCalls() {  return ++i; }
};
int Derived2::i;

int main()
{
  Derived1 d1;
  Derived2 d2;
  int d1Calls = d1.countCalls(); //d1Calls = 1
  int d2Calls = d2.countCalls(); //d2Calls also = 1
  return 0;
}
```

Static variables are problematic in a multithreaded environment because they are
shared and have to be accessed by means of a lock.

Global Anonymous Unions

An *anonymous union* (anonymous unions are discussed in Chapter 12, "Optimizing Your Code") that is declared in a named namespace or in the global namespace has to be explicitly declared `static`. For example

```
static union //anonymous union in global namespace
{
  int num;
  char *pc;
};
namespace NS
{
  static union { double d; bool b;}; //anonymous union in a named namespace
}
int main()
{
  NS::d = 0.0;
  num = 5;
  pc = "str";
  return 0;
}
```

The `const` and `volatile` Properties of an Object

There are several phases that comprise the construction of an object, including the construction of its base and embedded objects, the assignment of a `this` pointer, the creation of the virtual table, and the invocation of the constructor's body. The construction of a cv-*qualified* (`const` or `volatile`) object has an additional phase, which turns it into a `const/volatile` object. The cv qualities are effected after the object has been fully constructed.

Conclusions

The complex memory model of C++ enables maximal flexibility. The three types of data storage—automatic, static, and free store—offer a level of control that normally exists only in assembly languages.

The fundamental constructs of dynamic memory allocation are operators `new` and `delete`. Each of these has no fewer than six different versions; there are plain and array variants, each of which comes in three flavors: exception throwing, exception free, and placement.

Many object-oriented programming languages have a built-in *garbage collector*, which is an automatic memory manager that detects unreferenced objects and reclaims their storage (see also Chapter 14, "Concluding Remarks and Future Directions," for a discussion on garbage collection). The reclaimed storage can then be used to create new objects, thereby freeing the programmer from having to explicitly release dynamically-allocated memory. Having an automatic garbage collector is handy because it eliminates a large source of bugs, runtime crashes, and memory leaks. However, garbage collection is not a panacea. It incurs additional runtime overhead due to repeated compaction, reference counting, and memory initialization operations, which are unacceptable in time-critical applications. Furthermore, when garbage collection is used, destructors are not necessarily invoked immediately when the lifetime of an object ends, but at an indeterminate time afterward (when the garbage collector is sporadically invoked). For these reasons, C++ does not provide a garbage collector. Nonetheless, there are techniques to minimize—and even eliminate—the perils and drudgery of manual memory management without the associated disadvantages of garbage collection. The easiest way to ensure automatic memory allocation and deallocation is to use automatic storage. For objects that have to grow and shrink dynamically, you can use STL containers that automatically and optimally adjust their size. Finally, in order to create an object that exists throughout the execution of a program, you can declare it `static`. Nonetheless, dynamic memory allocation is sometimes unavoidable. In such cases, `auto_ptr` (discussed in Chapters 6 and 11, "Memory Management") simplifies the usage of dynamic memory.

Effective and bug-free use of the diversity of C++ memory handling constructs and concepts requires a high level of expertise and experience. It isn't an exaggeration to say that most of the bugs in C/C++ programs are related to memory management. However, this diversity also renders C++ a multipurpose, no compromise programming language.

12

Optimizing Your Code

Introduction

One often-heard claim during the past 30 years is that performance doesn't matter because the computational power of hardware is constantly increasing. Therefore, buying a stronger machine or extending the RAM of an existing one can make up for the sluggish performance of software written in a high-level programming language. In other words, a hardware upgrade is more cost-effective than the laborious task of hand-tuning code. That might be correct for client applications that execute on a standard personal computer. A modestly priced personal computer these days offers higher computational power than a mainframe did two decades ago, and the computational power still grows exponentially every 18 months or so. However, in many other application domains, a hardware upgrade is less favorable because it is too expensive or because it simply is not an option. In proprietary embedded systems with 128K of RAM or less, extending the RAM requires redesigning the entire system from scratch, as well as investing several years in the development and testing of the new chips. In this case, code optimization is the only viable choice for satisfactory performance.

But optimization is not confined to esoteric application domains such as embedded systems or hard core real-time applications. Even in mainstream application domains such as financial and billing systems, code optimization is sometimes necessary. For a bank that owns a $1,500,000 mainframe computer, buying a faster machine is less preferable than rewriting a few thousand lines of critical code. Code optimization is also the primary tool for achieving satisfactory performance from server applications that support numerous users, such as Relational Database Management Systems and Web servers.

Another common belief is that code optimization implies less readable and harder to maintain software. This is not necessarily true. Sometimes, simple code modifications such as relocating the declarations in a source file or choosing a different container type can make all the difference in the world. Yet none of these changes entails unreadable code, nor do they incur any additional maintenance overhead. In fact, some of the optimization techniques can even improve the software's extensibility and readability. More aggressive optimizations can range from using a simplified class hierarchy, through the combination of inline assembly code. The result in this case is less readable, harder to maintain, and less portable code. Optimization can be viewed as a continuum; the extent to which it is applied depends on a variety of considerations.

Scope of This Chapter

Optimization is a vast subject that can easily fill a few thick volumes. This chapter discusses various optimization techniques, most of which can be easily applied in C++ code without requiring a deep understanding of the underlying hardware architecture of a particular platform. The intent is to give you a rough estimate of the performance cost of choosing one programming strategy over another (you can experiment with the programs that are discussed in the following sections on your computer). The purpose is to provide you with practical guidelines and notions, rather than delve into theoretical aspects of performance analysis, efficiency of algorithms, or the Big Oh notation.

Before Optimizing Your Software

Detecting the bottlenecks of a program is the first step in optimizing it. It is important, however, to profile the release version rather than the debug version of the program because the debug version of the executable contains additional code. A debug-enabled executable can be about 40% larger than the equivalent release executable. The extra code is required for symbol lookup and other debug "scaffolding". Most implementations provide distinct debug and release versions of operator new and other library functions. Usually, the debug version of new initializes the allocated memory with a unique value and adds a header at block start; the release version of new doesn't perform either of these tasks. Furthermore, a release version of an executable might have been optimized already in several ways, including the elimination of unnecessary temporary objects, loop unrolling (see the sidebar "A Few Compiler Tricks"), moving objects to the registers, and inlining. For these reasons, you cannot assuredly deduce from a debug version where the performance bottlenecks are actually located.

A Few Compiler Tricks

A compiler can automatically optimize the code in several ways. The *named return value* and *loop unrolling* are two instances of such automatic optimizations.

Consider the following code:

```
int *buff = new int[3];
for (int i =0; i<3; i++)
   buff[i] = 0;
```

This loop is inefficient: On every iteration, it assigns a value to the next array element. However, precious CPU time is also wasted on testing and incrementing the counter's value and performing a jump statement. To avoid this overhead, the compiler can unroll the loop into a sequence of three assignment statements, as follows:

```
buff[0] = 0;
buff[1] = 0;
buff[2] = 0;
```

The named return value is a C++-specific optimization that eliminates the construction and destruction of a temporary object. When a temporary object is copied to another object using a copy constructor, and when both these objects are cv-unqualified, the Standard allows the implementation to treat the two objects as one, and not perform a copy at all. For example

```
class A
{
public:
  A();
  ~A();
  A(const A&);
  A operator=(const A&);
};

A f()
{
  A a;
  return a;
}

A a2 = f();
```

The object a does not need to be copied when f() returns. Instead, the return value of f() can be constructed directly into the object a2, thereby avoiding both the construction and destruction of a temporary object on the stack.

Remember also that debugging and optimization are two distinct operations. The debug version needs to be used to trap bugs and to verify that the program is free from logical errors. The tested release version needs to be used in performance tuning and optimizations. Of course, applying the code optimization techniques that are presented in this chapter can enhance the performance of the debug version as well, but the release version is the one that needs to be used for performance evaluation.

Declaration Placement

The placing of declarations of variables and objects in the program can have significant performance effects. Likewise, choosing between the postfix and prefix operators can also affect performance. This section concentrates on four issues: initialization versus assignment, relocation of declarations to the part of the program that actually uses them, a constructor's member initialization list, and prefix versus postfix operators.

Prefer Initialization to Assignment

C allows declarations only at a block's beginning, before any program statements. For example

```
void f();

void g()
{
  int i;
  double d;
  char * p;
  f();
}
```

In C++, a declaration is a statement; as such, it can appear almost anywhere within the program. For example

```
void f();

void g()
{
 int i;
 f();
 double d;
 char * p;
}
```

> **Note**
>
> It is not uncommon to find a "phantom bottleneck" in the debug version, which the programmer strains hard to fix, only to discover later that it has disappeared anyway in the release version. Andrew Koenig wrote an excellent article that tells the story of an evasive bottleneck that automatically dissolved in the release version ("An Example of Hidden Library Overhead", *C++ Report* vol. 10:2, February 1998, page 11). The lesson that can be learned from this article is applicable to everyone who practices code optimization.

The motivation for this change in C++ was to allow for declarations of objects right before they are used. There are two benefits to this practice. First, this practice guarantees that an object cannot be tampered with by other parts of the program before it has been used. When objects are declared at the block's beginning and are used only 20 or 50 lines later, there is no such guarantee. For instance, a pointer to an object that was allocated on the free store might be accidentally deleted somewhere before it is actually used. Declaring the pointer right before it is used, however, reduces the likelihood of such mishaps.

The second benefit in declaring objects right before their use is the capability to initialize them immediately with the desired value. For example

```
#include <string>
using namespace std;
void func(const string& s)
{
  bool emp = s.empty(); //local declarations enables immediate initialization
}
```

For fundamental types, initialization is only marginally more efficient than assignment; or it can be identical to late assignment in terms of performance. Consider the following version of func(), which applies assignment rather than initialization:

```
void func2() //less efficient than func()? Not necessarily
{
  string s;
  bool emp;
  emp = s.empty(); //late assignment
}
```

My compiler produces the same assembly code as it did with the initialization version. However, as far as user-defined types are concerned, the difference between initialization and assignment can be quite noticeable. The following example demonstrates the performance gain in this case (by modifying the preceding example). Instead of a bool variable, a full-blown class object is used, which has all the four special member functions defined:

```
int constructor, assignment_op, copy, destr; //global counters
class C
{
public:
  C();
  C& operator = (const C&);
  C(const C&);
  ~C();
};

C::C()
{
  ++constructor;
```

```
}

C& C::operator = (const C& other)
{
  ++assignment_op;
  return *this;
}

C::C(const C& other)
{
  ++copy;
}

C::~C()
{
  ++destr;
}
```

As in the previous example, two different versions of the same function are compared; the first uses object initialization and the second uses assignment:

```
void assign(const C& c1)
{
 C c2;
 c2 = c1;

}

void initialize(const C& c1)
{
 C c2 = c1;
}
```

Calling `assign()` causes three member function invocations: one for the constructor, one for the assignment operator, and one for the destructor. `initialize()` causes only two member function invocations: the copy constructor and the destructor. Initialization saves one function call. For a nonsensical class such as `C`, the additional runtime penalty that results from a superfluous constructor call might not be crucial. However, bear in mind that constructors of real-world objects also invoke constructors of their base classes and embedded objects. When there is a choice between initialization and assignment, therefore, initialization is always preferable.

Relocating Declarations

Preferring initialization of objects over assignment is one aspect of localizing declarations. On some occasions, the performance boost that can result from moving declarations is even more appreciable. Consider the following example:

```
bool is_C_Needed();
void use()
{
```

```
   C c1;
   if (is_C_Needed() == false)
   {
      return; //c1 was not needed
   }
   //use c1 here
   return;
}
```

The local object c1 is unconditionally constructed and destroyed in use(), even if it is not used at all. The compiler transforms the body of use() into something that looks like this:

```
void use()
{
   C c1;
   c1.C::C(); //1. compiler-added constructor call
   if (is_C_Needed() == false)
   {
      c1.C::~C(); //2. compiler-added destructor call
      return; //c1 was not needed but was constructed and destroyed still
   }
   //use c1 here
   c1.C::~C(); //3. compiler-added destructor call
   return;
}
```

As you can see, when is_C_Needed() returns false, the unnecessary construction and destruction of c1 are still unavoidable. Can a clever compiler optimize away the unnecessary construction and destruction in this case? The Standard allows the compiler to suppress the creation (and consequently, the destruction) of an object if it is not needed, and if neither its constructor nor its destructor have any side effects. In this example, however, the compiler cannot perform this feat for two reasons. First, both the constructor and the destructor of c1 have side effects—they increment counters. Second, the result of is_C_Needed() is unknown at compile time; therefore, there is no guarantee that c1 is actually unnecessary at runtime. Nevertheless, with a little help from the programmer, the unnecessary construction and destruction can be eliminated. All that is required is the relocation of the declaration of c1 to the point where it is actually used:

```
void use()
{
   if (is_C_Needed() == false)
   {
      return; //c1 was not needed
   }
   C c1; //moved from the block's beginning
   //use c1 here
   return;
}
```

Consequently, the object c1 is constructed only when it is really needed—that is, when is_C_Needed() returns true. On the other hand, if is_C_Needed() returns false, c1 is neither constructed nor destroyed. Thus, simply by moving the declaration of c1, you managed to eliminate two unnecessary member function calls! How does it work? The compiler transforms the body of use() into something such as the following:

```
void use()
{
  if (is_C_Needed() == false)
  {
    return; //c1 was not needed
  }
  C c1; //moved from the block's beginning
  c1.C::C(); //1 compiler-added constructor call
  //use c1 here
  c1.C::~C(); //2 compiler-added destructor call
  return;
}
```

To realize the effect of this optimization, change the body of use(). Instead of constructing a single object, you now use an array of 1000 C objects:

```
void use()
{
  if (is_C_Needed() == false)
  {
    return; //c1 was not needed
  }
  C c1[1000];
  //use c1 here
  return;
}
```

In addition, you define is_C_Needed() to return false:

```
bool is_C_Needed()
{
  return false;
}
```

Finally, the main() driver looks similar to the following:

```
int main()
{
  for (int j = 0; j<100000; j++)
    use();
  return 0;
}
```

The two versions of use() differ dramatically in their performance. They were compared on a Pentium II, 233MHz machine. To corroborate the results, the test was repeated five times. When the optimized version was used, the for loop in main() took less than 0.02 of a second, on average. However, when the same for loop was executed with the original, the nonoptimized version of use() took 16 seconds. The dramatic variation in these results isn't too surprising; after all, the nonoptimized version incurs 100,000,000 constructor calls as well as 100,000,000 destructor calls, whereas the optimized version calls none. These results might also hint at the performance gain that can be achieved simply by preallocating sufficient storage for container objects, rather than allowing them to reallocate repeatedly (see also Chapter 10, "STL and Generic Programming").

Member-Initialization Lists

As you read in Chapter 4, "Special Member Functions: Default Constructor, Copy Constructor, Destructor, and Assignment Operator," a member initialization list is needed for the initialization of const and reference data members, and for passing arguments to a constructor of a base or embedded subobject. Otherwise, data members can either be assigned inside the constructor body or initialized in a member initialization list. For example

```
class Date //mem-initialization version
{
private:
  int day;
  int month;
  int year;
  //constructor and destructor
public:
  Date(int d = 0, int m = 0, int y = 0) : day(d), month(m), year(y) {}
};
```

Alternatively, you can define the constructor as follows:

```
Date::Date(int d, int m, int y) //assignment within the constructor body
{
  day   = d;
  month = m;
  year  = y;
}
```

Is there a difference in terms of performance between the two constructors? Not in this example. All the data members in Date are of a fundamental type. Therefore, initializing them by a mem-initialization list is identical in terms of performance to assignment within the constructor body. However, with user-defined types, the difference between the two forms is significant. To demonstrate that, return to the member function counting class, C, and define another class that contains two instances thereof:

```
class Person
{
private:
  C c_1;
  C c_2;
public:
  Person(const C& c1, const C& c2 ): c_1(c1), c_2(c2) {}
};
```

An alternative version of `Person`'s constructor looks similar to the following:

```
Person::Person(const C& c1, const C& c2)
{
  c_1 = c1;
  c_2 = c2;
}
```

Finally, the `main()` driver is defined as follows:

```
int main()
{
  C c; //created only once, used as dummy arguments in Person's constructor
  for (int j = 0; j<30000000; j++)
  {
    Person p(c, c);
  }
  return 0;
}
```

The two versions were compared on a Pentium II, 233MHz machine. To corroborate the results, the test was repeated five times. When a member initialization list was used, the `for` loop in `main()` took 12 seconds, on average. The nonoptimized version took 15 seconds, on average. In other words, the assignment inside the constructor body is slower by a factor of 25% compared to the member-initialized constructor. The member function counters can give you a clue as to the reasons for the difference. Table 12.1 presents the number of member function calls of class `C` for the member initialized constructor and for the assignment inside the constructor's body.

Table 12.1   Comparison Between Member Initialization and Assignment Within the Constructor's Body for Class `Person`

Initialization Method	Default Constructor Calls	Assignment Operator Calls	Copy Constructor Calls	Destructor Calls
Member initialization list	0	0	60,000,000	60,000,000
Assignment within Constructor	60,000,000	60,000,000	0	60,000,000

When a member initialization list is used, only the copy constructor and the destructor of the embedded object are called (note that Person has two embedded members), whereas the assignment within the constructor body also adds a default constructor call per embedded object. In Chapter 4, you learned how the compiler inserts additional code into the constructor's body before any user-written code. The additional code invokes the constructors of the base classes and embedded objects of the class. In the case of polymorphic classes, this code also initializes the vptr. The assigning constructor of class Person is transformed into something such as the following:

```
Person::Person(const C& c1, const C& c2) //assignment within constructor body
{
 //pseudo C++ code inserted by the compiler before user-written code
  c_1.C::C(); //invoke default constructor of embedded object c_1
  c_2.C::C(); //invoke default constructor of embedded object c_2
//user-written code comes here:
  c_1 = c1;
  c_2 = c2;
}
```

The default construction of the embedded objects is unnecessary because they are reassigned new values immediately afterward. The member initialization list, on the other hand, appears before any user-written code in the constructor. Because the constructor body does not contain any user-written code in this case, the transformed constructor looks similar to the following:

```
Person::Person(const C& c1, const C& c2) // member initialization list ctor
{
 //pseudo C++ code inserted by the compiler before user-written code
  c_1.C::C(c1); //invoke copy constructor of embedded object c_1
  c_2.C::C(c2); //invoke copy constructor of embedded object c_2
//user-written code comes here (note: there's no user code)
}
```

You can conclude from this example that for a class that has subobjects, a member initialization list is preferable to an assignment within the constructor's body. For this reason, many programmers use member initialization lists across the board, even for data members of fundamental types.

Prefix Versus Postfix Operators

The prefix operators ++ and − tend to be more efficient than their postfix versions because when postfix operators are used, a temporary copy is needed to retain the value of the operand before it is changed. For fundamental types, the compiler can eliminate the extra copy. However, for user-defined types, this is nearly impossible. A typical implementation of the overloaded prefix and postfix operators demonstrates the difference between the two:

```
class Date
{
private:
  //...
  int AddDays(int d);
public:
```

```
    Date operator++(int unused);
    Date& operator++();
};

Date Date::operator++(int unused)  //postfix
{
  Date temp(*this); //create a copy of the current object
  this->AddDays(1); //increment  current object
  return temp; //return by value a copy of the object before it was incremented
}
Date& Date::operator++()    //prefix
{
  this->AddDays(1); //increment  current object
  return *this; //return by reference the current object
}
```

The overloaded postfix ++ is significantly less efficient than the prefix for two reasons: It requires the creation of a temporary copy, and it returns that copy by value. Therefore, whenever you are free to choose between postfix and prefix operators of an object, choose the prefix version.

Inline Functions

Inline functions can eliminate the overhead incurred by a function call and still provide the advantages of ordinary functions. However, inlining is not a panacea. In some situations, it can even degrade the program's performance. It is important to use this feature judiciously.

Function Call Overhead

The exact cost of an ordinary function call is implementation-dependent. It usually involves storing the current stack state, pushing the arguments of the function onto the stack and initializing them, and jumping to the memory address that contains the function's instructions—only then does the function begin to execute. When the function returns, a sequence of reverse operations also takes place. In other languages (such as Pascal and COBOL), the overhead of a function call is even more noticeable because there are additional operations that the implementation performs before and after a function call. For a member function that merely returns the value of a data member, this overhead can be unacceptable. Inline functions were added to C++ to allow efficient implementation of such accessor and mutator member functions (*getters* and *setters*, respectively). Nonmember functions can also be declared `inline`.

Benefits of Inline Functions

The benefits of inlining a function are significant: From a user's point of view, the inlined function looks like an ordinary function. It can have arguments and a return value; furthermore, it has its own scope, yet it does not incur the overhead of a full-blown function call. In addition, it is remarkably safer and easier to debug than using a macro. But there are even more benefits. When the body of a function is inlined, the compiler can optimize the resultant code even further by applying context-specific optimizations that it cannot perform on the function's code alone. All member functions that are implemented inside the class body are implicitly declared `inline`. In addition, compiler synthesized constructors, copy constructors, assignment operators, and destructors are implicitly declared `inline`. For example

```
class A
{
private:
  int a;
public:
  int Get_a() { return a; } // implicitly inline
  virtual void Set_a(int aa) { a = aa; } //implicitly inline
  //compiler synthesized canonical member functions also declared inline
};
```

It is important to realize, however, that the `inline` specifier is merely a recommendation to the compiler. The compiler is free to ignore this recommendation and *outline* the function; it can also inline a function that was not explicitly declared `inline`. Fortunately, C++ guarantees that the function's semantics cannot be altered by the compiler just because it is or is not inlined. For example, it is possible to take the address of a function that was not declared `inline`, regardless of whether it was inlined by the compiler (the result, however, is the creation of an outline copy of the function). How do compilers determine which functions are to be inlined and which are not? They have proprietary heuristics that are designed to pick the best candidates for inlining, depending on various criteria. These criteria include the size of the function body, whether it declares local variables, its complexity (for example, recursion and loops usually disqualify a function from inlining), and additional implementation- and context-dependent factors.

What Happens When a Function That Is Declared `inline` Cannot Be Inlined?

Theoretically, when the compiler refuses to inline a function, that function is then treated like an ordinary function: The compiler generates the object code for it, and invocations of the function are transformed into a jump to its memory address. Unfortunately, the implications of outlining a function are more complicated than that. It is a common practice to define inline functions in the class declaration. For example

```
    // filename Time.h
#include<ctime>
#include<iostream>
using namespace std;
class Time
{
```

```
public:
  inline void Show() { for (int i = 0; i<10; i++) cout<<time(0)<<endl;}
};
   // filename Time.h
```

Because the member function `Time::Show()` contains a local variable and a `for` loop, the compiler is likely to ignore the `inline` request and treat it as an ordinary member function. However, the class declaration itself can be `#included` in separately compiled translation units:

```
    // filename f1.cpp
#include "Time.h"
void f1()
{
  Time t1;
  t1.Show();
}
    // f1.cpp

// filename f2.cpp
#include "Time.h"
void f2()
{
  Time t2;
  t2.Show();
}
    // f2.cpp
```

As a result, the compiler generates two identical copies of the same member function for the same program:

```
void f1();
void f2();
int main()
{
  f1();
  f2();
  return 0;
}
```

When the program is linked, the linker is faced with two identical copies of `Time::Show()`. Normally, function redefinition causes a link-time error. Un-inlined functions are a special case, however. Older implementations of C++ coped with this situation by treating an un-inlined function as if it had been declared `static`. Consequently, each copy of the compiled function was only visible within the translation unit in which it was declared. This solved the name clashing problem at the cost of multiple local copies of the same function. In this case, the `inline` declaration did not boost performance; on the contrary, every call of the un-inlined function was resolved as an ordinary function call with the regular overhead. Even worse, the multiple copies of the function code increased compilation and linkage time and bloated the size of the executable. Ironically, *not* declaring `Time::Show()` `inline` might have yielded better performance! Remember that the programmer is generally not aware of all the actual costs of this—the compiler strains quietly, the linker sighs silently, and the resultant executable is more bloated and sluggish than ever. But it still works, and the users scratch their heads, saying, "This object-oriented programming is really awful! I'm sure this app would run much faster if I'd written it in C!"

Fortunately, the Standard's specification regarding un-inlined functions was recently changed. A Standard compliant implementation generates only a single copy of such a function, regardless of the number of translation units that define it. In other words, an un-inlined function is treated similarly to an ordinary function. However, it might take some time for all compiler vendors to adopt the new specifications.

Additional Issues of Concern

There are two more conundrums that are associated with inline functions. The first has to do with maintenance. A function can begin its life as a slim inline function, offering the benefits that were previously described. At a later phase in the lifetime of the system, the function body can be extended to include additional functionality, resulting from changes in the implementation of its class. Suddenly, the inline substitution can become inefficient or even impossible. It is therefore important to reconsider the removal of the `inline` specifier from such functions. For member functions that are defined in the class body, the change is more complicated because the function definition has to be moved to a separate source file.

Another problem might arise when inline functions are used in code libraries. It is impossible to maintain binary compatibility if the definition of an inline function changes. In this case, the users must recompile their code to reflect the change. For a non-inline function, the users only need to relink their code, which is considerably less of a burden than a massive recompilation and relink.

The Do's and Don'ts of `inline`

The lesson here is that `inline` is not a magical potion for enhancing performance. For very short functions—for example, accessors, mutators, and function wrappers (see Chapter 13, "C Language Compatibility Issues")—the `inline` specifier can be profitable in terms of both execution speed and program size. If the inlined function is not very short and it is called extensively, however, the result can be an increase in the size of the executable. Furthermore, many processors cache the machine instructions of frequently used parts of the program; excessive inlining can cause a reduced instruction cache hit and, consequently, poorer overall performance. The real annoyance occurs when the compiler refuses to inline a function even though it was declared `inline`. On older implementations, the result was quite painful. On Standard compliant implementations, the consequences of un-inlining are less detrimental, but they are still undesirable. Some compilers are clever enough to figure out on their own which functions are to be inlined. However, most compilers are less inline-savvy so it is best to examine the effect of an inline declaration empirically. If the inline declaration does not enhance performance, avoid it.

Optimizing Memory Usage

Optimization has several aspects: faster execution speed, efficient usage of system resources, and minimal usage of memory. In general, code optimization attempts to improve all these aspects. The declaration relocation technique that was demonstrated earlier eliminates the unnecessary creation and destruction of objects, thereby reducing the program's size and accelerating its runtime speed. However, other optimization techniques are heavily biased toward one direction—speedier code or a smaller memory footprint. Sometimes, though, these goals are mutually exclusive; that is, compacting the memory footprint engenders slower code, whereas a faster code implies a larger memory footprint. This section presents various techniques for optimizing, or compacting, the memory requirements of a program.

Bit Fields

In both C and C++ it is possible to store and access data directly in the tiniest possible unit: a single bit. Because a bit is not the natural storage unit for C/C++ implementations, the use of bit fields can increase the size of the executable due to the additional maneuvers that are exercised by the processor in accessing a sequence of one or more bits. This is a clear-cut case of sacrificing runtime speed for the sake of minimizing memory usage.

Normally, you don't use bit fields just to save a few more bytes. For some applications, however, the tradeoff between execution speed and storage compaction is definitely worth its while. For example, the billing system of an average international telephone company stores every phone call as a record in a relational database. These records are processed in batch periodically to calculate the customer's monthly bill. The database stores millions of new records every day, and it has to keep the customer's billing information for at least one year. The complete database contains around one billion records at any given time. Because the database is also backed up periodically, and because it might also be a distributed database, every record is stored in more than one physical location. In fact, there might be 20 billion records stored in different backup generations and distributed portions of the database at any given time. A minimal billing record contains the customer's ID, a timestamp, codes that indicate the type of the call (for example, local or long distance) and the tariff (off peak, peak time). Literally, every bit counts here—one redundant bit implies 2.5GB of wasted storage!

> **Note**
>
> Note, however, that some hardware architectures provide special processor instructions for accessing bits. Therefore, whether bit fields affect the program's speed or not is very much platform-dependent.

A non–space-optimizing definition of the billing record might look like this:

```
struct BillingRec
{
  long cust_id;
  long timestamp;
  enum CallType
  {
    toll_free,
    local,
    regional,
    long_distance,
    international,
    cellular
  } type;
  enum CallTariff
  {
    off_peak,
    medium_rate,
    peak_time
  } tariff;
};
```

A `BillingRec` occupies no fewer than 16 bytes of memory on my 32-bit machine. Clearly, space is wasted here. The first two fields occupy four bytes each, as expected. However, the two `enum` variables occupy an additional eight bytes, even though they both can be safely represented in less than a single byte. A tweaked version of `BillingRec` can squeeze the enum values into two bit fields:

```
struct BillingRec
{
  long cust_id;
  long timestamp;
  enum CallType
  {
    toll_free,
    local,
    regional,
    long_distance,
    international,
    cellular
  };

  enum CallTariff
  {
    off_peak,
    medium_rate,
    peak_time
  };
  unsigned call: 3; //three bits
  unsigned tariff: 2; //two bits
};
```

The size of `BillingRec` is now 12 bytes. The four bytes that are saved are equal to megabytes of data storage per day. Still, the size can be reduced even more. The two bit fields occupy five bits in total, which is less than a byte. One might therefore expect `BillingRec` to occupy 9 bytes rather than 12. The problem is that the compiler inserts three additional padding bytes after the bit fields to align the size of `BillingRec` on a word boundary (more on member alignment in Chapter 11, "Memory Management"). The additional padding bytes ensure faster access time—at the cost of three wasted bytes. There are two ways to overcome this problem: You can change the compiler's setting to allow alignment on a byte boundary, or you can change the size of the other members so that—in total—they reach exactly eight bytes.

Changing the size of the members is somewhat tricky because the first two members have to become bit fields as well:

```
struct BillingRec
{
  int cust_id: 24; // 23 bits + 1 sign bit
  int  timestamp: 24;
  enum CallType
  {//...
  };

  enum CallTariff
  {//...
  };
  unsigned call: 3;
  unsigned tariff: 2;
};
```

This time, `BillingRec` occupies eight bytes in total, which is half of its original size. The storage that is saved in this example can amount to 10GB annually. Considering the cheap prices of magnetic storage media these days, saving a few thousand dollars might not seem to be a compelling argument—but there is another reason for favoring smaller data storage: the costs of digital communication. A distributed database has synchronized copies in multiple sites. The synchronization process is usually done by means of digital data transfer from the central database to its synchronized copies, and vice versa. The transmission of millions of records on leased lines is pretty expensive. For a phone company that owns these lines, this is not an issue of special concern; suppose, however, that the company is an international bank that pays hundreds of dollars for every hour of data transfer. In this case, halving the data volume is unquestionably profitable. Another point to remember is the Web; if the telephone company has a Web site that enables its customers to view their billing information online, the download time of hundreds of records through analog dialup lines can be cut in half by this tweak.

Note

Note that both solutions might not be portable, and on some hardware architectures, the compiler will nonetheless insist on word boundary alignment. Check your compiler's specifications regarding member alignment settings.

Unions

Unions can also be used to minimize memory waste by locating two or more data members at the same memory address, where the value of (at most) one of the data members is active at any time. The size of a union is sufficient to hold the largest of its data members. A union can have member functions, including a constructor and destructor, but it cannot have virtual member functions. A union cannot serve as a base class of, nor can it inherit from, another class. In addition, a union cannot store objects that have nontrivial special member functions. C++ also supports *anonymous unions*. An anonymous union is an unnamed object of an unnamed type (anonymous unions are also discussed in Chapter 11). For example

```
union { long n; void * p}; // anonymous
n = 1000L;  // members are directly accessed
p = 0; // n is now also 0
```

Unlike a named union, an anonymous one cannot have member functions or nonpublic data members.

When are unions useful? The following class retrieves a person's data from a database. The key can be either a unique ID number or a person's last name, but never both
at once:

```
class PersonalDetails
{
private:
  char * name;
  long ID;
  //...
public:
  PersonalDetails(const char *nm); //key is of type char * used
  PersonalDetails(long id) : ID(id) {} //numeric key used
};
```

Memory is wasted here because only one of the keys can be used at a time. An anonymous union can be used in this case to minimize memory usage. For example

```
class PersonalDetails
{
private:
  union  //anonymous
  {
    char * name;
    long ID;
  };
public:
  PersonalDetails(const char *nm);
  PersonalDetails(long id) : ID(id) {/**/}  // direct access to a member
  //...
};
```

By using a union, the size of class `PersonalDetails` is halved. Again, saving four bytes of memory is not worth the trouble unless this class serves as a mold for millions of database records or if the records are transmitted on slow communication lines.

Note that unions do not incur any runtime overhead, so there is no speed tradeoff in this case. The advantage of an anonymous union over a named one is that its members can be accessed directly.

Speed Optimizations

In time-critical applications, every CPU cycle counts. This section presents a few simple guidelines for speed optimization. Some of them have been around since the early days of C; others are C++ specific.

Using a Class to Pack a Long Argument List

The overhead of a function call is increased when the function has a long list of arguments. The runtime system has to initialize the stack with the values of the arguments; naturally, this operation takes longer when there are more arguments. For example, executing the following function 100,000,000 times takes 8.5 seconds on average on my machine:

```
void retrieve(const string& title, //5 arguments
              const string& author,
              int ISBN,
              int year,
              bool& inStore)
{}
```

Packing the argument list into a single class and passing it by reference as the only argument reduces the result to five seconds, on average. Of course, for functions that take a long time to execute, the stack initialization overhead is negligible. However, for short and fast functions that are called very often, packing a long parameter list within a single object and passing it by reference can improve performance.

Register Variables

The storage specifier `register` can be used as a hint to the compiler that an object will be heavily used in the program. For example

```
void f()
{
  int *p = new int[3000000];
  register int *p2 = p; //store the address in a register
  for (register int j = 0; j<3000000; j++)
  {
    *p2++ = 0;
  }
  //...use  p
  delete [] p;
}
```

Loop counters are good candidates for being declared as register variables. When they are not stored in a register, a substantial amount of the loop's execution time is wasted in fetching the variable from memory, assigning a new value to it, and storing it back in memory repeatedly. Storing it in a machine register reduces this overhead. Note, however, that register is only a recommendation to the compiler. As with function inlining, the compiler can refuse to store the object in a machine register. Furthermore, modern compilers optimize loop counters and move them to the machine's registers anyway. The register storage specification is not confined to fundamental types. Rather, it can be used for any type of object. If the object is too large to fit into a register, the compiler can still store the object in a faster memory region, such as the cache memory (cache memory is about ten times faster than the main memory).

Declaring function parameters with the register storage specifier is a recommendation to pass the arguments on the machine's registers rather than passing them on the stack. For example

```
void f(register int j, register Date d);
```

Declaring Constant Objects as const

In addition to the other boons of declaring constant objects as const, an optimizing compiler can take advantage of this declaration, too, and store such an object in a machine register instead of in ordinary memory. Note that the same optimization can be applied to function parameters that are declared const. On the other hand, the volatile qualifier disables such an optimization (see Appendix A, "Manual of Programming Style"), so use it only when it is unavoidable.

Runtime Overhead of Virtual Functions

When a virtual function is called through a pointer or a reference of an object, the call doesn't necessarily impose additional runtime penalties. If the compiler can resolve the call statically, no extra overhead is incurred. Furthermore, a very short virtual function can be inlined in this case. In the following example, a clever compiler can resolve the calls of the virtual member functions statically:

```
#include <iostream>
using namespace std;

class V
{
public:
  virtual void show() const { cout<<"I'm V"<<endl; }
```

> **Note**
>
> Some compilers ignore the register specification altogether and automatically store the program's variables according to a set of built-in optimization rules. Please consult your vendor's specifications for more details on the compiler's handling of register declarations.

```
};
class W : public V
{
public:
  void show() const { cout<<"I'm W"<<endl; }
};

void f(V & v, V *pV)
{
  v.show();
  pV->show();
}
void g()
{
  V v;
  f(v, &v);
}
int main()
{
  g();
  return 0;
}
```

If the entire program appears in a single translation unit, the compiler can perform an inline substitution of the call of the function g() in main(). The invocation of f() within g() can also be inlined, and because the dynamic type of the arguments that are passed to f() is known at compile time, the compiler can resolve the virtual function calls inside f() statically. There is no guarantee that every compiler actually inlines all the function calls; however, some compilers certainly take advantage of the fact that the dynamic type of the arguments of f() can be determined at compile time, and avoid the overhead of dynamic binding in this case.

Function Objects Versus Function Pointers

The benefits of using function objects instead of function pointers (function objects are discussed in Chapter 10 and in Chapter 3, "Operator Overloading") are not limited to genericity and easier maintenance. Furthermore, compilers can inline the call of a function object, thereby enhancing performance even further (inlining a function pointer call is rarely possible).

A Last Resort

The optimization techniques that have been presented thus far do not dictate design compromises or less readable code. In fact, some of them *improve* the software's robustness and the ease of maintenance. Packing a long argument list within a class object, const declarations, and using function objects rather than function pointers provide additional benefits on top of the performance boost. Under strict time and memory constraints, however, these techniques might not suffice; additional tweaks are sometimes required, which affect the portability and extensibility of the software. The techniques that are presented in this section are to be used only as a last resort, and only after all the other optimizations have been applied.

Disabling RTTI and Exception Handling Support

When you port pure C code to a C++ compiler, you might discover a slight performance degradation. This is not a fault in the programming language or the compiler, but a matter of compiler tuning. All you have to do to gain the same (or better) performance that you might get from a C compiler is switch off the compiler's RTTI and exception handling support. Why is this? In order to support RTTI or exception handling, a C++ compiler inserts additional "scaffolding" code to the original source file. This increases the executable size a little, and imposes slight runtime overhead (the overhead of exception handling and RTTI are discussed in Chapter 6, "Exception Handling," and Chapter 7, "Runtime Type Information," respectively). When pure C is used, this additional code is unnecessary. Please note, however, that you should not attempt to apply this tweak with C++ code or C code that uses any C++ constructs such as operator new and virtual functions.

Inline Assembly

Time-critical sections of C++ code can be rewritten in native assembly code. The result can be a significant increase in speed. Note, however, that this measure is not to be taken lightly because it makes future modifications much more difficult. Programmers who maintain the code might not be familiar with the particular assembly language that is used, or they might have no prior experience in assembly language at all. Furthermore, porting the software to other platforms requires rewriting of the assembly code parts (in some instances, upgrading the processor can also necessitate rewriting). In addition, developing and testing assembly code is an arduous task that can take much more time than developing and testing code that is written in a high-level language.

Generally, operations that are coded in assembly are low-level library functions. On most implementations, for example, the standard library functions memset() and strcpy() are written in native assembly code. C and C++ enable the programmer to embed inline assembly code within an asm block. For example

```
asm
{
  mov a, ecx
  //...
}
```

Interacting with the Operating System Directly

API functions and classes enable you to interact with the operating system. Sometimes, however, executing a system command directly can be much faster. For this purpose, you can use the standard function `system()` that takes a shell command as a `const char *`. For example, on a DOS/Windows system, you can display the files in the current directory as follows:

```
#include <cstdlib>
using namespace std;

int main()
{
  system("dir");  //execute the "dir" command
}
```

Here again, the tradeoff is between speed on the one hand and portability and future extensibility on the other hand.

Conclusions

In an ideal world, software designers and developers might focus their efforts on robust, extensible, and readable code. Fortunately, the current state of affairs in the software world is much closer to that ideal than it was 15, 30, or 50 years ago. Notwithstanding that, performance tuning and optimizations will probably remain a necessity for a long time. The faster hardware becomes, the more the software that runs on it is required to meet higher demands. Speech recognition, online translation of natural languages, neural networks, and complex mathematical computations are only a few examples of resource-hungry applications that will evolve in the future and require careful optimizations.

Textbooks often recommend that you put off optimization consideration to the final stages of testing. Indeed, the primary goal is to get the system to work correctly. Nonetheless, some of the techniques presented here—such as declaring objects locally, preferring prefix to postfix operators, and using initialization instead of assignment— need to become a natural habit. It is a well-known fact that programs usually spend 90% of their time executing only 10% of their code (the numbers might vary, but they range between 80%/20% and 95%/5%). The first step in optimization is, therefore, identifying that 10% of your programs and optimizing them. Many automated profiling and optimization tools can assist you in identifying these critical code parts. Some of these tools can also suggest solutions to enhance performance. Still, many of the optimization techniques are implementation-specific and always require human expertise. It is important to empirically verify your suspicions and to test the effect of suggested code modifications to ensure that they indeed improve the program's performance. Programmers' intuitions regarding the cost of certain operations are often misleading. For example, shorter code is not necessarily faster code. Similarly, writing convoluted code to avoid the cost of a simple `if` statement is not worth the trouble because it saves only one or two CPU cycles.

13

C Language Compatibility Issues

Introduction

C is a subset of C++. Theoretically, every valid C program is also a valid C++ program. In practice, however, there are some subtle incompatibilities and silent differences between the seemingly common portion of both languages. Most of these differences can be diagnosed by the compiler. Others are more evasive and, in rare conditions, they can have surprising effects.

Although it seems that most of the time legacy C code is combined with newer C++ code, the opposite is also true: C++ code is used in C-based applications. For example, transaction-processing monitors of relational databases that are written in C interact with code modules that are written in C++. This chapter first discusses the differences between ISO C and the C subset of ANSI/ISO C++, and it demonstrates how to migrate legacy C code to a C++ environment. Next, you will explore the underlying object model of C++, including the memory layout of objects, member functions, virtual member functions, virtual base classes, and access specifiers, and you will learn how C code can access C++ objects.

Differences Between ISO C and the C Subset of ANSI/ISO C++

With a few minor differences, C++ is a superset of C. The following sections outline the differences between the C subset of C++ and ISO C.

Function Parameter List

In pre-Standard C, the parameter list of a function was declared as follows:

```
/* pre-standard C, still valid in ISO C, invalid in C++*/
int negate (n)
int n; /* parameter declaration  appears here*/
{
   return -n;
}
```

In other words, only the parameters' names appeared in the parentheses, whereas their types were declared before the opening brace. Undeclared parameters defaulted to int. In ISO C, as in C++, both the names and types of the parameters must appear in the parentheses:

```
/* ISO C and C++ */
int negate (int n)
{
   return -n;
}
```

The old-style parameter list is still legal in ISO C, but it is deprecated. In C++, it is illegal. Legacy C code that contains an old-style parameter list has to be changed to become valid in C++.

Function Declaration

In C, functions can be called without having to be declared first. In C++, a function cannot be called without a previous declaration or definition. For example

```
/* valid in C but not in C++ */
int main()
{
  int n;
  n = negate(5); /* undeclared function; valid in C but not in C++ */
  return 0;
}
```

Functions can be declared in C, just as in C++:

```
/* C/C++ */
int negate(int n);
int main()
{
  int n;
  n= negate(5);
  return 0;
}
```

The use of a function declaration (also called a *function prototype*) in C is recommended because it enables the compiler to detect mismatches in type and argument number. However, it is not a requirement.

Empty Parameter List

In C, a function that is declared with an empty list of parameters such as

```
int f();
void g( int i)
{
  f(i)  /* valid in C but not in C++ */
}
```

can take any number of arguments of any type. In C++, such a function does not take any arguments.

Implicit `int` Declarations

In C and in pre-Standard C++, the default type for missing declarations is `int`. For example

```
/* valid in C but not in C++ */
void  func()
{
  const k =0; /*int type assumed in C; invalid in C++*/
}
```

ISO C is currently being revised to disallow implicit `int` declarations.

Repeated Declarations of Global Variables

In C, global variables can be declared more than once without the `extern` specifier. As long as a single initialization (at most) for the same variable is used, the linker resolves all the repeated declarations into a single entity:

```
/* valid in C but not in C++ */
int flag;
int num;
int flag; /* repeated declaration of a global variable */
void func()
{
  flag = 1;
}
```

In C++, an entity must be defined exactly once.

Implicit Casting of `void` Pointers

In C, a `void` pointer is implicitly cast to any other pointer type in assignments and initializations. For example

```
/* valid in C but not C++*/
#include <stdlib.h>
long * p_to_int()
{
```

```
  long * pl = malloc(sizeof(long)); /* implicit conversion of void* to long* */
  return pl;
}
```

In general, implicit conversion of void * is undesirable because it can result in bugs that can otherwise be detected by the compiler. Consider the following example:

```
/* valid in C but not C++*/
#include <stdlib.h>
long * p_to_int()
{
  long * pl = malloc(sizeof(short)); /* oops!  */
  return pl;
}
```

In C++, void pointers have to be cast explicitly to the desired type. The explicit cast makes the programmer's intention clearer and reduces the likelihood of unpleasant surprises.

The Underlying Representation of NULL Pointers

NULL is an implementation-defined const null pointer. C implementations usually define NULL as follows:

```
#define NULL  ((void*)0)
```

However, In C++, NULL is usually defined as the literal 0 (or 0L), but never as void *:

```
const int NULL = 0; //some C++ implementations use this convention
#define NULL 0; //others might use this convention
```

The difference in the underlying representations of NULL pointers between C and C++ derives from the fact that C++ pointers are strongly typed, whereas in C they are not. If C++ retained C's convention, a C++ statement such as

```
char * p = NULL;
```

would be expanded into something similar to

```
char * p = (void*) 0;    // compile time error: incompatible pointer types
```

Because 0 is the universal initializer for all pointer types in C++, it is used instead of the traditional C convention; in fact, many programmers simply use the literal 0 or 0L instead of NULL.

Default Linkage Type of Global const Variables

In C, the default linkage of global const variables is extern. An uninitialized const variable is implicitly zero initialized. For example

```
/*** valid in C but not C++ ***/

/* file error_flag.h */
const int error; /*default extern linkage */
/*** end file ***/
#include"error_flag.h"
int func();
int main()
{
  int status = func();
  if( status == error)
  {
    /*do something */
  }
  return 0;
}
```

In C++, a global const variable that is not explicitly declared extern has static linkage. In addition, a const variable must be initialized.

Null-Terminated Character Arrays

In C, character arrays can be initialized with a string literal without the null-terminating character. For example

```
/*** valid in C but not C++ ***/
const char message[5] = "hello"; /* does not contain a null terminator */
```

In C++, character arrays that are initialized by a string literal must be large enough to contain a null terminator.

Assignment of Integers to an enum Type

In C, the assignment of integers to an enumerated type is valid. For example

```
/*** valid in C but not C++ ***/
enum Status {good, bad};
void func()
{
  Status stat = 1;  /* integer assignment */
}
```

In C++, enums are strongly typed. Only enumerators of the same enum type can be assigned to an enum variable. Explicit type casting is required otherwise. For example

```
//C++
enum Status {good, bad};
void func()
{
  Status stat = static_cast<Status> (1);  // stat = bad
}
```

Definition of Structs in a Function Parameter List and Return Type

In C, a struct can be defined in a function parameter list as well as in its return type. For example

```
/*** valid in C but not C++ ***/
/* struct definition in return type and parameter list of a function */
struct Stat { int code; char msg[10];}
    logon (struct User { char username[8];  char pwd[8];} u );
```

In C++, this is illegal.

Bypassing an Initialization

A *jump statement* unconditionally transfers control. A jump statement is one of the following: a `goto` statement, a transfer from the condition of a `switch` statement to a `case` label, a `break` statement, a `continue` statement, or a `return` statement. In C, the initialization of a variable can be skipped by a jump statement, as in the following example:

```
/*** valid in C but not C++ ***/
int main()
{
  int n=1;

  switch(n)
  {
  case 0:
    int j=0;
    break;
  case 1: /* skip initialization of j */
    j++;  /* undefined */
    break;
  default:
    break;
  }
  return 0;
}
```

In C++, bypassing an initialization is illegal.

Quiet Differences Between C and C++

The differences that have been presented thus far are easily diagnosed by a C++ compiler. There are, however, semantic differences between C and C++ in the interpretation of certain constructs. These differences might not result in a compiler diagnostic; therefore, it is important to pay attention to them.

The Size of an **enum** Type

In C, the size of an enumeration equals the `sizeof(int)`. In C++, the underlying type for an enumeration is not necessarily an `int`—it can be smaller. Furthermore, if an enumerator's value is too large to be represented as an `unsigned int`, the implementation is allowed to use a larger unit: for example, `enum { SIZE = 5000000000UL };` .

The Size of a Character Constant

In C, the result of applying the operator `sizeof` to a character constant—for example, `sizeof('c');`—equals `sizeof(int)`. In C++, on the other hand, the expression `sizeof('c');` equals `sizeof(char)`.

Predefined Macros

C and C++ compilers define the following macros:

```
__DATE__ /*a literal containing compilation date in the form "Apr 13 1998" */
__TIME__ /*a literal containing the compilation time in the form "10:01:07" */
__FILE__  /*a literal containing the name of the source file being compiled */
__LINE__ /* current line number in the source file */
```

C++ compilers exclusively define the following macro:

```
__cpluplus
```

Standard-compliant C compilers define the following macro symbol:

```
__STDC__
```

Whether a C++ compiler also defines the macro symbol `__STDC__` is implementation-dependent.

Default Value Returned from **main()**

In C, when control reaches the end of `main()` without encountering a `return` statement, the effect is that of returning an undefined value to the environment. In C++, however, `main()` implicitly executes a

```
return 0;
```

statement in this case.

Note

You might have noticed that the code listings throughout the book contain an explicit `return` statement at the end of `main()`, even though this is not necessary. There are two reasons for this: First, many compilers that do not comply with the Standard issue a warning message when a `return` statement is omitted. Secondly, the explicit `return` statement is used to return a nonzero value in the event of an error.

Migrating From C to C++

Resolving the syntactic and semantic differences between C and C++ is the first step
in migrating from C to C++. This process ensures that C code can compile under a
C++ compiler, and that the program behaves as expected. There is another clear
advantage of compiling C code under a C++ compiler: The tighter type checking that
is applied by a C++ compiler can detect potential bugs that a C compiler does not
detect. The list of discrepancies between C and C++ that was previously presented is
mostly a result of loopholes and potential traps in C that were fixed in C++. An issue
that is of concern, however, is performance—does a C++ compiler produce object
code that is less efficient than the code produced by a C compiler? This topic is discussed in more detail in Chapter 12, "Optimizing Your Code." However, it is important to note that a good C++ compiler can *outperform* a good C compiler because it
can exercise optimization techniques that C compilers normally do not support, such
as function inlining and the *named return value* (also discussed in Chapter 12).

Nonetheless, in order to benefit from the robustness of object-oriented programming, more substantial code modifications are required. Fortunately, the transition from
procedural to object-oriented programming can be performed gradually. The following section demonstrates a technique of wrapping bare functions with an additional
code layer to minimize the dependency on implementation details. Following that is a
discussion of how to use full-fledged classes that wrap legacy code in order to gain
more of the benefits of object-orientation.

Function Wrappers

Low-level code such as infrastructure routines and API functions can be used by different teams for the same project. Normally, this code is developed and maintained by
a third party vendor or a specific team in the project. For example

```
int retrievePerson (int key, Person* recordToBefilled); /* C function */
```

A problem can arise when the interface of `retrievePerson` () changes: Every
occurrence of a function `retrievePerson` call has to be tracked down and modified
accordingly. Consider how such a small change can affect existing programs:

```
/*
function modification: key is now a char * instead of an int
every call to this function has to modified accordingly
*/
int retrievePerson (const char * key, Person* recordToBefilled);
```

As you saw in Chapter 5, "Object-Oriented Programming and Design," one of the
most noticeable weaknesses of procedural programming is its vulnerability to such
changes; however, even in strict procedural programming you can localize their impact
by using a *wrapper function*. A wrapper function calls the vulnerable function and
returns its result. Following is an example:

```
/* A wrapper function */
int WrapRetrievePerson(int key, Person* recordToBefilled)
{
    return retrievePerson (key, recordToBefilled);
}
```

A wrapper provides a stable interface to a code fragment that is used extensively and that is vulnerable to changes. When using a wrapper function, a change in the interface of an API function is reflected only in the definition of its corresponding wrapper function. Other parts of the program are not affected by the change. This is very similar to the way in which a class's accessors and mutators provide indirect access to its nonpublic members. In the following example, the function wrapper's body has been modified due to the change in the type of key from int to char *. Note, however, that its interface remains intact:

```
/*** file DB_API.h ***/
int retrievePerson (const char *strkey, Person* precordToBefilled);

typedef struct
{
    char first_name[20];
    char last_name[20];
    char address [50];
} Person;

/*** file DB_API.h ***/

#include <stdio.h>
#include " DB_API.h "

int WrapRetrievePerson(int key, Person* precordToBefilled) //remains intact
{
    /* wrapper's implementation modified according to API's modification */
    char strkey[100];
    sprintf (strkey, "%d", key);  /* convert int to a string */
    return retrievePerson (strkey, precordToBefilled);
}
```

By systematically applying this technique to every function that is maintained by other teams or vendors, you can ensure a reasonable level of interface stability even when the underlying implementation changes.

Although the function wrapper technique offers protection from changes in implementation details, it does not provide other advantages of object-oriented programming, including encapsulation of related operations in a single class, constructors and destructors, and inheritance. The next phase in the migration process is to encapsulate a collection of related functions into a single wrapper class. This technique, however, requires familiarity with object-oriented concepts and principles.

Designing Legacy Code Wrapper Classes

In many frameworks that were originally written in C and then ported to C++, a common—but wrong—practice was to wrap C functions in a single *wrapper class*. Such a wrapper class provides as its interface a series of operations mapped directly to the legacy functions. The following networking functions provide an example:

```
/*** file: network.h ***/

#ifndef NETWORK_H
#define NETWORK_H
    /* functions related to UDP protocol */
int UDP_init();
int UDP_bind(int port);
int UDP_listen(int timeout);
int UDP_send(char * buffer);
    /* functions related to X.25 protocol */
int X25_create_virtual_line();
int X25_read_msg_from_queue(char * buffer);
    /* general utility functions */
int hton(unsigned int); //reverse bytes from host to network order
int ntoh(unsigned int); //reverse bytes from network to host order

#endif

/*** network.h ***/
```

A naive implementation of a class wrapper might simply embed all these functions in a single class as follows:

```
#include "network.h"

class Networking
{
private:
//...stuff

public:

  //constructor and destructor
  Networking();
  ~Networking();

  //members
  int UDP_init();
  int UDP_bind(int port);
  int UDP_listen(int timeout);
  int UDP_send(char * buffer);

  int X25_create_virtual_line();
  int X25_read_msg_from_queue(char * buffer);
```

```
    int hton(unsigned int); //reverse bytes from host to network order
    int ntoh(unsigned int); //reverse bytes from network to host order
};
```

However, this method of implementing a wrapper class is not recommended. X.25 and UDP protocols are used for different purposes and have almost nothing in common. Bundling the interfaces of these two protocols together can cause maintenance problems in the long term—and it undermines the very reason for moving to an object-oriented design in the first place. Furthermore, due to its amorphous interface, Networking is not an ideal base for other derived classes. The problem with Networking and similar classes is that they do not genuinely embody an object-oriented policy. They are merely a collection of unrelated operations. A better design approach is to divide the legacy functions into meaningful, self-contained units and wrap each unit by a dedicated class. For example

```
#include "network.h"

class UDP_API
{
private:
//...stuff

public:
  //constructor and destructor
  UDP_API();
  ~UDP_API();
  //members
  int UDP_init();
  int UDP_bind(int port);
  int UDP_listen(int timeout);
  int UDP_send(char * buffer);
};

class X25_API
{
private:
//...stuff
public:
  //constructor and destructor
  X25_API();
  ~X25_API();
  //members
  int X25_create_virtual_line();
  int X25_read_msg_from_queue(char * buffer);
};

class Net_utility
{
    private:
//...stuff
```

```
public:
  //constructor and destructor
  Net_utility();
  ~Net_utility();
  //members
  int hton(unsigned int); //reverse bytes from host to network order
  int ntoh(unsigned int); //reverse bytes from network to host order
};
```

Now each class offers a coherent interface. Another advantage is a simpler usage protocol; users of class X25_API, for instance, are not forced to accept the interface of UDP protocol, and vice versa.

Multilingual Environments

Thus far, this chapter has concentrated on a unidirectional migration process: from C to C++. Nevertheless, many systems are not confined to a single programming language. A typical information system can simultaneously use one programming language for the graphical interface, another language for accessing data from a database, and a third language for server applications. Often, these languages have to share data and code with one another. This section focuses on how to combine C and C++ code in a bilingual system that uses both these languages simultaneously.

The easiest way to ensure compatibility between code modules that are written in C and C++ is to adhere to the common denominator of these languages. Then again, using C++ as a procedural language ("better C") isn't worth the bother—you can simply stick to C. Combining object-oriented C++ code with procedural C code into a seamless executable is more challenging—but it offers many advantages.

C and C++ Linkage Conventions

By default, C++ functions have C++ linkage, which is incompatible with C linkage. Consequently, global C++ functions cannot be called from C code unless they are explicitly declared as having a C linkage.

> **Note**
> In this section, the distinction between C code and C++ is indicated explicitly by file extensions. The .h extension is used for C header files, whereas C++ header files are indicated by the .hpp extension. Similarly, .c and .cpp extensions are used for C and C++ source files, respectively. In addition, only C-style comments are used in C files.

Forcing C Linkage on a C++ Function

To override the default C++ linkage, a C++ function has to be declared `extern "C"`. For example

```
// filename decl.hpp

extern "C" void f(int n); //force C linkage so that f() can be called from C
                          // code although it is compiled by a C++ compiler

// decl.hpp
```

The `extern "C"` prefix instructs a C++ compiler to apply C linkage to the function `f()` rather than the default C++ linkage. This means that a C++ compiler does not apply *name mangling* to `f()`, either (see the following sidebar, "What's in Name Mangling?"). Consequently, a call to `f()` from C code is properly resolved by a C linker. A C++ linker can also locate the compiled version of `f()` even though it has a C linkage type. In other words, declaring C++ functions as `extern "C"` guarantees interoperability between C++ and C (as well as other procedural languages that use the C calling convention). However, forcing C linkage has a price: It is impossible to overload another version of `f()` that is also declared as `extern "C"`. For example

```
// filename decl.hpp

extern "C" void f(int n);
extern "C" void f(float f); //error, second C linkage of f is illegal

// decl.hpp
```

Note that you can declare additional overloaded versions of `f()` as long as they are not declared `extern "C"`:

```
// filename decl.hpp

extern "C" void f(int n); //OK, can be called from C and C++ code
void f(float f); //OK, no C linkage used. Can be called only from C++ code
void f(char c); //OK, no C linkage used. Can be called only from C++ code

// decl.hpp
```

How does it work? A call to the function from C code is translated to a CALL assembly directive, followed by the function name. Declaring a C++ function as `extern "C"` ensures that the name that is generated for it by a C++ compiler is identical to the name that a C compiler expects. On the other hand, if the called function is compiled by a C++ compiler without the `extern "C"` specifier, it has a mangled name but a C compiler still places the nonmangled name after the CALL directive, resulting in a link-time error.

Calling C++ Code from C Code

Up until now, you have observed the C++ side of the story. A C program cannot #include the header file decl.hpp because the extern "C" specifier is not recognized by a C compiler. To ensure that the declaration can be parsed by a C compiler, extern "C" needs to be visible to a C++ compiler—but not to a C compiler. A C++ function with C linkage has to be declared in two distinct forms, one for C++ and another for C. This can be achieved by using separate C and C++ header files. The C header file looks similar to the following:

What's in Name Mangling?

Name mangling (the more politically correct term, although rarely used, is *name decoration*) is a method used by a C++ compiler to generate unique names for identifiers in a program. The exact details of the algorithm are compiler-dependent, and they might vary from one version to another. Name mangling ensures that entities with seemingly identical names get unique identifications. The resultant mangled name contains all the information that might be needed by the linker, including linkage type, scope, calling convention, and so on. For instance, when a global function is overloaded, the generated mangled name for each overloaded version is unique. Name mangling is also applied to variables. Thus, a local variable and a global variable with the same user-given name still get distinct mangled names. How is the mangled name synthesized? The compiler picks the user-given name of an identifier and decorates it with additional affixes to indicate a variable of a fundamental type, a class, or a function. For a function, the mangled name embeds its scope and linkage type, the namespace in which it is declared, the list of parameters, the parameters' passing mechanism, and the parameters' cv-qualifications. A mangled name of a member function incorporates additional information such as the class name, whether it is a const member function, and other implementation-dependent details that the linker and the runtime environment might need. Following is an example: For a global function void func(int);, a given compiler can generate the corresponding mangled name __x_func@i@, where the affix x indicates a function, func is the function's user-given name, @ indicates the beginning of the parameter list, i indicates the type of the parameter, and the closing @ sign signals the end of the parameter list. An overloaded version of f() has a different mangled name because it has a different parameter list. The original user-given name can be reproduced from the mangled name, so linkers in general can issue error messages in a human-readable format.

As was previously stated, the name mangling scheme of a given compiler can change from one version to another (for example, if the new version supports namespaces, whereas the previous one did not). This is one of the reasons you often have to recompile your code with every compiler upgrade. Another important implication is that, usually, the linker and the compiler need to come from the same vendor and have compatible versions. This ensures that they share the same naming conventions and that they produce compatible binary code.

```
/*** filename decl.h ***/

void f(int n);  /* identical to the C++ header but no extern "C" here */

 /*** decl.h ***/
```

The header file can be #included in the C source file that calls the function f().
For example

```
/*** filename do_something.c ***/

#include "decl.h"
void do_something()
{
   f(5);
}


/*** do_something.c ***/
```

Keeping separate header files for C and C++ is not an elegant solution, however.
The header files have to remain in sync all the time, and when many header files are
used, this can turn into a serious maintenance problem. A better alternative is to use
one or more C header files for the declarations. For example

```
/*** filename f.h ***/

void f(int n);  /* identical to the C++ header but no extern "C" here */

 /*** f.h ***/
/*** filename g.h ***/

void g(const char * pc, int n);

 /*** g.h ***/
```

Next, the C header files are #included in a C++ header file that contains an
extern "C" block:

```
// filename decl.hpp

extern "C"
{
#include "f.h"
#include "g.h"
}

// filename decl.hpp
```

The effect of an extern "C" block is as if every declaration in the #included
header files had a preceding extern "C" specifier. Another alternative is to modify the
C header file directly by adding an #ifdef directive to make the extern "C" declaration visible only to a C++ compiler. For example

```
/*** filename decl.h ***/

#ifdef __cplusplus
extern "C"  { //visible only to a C++ compiler
#endif

void g(const char * pc, int n);
void f(int n);

#ifdef __cplusplus
} //visible only to a C++ compiler
#endif

 /*** g.h ***/
```

This way, only one header file is needed. However, it is not always possible to modify the C header files directly. In such cases, the preceding technique needs to be used. Please note that a C++ function called from C code is an ordinary C++ function. It can instantiate objects, invoke their member functions, or use any other C++ feature. However, some implementations might require special configuration settings to ensure that the linker has access to the C++ libraries and template codes.

Compiling `main()`

Functions can be compiled by either a C compiler or a C++ compiler. However, a C++ compiler should compile `main()`. This enables a C++ compiler to take care of templates, static initialization, and additional implementation-dependent operations for which `main()` is responsible. Compiling `main()` under a C compiler will most likely result in link-time errors due to the different semantics of `main()` in C and C++.

Minimize the Interface Between C and C++ Code

In general, you can call a C function from C++ code without special adjustments. The opposite, as you have seen, is also possible—but it requires additional adjustments. It is therefore recommended that you keep the interface between the two languages at a minimum. Declaring every C++ function as `extern "C"`, for example, is not recommended. Not only does this convention imply additional modifications to the header files, it also disables overloading. Remember also that you cannot declare a member function `extern "C"`. For C++ functions that have to be called from C code, it might be advantageous to use a function wrapper that has an `extern "C"` specifier. In this case, the wrapped C++ functions can have the C++ linkage. For example

```
void g(const char * pc, int n);  //extern "C" is unnecessary
void f(int n);

extern "C" void f_Wrapper(int n) //only the wrapper function is called from C
```

```
{
  f(n);
}
extern "C" void g_Wrapper(const char *pc,  int n)
{
  g(pc, n);
}
```

Mixing `<iostream>` Classes with `<stdio.h>` Functions

It is possible to use both `<iostream>` classes and `<stdio.h>` library functions in the same program, as long as they do not access the same file. For example, you can use the `<iostream>` object `cin` to read data from the keyboard, and then use `<stdio.h>` functions to write the data to a disk file, as in the following program:

```
#include <iostream>
#include <cstdio>
using namespace std;

int main()
{
  int num;
  cin>>num;
  cout<<"you enetred: "<< num <<endl;
  FILE *fout = fopen("data.dat", "w");
  if (fout) //write num to a disk file
  {
    fprintf(fout, "%d\n", num);
  }
  fclose(fout);
  return 0;
}
```

It is even possible to use `<iostream>` and `<stdio.h>` to manipulate the same file; for instance, a program can send output to both `stdout` and `cout`, although this is not recommended. To enable simultaneous access to the same file, you first have to call `ios::sync_with_stdio(true);` to synchronize the I/O operations. Note, however, that this synchronization degrades performance. Therefore, only use it when `<iostream>` and `<stdio.h>` access the same file. For example

```
#include <iostream>
#include <cstdio>
using namespace std;
int main()
{
  ios::sync_with_stdio(true);//enable mixed I/O
  int num;
  printf("please enter a number\n");
  cin>>num;
```

```
cout<<"you entered: "<< num << "please enter another one " << endl;
scanf("%d", &num);
return 0;
}
```

Normally, you won't write such code. However, when a large application combines legacy C functions that use <stdio.h> and C++ objects that use <iostream>, I/O synchronization is unavoidable because, ultimately, the same low-level system resources are used by both <stdio.h> and <iostream>.

The fact that <iostream> and <stdio.h> can be combined is a major advantage. Otherwise, the migration process from C to C++ might be much fussier, and making C and C++ code work together might prove to be very difficult.

Accessing a C++ Object in C Code

Can C code, which of course is unaware of object semantics, access the data members of a C++ object directly? The short answer is, "Yes, but...". There are some guarantees about the underlying memory layout of an object; C code can take advantage of these guarantees and treat a C++ object as an ordinary data struct, provided that all the following restrictions apply to the class of the object in question:

- The class has no virtual member functions (including inherited virtual functions of a base class).
- The class has no virtual base classes in the entire inheritance chain.
- The class has no member objects that have either a virtual base class or virtual member functions.
- All the data members of the class are declared without an intervening access specifier.

The Underlying Representation of an Object in Memory

Examine these restrictions in more detail, given the following declaration of the class Date:

```
class Date
{
public:
  int day;
  int month;
  int year;
  //constructor and destructor
  Date(); //current date
  ~Date();
  //a non-virtual member function
  bool isLeap() const;
  bool operator == (const Date& other);
};
```

The Standard guarantees that within every instance of class `Date`, data members are set down in the order of their declarations (static data members are stored outside the object and are therefore ignored). There is no requirement that members be set down in contiguous memory regions; the compiler can insert additional padding bytes (more on this in Chapter 11, "Memory Management") between data members to ensure proper alignment. However, this is also the practice in C, so you can safely assume that a `Date` object has a memory layout that is identical to that of the following C struct:

```
/*** filename POD_Date.h***/
struct POD_Date
/* the following struct has memory layout that is identical
to a Date object */
{
  int day;
  int month;
  int year;
};
/*** POD_Date.h***/
```

Consequently, a `Date` object can be passed to C code and treated as if it were an instance of `POD_Date`. That the memory layout in C and C++ is identical in this case might seem surprising; class `Date` defines member functions in addition to data members, yet there is no trace of these member functions in the object's memory layout. Where are these member functions stored? C++ treats nonstatic member functions as static functions. In other words, member functions are ordinary functions. They are no different from global functions, except that they take an implicit `this` argument, which ensures that they are called on an object and that they can access its data members. An invocation of a member function is transformed to a function call, whereby the compiler inserts an additional argument that holds the address of the object. Consider the following example:

```
void func()
{
  Date d;
  bool leap = d.isLeap(); //1
}
```

The invocation of the member function `isLeap()` in (1) is transformed by a C++ compiler into something such as

```
_x_isLeap?Date@KPK_Date@(&d); //pseudo C++ code
```

What was that again? Parse it carefully. The parentheses contain the `this` argument, which is inserted by the compiler in every nonstatic member function call. As you already know, function names are mangled. `_x_isLeap?Date@KPK_Date@` is a hypothetical mangled name of the member function `bool Date::isLeap() const;`. In the hypothetical C++ compiler, every mangled name begins with an underscore to minimize the potential for conflicts with user-given names. Next, the x indicates a function, as opposed to a data variable. `isLeap` is the user-given name of the function. The

? is a delimiter that precedes the name of the class. The @ that follows the class name indicates the parameter list, which begins with a KPK and Date to indicate a const pointer to a const Date (the this argument of a const member function is a const pointer to a const object). Finally, a closing @ indicates the end of the parameter list. _x_isLeap?Date@KPK_Date@ is, therefore, the underlying name of the member function bool Date::isLeap() const;. Other compilers are likely to use different name mangling schemes, but the details are quite similar to the example presented here. You must be thinking: "This is very similar to the way procedural programming manipulates data." It is. The crucial difference is that the compiler, rather than the human programmer, takes care of these low-level details.

The C++ Object Model Is Efficient

The object model of C++ is the underlying mechanism that supports object-oriented concepts such as constructors and destructors, encapsulation, inheritance, and polymorphism. The underlying representation of class member functions has several advantages. It is very efficient in terms of execution speed and memory usage because an object does not store pointers to its member functions. In addition, the invocation of a nonvirtual member function does not involve additional lookup and pointer dereferencing. A third advantage is backward compatibility with C; an object of type Date can be passed to C code safely because the binary representation of such an object complies with the binary representation of a corresponding C struct. Other object-oriented languages use a radically different object model, which might not be compatible with either C or C++. Most of them use *reference semantics*. In a reference-based object model, an object is represented as a reference (a pointer or a handle) that refers to a memory block in which data members and pointers to functions are stored. There are some advantages to reference semantics; for example, reference counting and garbage collection are easier to implement in such languages, and indeed such languages usually provide automatic reference counting and garbage collection. However, garbage collection also incurs additional runtime overhead, and a reference-based model breaks down backward compatibility with C. The C++ object model, on the other hand, enables C++ compilers to be written in C, and (as you read in Chapter 6, "Exception Handling,") early C++ compilers were essentially C++-to-C translators.

Memory Layout of Derived Objects

The Standard does not specify the memory layout of base class subobjects in a derived class. In practice, however, all C++ compilers use the same convention: The base class subobject appears first (in left-to-right order in the event of multiple inheritance), and data members of the derived class follow. C code can access derived objects, as long as the derived class abides by the same restrictions that were specified previously. For example, consider a nonpolymorphic class that inherits from Date and has additional data members:

```
class DateTime: public Date
{
public: //additional members
long time;
bool PM; //display time in AM or PM?
DateTime();
~DateTime();
long getTime() const;
};
```

The two additional data members of DateTime are appended after the three members of the base class Time, so the memory layout of a DateTime object is equivalent to the following C struct:

```
/*** filename POD_Date.h***/
struct POD_DateTime
{
  int day;
  int month;
  int year;
  long time
  bool PM;
};
/*** POD_Date.h***/
```

In a similar vein, the nonpolymorphic member functions of DateTime have no effect on the size or memory layout of the object.

The compatible memory layout of nonpolymorphic C++ objects and C structs has many useful applications. For example, it enables relational databases to retrieve and insert objects into a database table. Data Manipulation Languages, such as SQL, that do not support object semantics, can still treat a "live" object as a raw chunk of memory. In fact, several commercial databases rely on this compatibility to provide an object-oriented interface with an underlying relational data model. Another application is the capability to transmit objects as a stream of bytes from one machine to another.

Support for Virtual Member Functions

What happens when an object becomes polymorphic? In this case, backward compatibility with C is trickier. As was noted previously, the compiler is allowed to insert additional data members to a class in addition to user-declared data members. These members can be padding bytes that ensure proper alignment. In the case of virtual functions, an additional member is inserted into the class: a pointer to the virtual table, or vptr. The vptr holds the address of a static table of function pointers (as well as the runtime type information of a polymorphic class; see Chapter 7, "Runtime Type Information"). The exact position of the _vptr is implementation-dependent. Traditionally, it was placed after the class's user-declared data members. However, some compilers have moved it to the beginning of the class for performance reasons. Theoretically, the _vptr can be located anywhere inside the class—even among user-declared members.

A virtual member function, like a nonvirtual member function, is an ordinary function. When a derived class overrides it, however, multiple distinct versions of the function exist. It is not always possible to determine at compile time which of these functions needs to be invoked. For example

```
#include <iostream>
using namespace std;
class PolyDate
{
public:
//PolyDate has the same members as Date but it's polymorphic
virtual void name() const { cout<<"PolyDate"<<endl;}
};
class PolyDateTime: public PolyDate
{
public:
// the same members as DateTime but it's polymorphic
void name() const { cout<<"PolyDateTime"<<endl;} //override PolyDate::name()
};
```

When these classes are compiled, the hypothetical compiler generates two underlying functions that correspond to PolyDate::name() and PolyDateTime()::name():

```
        // mangled name of void PolyDate::name() const
_x_name?PolyDate@KPK_PolyDate@
        // mangled name of void PolyDateTime::name() const;
_x_name?PolyDateTime@KPK_PolyDateTime@
```

So far, there's nothing unusual about this. You already know that a member function is an ordinary function that takes an implicit this argument. Because you have defined two versions of the same virtual function, you also expect to find two corresponding functions, each of which has a distinct mangled name. However, unlike nonvirtual functions, the compiler cannot always transform an invocation of a virtual member function into a direct function call. For example

```
void func(const PolyDate* pd)
{
  pd->name();
}
```

func() can be located in a separate source file, which might have been compiled before class PolyDateTime was defined. Therefore, the invocation of the virtual function name() has to be deferred until runtime. The compiler transforms the function call into something such as

```
(* pd->_vptr[2]) (pd);
```

Analyze it; the member vptr points to the internally-generated virtual table. The first member of the virtual table is usually saved for the address of the destructor, and the second might store the address of the class's type_info. Any other user-defined virtual member functions are located in higher positions. In this example, the address of name() is stored at the third position in the virtual table (in practice, the name of the `vptr` is also mangled). Thus, the expression `pd->_vptr[2]` returns the address of the function `name()` associated with the current object. `pd`, in the second occurrence, represents the `this` argument.

Clearly, defining a corresponding C struct is more precarious in this case and requires intimate acquaintance with the compiler's preferred position of the `vptr` as well as with its size. There is another hazard here: The value of the `vptr` is transient, which means that it might have a different value, according to the address space of the process that executes the program. Consequently, when an entire polymorphic object is stored in a file and retrieved later, the retrieved data cannot be used as a valid object. For all these reasons, accessing polymorphic objects from C code is dangerous and generally needs to be avoided.

Virtual Inheritance

C code should not access objects that have a virtual base class either. The reason is that a virtual base is usually represented in the form of a pointer to a shared instance of the virtual subobject. Here again, the position of this pointer among user-defined data members is implementation-dependent. Likewise, the pointer holds a transient value, which can change from one execution of the program to another.

Different Access Specifiers

The fourth restriction on the legality of accessing C++ objects from C code states that all the data members of the class are declared without an intervening access specifier. This means, theoretically, that the memory layout of a class that looks similar to the following

```
class AnotherDate
{
private:
  int day;
private:
  int month;
private:
  int year;
public:
  //constructor and destructor
  AnotherDate(); //current date
  ~AnotherDate();
  //a non-virtual member function
  bool isLeap() const;
  bool operator == (const Date& other);
};
```

might differ from a class that has the same data members declared in the same order, albeit without any intervening access specifiers. In other words, for class `AnotherDate`, an implementation is allowed to place the member `month` before the member `day`, year before month, or whatever. Of course, this nullifies any compatibility with C code. However, in practice, all current C++ compilers ignore the access specifiers and store the data members in the order of declaration. So C code that accesses a class object that has multiple access specifiers might work—but there is no guarantee that the compatibility will remain in the future.

Conclusions

The creators of C++ have attempted to preserve, as closely as possible, backward compatibility with C. Indeed, almost without exception, every C program is also a valid C++ program. Still, there are some subtle differences between the seemingly common denominator of the two languages. Most of them, as you might have noted, derive from the improved type-safety of C++—for example, the obligatory declaration of a function prior to its usage, the need to use explicit cast of void pointers to the target pointer, the deprecation of implicit int declarations, and the enforcement of a null terminator in a string literal. Other discrepancies between the two languages derive from the different rules of type definition.

C code can be called directly from C++ code. Calling C++ code from C is also possible under certain conditions, but it requires additional adjustments regarding the linkage type and it is confined to global functions exclusively. C++ objects can be accessed from C code, as you have seen, but here again, there are stringent constraints to which you must adhere.

"Hey, we're done!"

(JOSEE LAJOIE'S WORDS RIGHT AFTER THE
APPROVAL OF THE C++ FINAL DRAFT
INTERNATIONAL STANDARD IN THE NOVEMBER
1997 MEETING OF THE ANSI/ISO C++
STANDARDIZATION COMMITTEE IN MORRISTOWN,
NEW JERSEY)

14

Concluding Remarks & Future Directions

Introduction

The previous chapters have told the past and the present of C++. In nearly 20 years, C++ has evolved from an experimental language into the most widely used object-oriented programming language worldwide. The importance of standardizing C++ cannot be overemphasized. Having the ANSI/ISO endorsement has several advantages:

- **Language stability**—C++ is probably the largest programming language in commercial use today. Learning it from scratch is a demanding and time-consuming process. It is guaranteed that, henceforth, learning C++ is a one-time investment rather than an iterative process.

- **Code stability**—The Standard specifies a set of deprecated features that might become obsolete in the future. Other than that, fully ANSI-compliant code is guaranteed to work in the future.

- **Manpower portability**—C++ programmers can switch more easily to different environments, projects, compilers, and companies.

- **Easier portability**—The Standard defines a common denominator for all platforms and compiler vendors, enabling easier porting of software across various operating systems and hardware architectures.

The following code sample is Standard-compliant; however, some compilers will reject it, whereas others will compile it without complaints:

```cpp
#include <iostream>
using namespace std;

void detect_int(size_t size)
{
 switch(size)
 {
   case sizeof(char):
     cout<<"char detected"<<endl;
   break;
   case sizeof(short):
     cout<<"short detected"<<endl;
   break;
   case sizeof(int):
     cout<<"int detected"<<endl;
   break;
   case sizeof(long):
     cout<<"int detected"<<endl;
   break;
 }
}
```

On platforms that have distinct sizes for all four integral types (for example, architectures that use 16 bits for short, 32 bits for int, and 64 bits for long) this code will compile and work as expected. On other platforms, where the size of int overlaps with the size of another integral type, the compiler will complain on identical case labels.

The point to take home from this example is that the Standard does not guarantee absolute code portability, nor does it ensure binary compatibility. However, it facilitates software porting from one platform to another by defining a common ground for the language, which an implementation is allowed to extend. This practice is almost universal: Platform-specific libraries and keywords are added to almost every C++ implementation. However, an implementation cannot alter the specifications of the Standard (otherwise, such an implementation is not Standard-compliant). As you will read in the following sections, allowing platform-specific extensions is an important factor in the success of programming languages in general; languages that have attempted to prohibit platform-specific extensions have failed to obtain a critical mass of users due to a lack of vendor support.

Scope of This Chapter

The previous chapters mostly focus on the hows of C++; this chapter explores the whys. It elucidates the philosophy behind the design and evolution of C++ and compares it to the evolution of other programming languages. Some features that almost made it into the Standard are then presented. Possible future additions to C++, including automatic garbage collection, object persistence, and concurrency, are discussed next. Finally, theoretical and experimental issues are discussed. The intent is not to predict the future of C++ (there is no guarantee that any of the features discussed here will ever become an integral part of the Standard), but rather to give you a broader view of the challenges of language design.

Some of the Features That Almost Made It into the Standard

The standardization of C++ lasted nine years. STL alone added at least one more year to the original agenda. However, STL was an exception. Other features that were proposed too late were not included in the Standard. The following section lists two such features: hashed associative containers and default type arguments of function templates.

Hashed Associative Containers

The Standard Template Library provides only one type of associative container—the *sorted associative container*. The STL sorted associated containers are `map`, `multimap`, `set`, and `multiset` (see Chapter 10, "STL and Generic Programming"). However, there is another type of associated container, the *hashed associative container*, that should really be in the Standard Library but isn't there because it was proposed too late. The difference between a sorted associative container and a hashed associative container is that the former keeps the keys sorted according to some total order. For example, in a `map<string, int>`, the elements are sorted according to the lexicographical order of the strings. A hashed associative container, on the other hand, divides the keys into a number of subsets, and the association of each key to its subset is done by a hash function. Consequently, searching a key is confined to its subset rather than the entire key space. Searching a hashed associative container can therefore be faster than searching a sorted associative container under some circumstances; but unlike sorted associated containers, the performance is less predictable. There are already vendors that include hashed associated containers as an extension, and it is likely that these containers will be added to the Standard in the next revision phase.

Default Type Arguments of Function Templates

As you read in Chapter 9, "Templates," class templates can take default type arguments. However, the Standard disallows default type arguments in function templates. This asymmetry between class templates and function templates is simply an unfortunate oversight that was discovered too late to be fixed. Default type arguments of function templates will most likely be added to C++ in the next revision of the Standard.

The Evolution of C++ Compared to Other Languages

Unlike other newer languages, C++ is not an artifact of a commercial company. C++ does not bear the trademark sign, nor do any of its creators receive royalties for every compiler that is sold. Thus, C++ is not subjected to the marketing ploys and dominance battles that rage among software companies these days. Another crucial factor that distinguishes C++ from some other "would-be perfect" programming languages is the way in which it has been designed and extended through the years.

Some of you might recall the tremendous hype that surrounded Ada in its early days. Ada was perhaps the most presumptuous endeavor to create a language that was free from the deficiencies of the other programming languages that existed at that time. Ada promised to be a 100% portable language, free of subsets and dialects. It also provided built-in support for multitasking and parameterized types. The design of Ada lasted more than a decade, but it was a *design by committee* process rather than the *design by community* process that characterizes C++. The facts are known: Ada never really became the general purpose, widely used programming language it intended to be. It is amusing to recall today that back in 1983, when Ada was released, many believed that it was the last third generation programming language to be created. Ironically, C++ was making its first steps at exactly that same time. Needless to say, the design and evolution of C++ have taken a radically different path. Other third generation languages have appeared since 1983 and—surely—new third generation languages will appear in the future. The factors that led to the failure of Ada as a universal and general purpose programming language can serve as a lesson in language design.

Users' Convenience

The failure of Ada can be attributed mostly to the design by committee approach. In addition, the prohibition of platform-specific extensions deterred vendors from developing libraries and tools that supported the new language. It is always surprising to learn how computer scientists and language users differ in their views about the important features of the language. C, which was created by programmers rather than by academia, offered convenience and efficiency at the expense of readability and safety. For example, the capability to write statements such as this one

```
if (n = v) //did the programmer mistake assignment for equality?
{
//...do something
}
```

has been a source of criticism. Still, it is this very feature that enables programmers to write a complete function that consists of a single statement such as the following:

```
void strcpy (char * dst, const char * src)
{
  while( *dst++ = *src++ );
}
```

The tedium of typing long keywords is also an issue of debate. "Academic languages" usually advocate the use of verbose statements that consist of complete keywords—for example, `integer` rather than `int`, `character` rather than `char` (as in Eiffel and other similar languages), and `call func();` rather than `func();`. Programmers, on the other hand, feel more comfortable with truncated keywords and symbols. Look at the following:

```
class Derived : Base {}; //inheritance indicated by :
```

In other languages, inheritance is expressed by explicit keywords:

```
class Derived extends Base {}; //Java; full keyword indicates inheritance
```

C++ adopts the policy of C in this respect. Furthermore, according to Bjarne Stroustrup, one of the principles in the design of C++ says that where there is a choice between inconveniencing the compiler writer and annoying the programmer, choose to inconvenience the compiler writer (*The Evolution of C++: Language Design in the Marketplace of Ideas*, p.50). The implementations of operator overloading, `enum` types, templates, default arguments, and Koenig lookup are instances of this approach. Programmers can get along without direct language support for these features, at the cost of inconvenience: Ordinary functions can be used instead of overloaded operators, constants can replace `enum` types, and fully qualified names can make up for the lack of Koenig lookup. Fortunately, this is not the case in C++. Other languages, however, have adopted the opposite approach, namely simple compiler writing at the cost of inconveniencing the programmers. Java, for instance, does not have `enum` types, operator overloading, and default arguments by design. Although these features do not incur overhead of any kind, and no one doubts their importance and usefulness, they make a compiler writer's work more difficult (originally, Java designers claimed that operator overloading was an unnecessary complexity).

"Pay as You Go"

The benefits of object-oriented programming are not free. The automatic invocation of constructors and destructors is very handy, but it incurs additional overhead in the speed and the size of the program. Likewise, dynamic binding and virtual inheritance also impose performance penalties. But none of these features is forced on the programmer. Pure procedural C++ code (legacy C code that is ported to a C++ compiler, for example) does not pay for these features. In other words, users—almost without exception—have a choice between higher-level features, which impose a performance penalty, and lower-level features, which are free from these performance penalties but are more susceptible to design modifications and are harder to maintain. The "pay as you go" principle enables programmers to use C++ in diverse application domains and apply different programming paradigms according to their needs and priorities.

Possible Future Additions to C++

It's hard to predict which new features will be added to C++ in the future, mostly because it's hard to predict what programming in general will be like five or ten years from now. However, automatic garbage collection, concurrency, and object persistence are already implemented in many other object-oriented programming languages; in the future, they might be added to C++ as well. Rule-based programming and better support for dynamically linked libraries are other such possible extensions that C++ might or might not have in the future. The following sections discuss these features, and their incurred complications, in greater detail.

Automatic Garbage Collection

"If the programmer's convenience is that important, why doesn't C++ have a garbage collector?" is an often-heard question (garbage collection is also discussed in Chapter 11, "Memory Management"). Clearly, an automated garbage collector can make the life of a programmer easier. However, unlike objects, virtual member functions, and dynamic casts, the programmer does not have the freedom of choice with garbage collection. If garbage collection is an automatic process that is hidden from the programmer, it violates the "pay as you go" principle. The cost of automatic garbage collection is forced on users, even if they prefer to manage dynamic memory manually.
Is it possible to add automated garbage collection as a switch (very much like the capability to turn off RTTI support in some compilers)? This is an interesting question. Surely, in programs that do not use dynamic memory allocation, the programmer might want to turn the garbage collector off. The real crux is with programs that allocate memory dynamically. Consider the following example:

```
void f()
{
  int * p = new int;
  //...use p
}
```

When the garbage collector is switched on, the implementation will mark the pointer p as unreferenced when f() exits. Consequently, in the next invocation of the garbage collector, the memory pointed to by p will be released. Adding a garbage collector for such simple cases is overkill, though. The programmer can use an `auto_ptr` (`auto_ptr` is discussed in Chapter 6, "Exception Handling," and in Chapter 11) to achieve the same effect. For example

```
void f()
{
  auto_ptr<int> p (new int);
  //...use p
} //auto_ptr's destructor releases p
```

Garbage collection is more useful when dynamic memory has to be released at a different scope from where it was allocated. For example, virtual constructors (which are discussed in Chapter 4, "Special Member Functions: Default Constructor, Copy Constructor, Destructor, and Assignment Operator") enable the user to instantiate a new object of the right type, without having to know the exact type of the source object (the example is repeated here for convenience):

```
class Browser
{
public:
  Browser();
  Browser( const Browser&);
  virtual Browser* construct()
    { return new Browser; } //virtual default constructor
  virtual Browser* clone()
    { return new Browser(*this); } //virtual copy constructor

  virtual ~Browser();
//...
};

class HTMLEditor: public Browser
{
public:
  HTMLEditor ();
  HTMLEditor (const HTMLEditor &);
  HTMLEditor * construct()
    { return new HTMLEditor; }//virtual default constructor
  HTMLEditor * clone()
    { return new HTMLEditor (*this); } //virtual copy constructor
  virtual ~HTMLEditor();
  //...
};
```

In a garbage collected environment, it is possible to use a virtual constructor in the following way:

```
void instantiate (Browser& br)
{
  br.construct()->view();
}
```

Here again, the system automatically registers the unnamed pointer that is returned from `br.construct()` and marks it as unreferenced so that the garbage collector can later destroy its associated object and recycle its storage. In a non-garbage collected environment, `instantiate()` causes a memory leak because the allocated object is never deleted (it might cause undefined behavior as well because the allocated object is never destroyed). To enable this programming practice, a garbage collector is mandatory rather than optional. You might suggest that `instantiate()` is to be written as follows:

```
void instantiate (Browser& br)
{
  Browser *pbr = br.construct();
  pbr->view();
```

```
    delete pbr;
  }
```

This way, `instantiate()` can be used in a non-garbage collected environment as well as in a garbage collected one: When the garbage collector is active, the `delete` statement is ignored (perhaps by some macro magic) and the dynamically allocated object is automatically released some time after `instantiate()` has exited. The `delete` statement is executed only when the garbage collector is inactive. However, there is another subtle problem here.

The Problem with Late Destructor Invocation

In a non-garbage collected environment, `pbr` is deleted right before `instantiate()` exits, which means that the destructor of the dynamically allocated object is also invoked at that point. Conversely, in a garbage collected environment, the destructor will be activated at an unspecified time after `instantiate()` exits. The programmer cannot predict when this will happen. It might take a few seconds, but it can also take hours or even days before the garbage collector is invoked the next time. Now suppose that the destructor of `Browser` releases a locked resource such as a database connection, a lock, or a modem. The program's behavior in a garbage collected environment is unpredictable—the locked resource can cause a deadlock because other objects might be waiting for it, too. In order to avert such a potential deadlock, destructors can perform only operations that do not affect other objects, and locked resources have to be released explicitly by calling another member function. For example

```
  void instantiate (Browser& br)
  {
    Browser *pbr = br.construct();
    pbr->view();
    pbr->release(); //release all locked resources
    delete pbr;
  }
```

This is, in fact, the predominant technique in garbage collected languages. Then again, to ensure interoperability between a garbage collected environment and a non-garbage collected one, programmers will have to write a dedicated member function that releases locked resources that the class acquires—even if that class is used in a non-garbage collected environment. This is an unacceptable burden and a violation of the "pay as you go" principle. The conclusion that can be drawn from this discussion is that garbage collection cannot be optional. It is nearly impossible to write efficient and reliable programs that work in both environments. Either automatic garbage collection needs to be an integral part of the language, or it is totally out (as is the case in C++ at present).

Time-Critical Applications

Garbage collection cannot be optional, as you have observed. Why not make it an integral part of the language? Real-time systems are based on deterministic time calculations. For example, a function that has to execute within a time slot of 500 microseconds should never exceed its allotted time slice. However, the garbage collection process is non-deterministic—it is impossible to predict when it will be invoked, and how long it will take. Therefore, languages that offer automatic garbage collection are usually disqualified for use in time-critical applications. Note that real-time programming is not confined to missile launching and low-level hardware manipulation; most modern operating systems include time-critical components that control the allocation of system resources among processes and threads. Many communication systems are also deterministic by nature. Adding an automated garbage collector to C++ would disqualify it from being used in such application domains. Because a t oggled garbage collector is also impractical, C++, by design, is not a garbage collected language at present. Notwithstanding the difficulties involved in garbage collection, there are some serious discussions of adding garbage collection to C++. It is too early to determine if and when this will happen.

Object Persistence

Persistent objects can be stored in nonvolatile storage and used later in other runs of the same program or in other programs. Storing the contents of an object in persistent storage is called *serialization*. The process of reconstituting a serialized object from a persistent repository is called *deserialization*, or *reconstitution*. Other object-oriented languages support object persistence directly by means of a library or built-in keywords and operators. C++ does not support object persistence directly. Designing an efficient, general purpose, platform-independent model of object persistence is quite a challenge. This section exemplifies handmade solutions that make up for the lack of language support for persistence. The difficulties and complications that are associated with a handmade object persistence model demonstrate the importance of language support.

Serialization and Deserialization of Concrete Objects

Consider the following class:

```
class Date
{
private:
  int day;
  int month;
  int year;
  //constructor and destructor
public:
  Date(); //current date
  ~Date();
```

```
//...
};
```

Storing a `Date` object is a rather straightforward operation: Every data member is
written to a persistent stream (usually this is a local disk file, but it can also be a file on
a remote computer). The data members can be read from the stream at a later stage.
For that purpose, two additional member functions are required, one for storing the
object and the other for reading the stored object:

```
#include<fstream>
using namespace std;

class Date
{
//...
  virtual ofstream& Write(ofstream& archive);
  virtual ifstream& Read(ifstream&  archive);
};

ofstream&  Date::Write(ofstream& archive)
{
  archive.write( reinterpret_cast<char*> (&day), sizeof(day));
  archive.write( reinterpret_cast<char*> (&month), sizeof(month));
  archive.write( reinterpret_cast<char*> (&month), sizeof(year));
  return archive;
}
ifstream&  Date::Read(ifstream& archive)
{
  archive.read( reinterpret_cast<char*> (&day), sizeof(day));
  archive.read( reinterpret_cast<char*> (&month), sizeof(month));
  archive.read( reinterpret_cast<char*> (&month), sizeof(year));
  return archive;
}
```

In addition to the member functions `Read()` and `Write()`, it is necessary to define a
reconstituting constructor, which reads a serialized object from a stream:

```
Date::Date(ifstream& archive) //reconstituting constructor
{
  Read(arcive);
}
```

Class Hierarchies

For concrete classes such as `Date`, whose members are fundamental types, making up
for the lack of standardized persistence facilities is rather straightforward. The serialization and deserialization operations merely store and read data members, respectively.
Note that the class's member functions are not serialized. This is not a major issue of
concern because the serialized object should be a close approximation of the binary
representation of the object in memory.

Handling derived classes and classes that contain member objects is more complicated: The member functions Read() and Write() need to be redefined in every class in the hierarchy. Likewise, a reconstituting constructor is required for every class, as in the following example:

```
class DateTime: public Date
{
private:
  int secs;
  int minutes;
  int hours;
public:
  //...
  DateTime::DateTime(ifstream& archive); //reconstituting constructor
  ofstream& Write(ofstream& archive);
  ifstream& Read(ifstream&  archive);
};

ofstream&  DateTime::Write(ofstream& archive)
{
  Date::Write(archive); //must invoke base class Write() first
  archive.write( reinterpret_cast<char*> (&), sizeof(day));
  archive.write( reinterpret_cast<char*> (&month), sizeof(month));
  archive.write( reinterpret_cast<char*> (&month), sizeof(year));
  return archive;
}
ifstream&  DateTime::Read(ifstream& archive)
{
  Date::Read(archive);
  archive.read( reinterpret_cast<char*> (&day), sizeof(day));
  archive.read( reinterpret_cast<char*> (&month), sizeof(month));
  archive.read( reinterpret_cast<char*> (&month), sizeof(year));
  return archive;
}
DateTime::DateTime(ifstream& archive) //reconstituting constructor
{
  Read(arcive);
}
```

Third Party Classes

Overriding the member functions Read() and Write() and serializing data members to and from a stream are error prone and can cause maintenance difficulties. Whenever data members are added or removed, or when their types are changed, the implementer has to modify these member functions accordingly—but this is still managable. However, deriving from classes that do not define a reconstituting constructor and the member functions Read() and Write() is more difficult to handle because a derived class can only serialize its own members—not members of its base classes. The same difficulties exist with embedded objects. How are such subobjects serialized? It might be possible to overcome these difficulties in some cases, albeit with considerable efforts. For example, a class that contains a `vector` can iterate through the vector's members and serialize them one by one. This is only half the story, though. A vector's state depends on other parameters, such as its capacity. Where can this information be stored if the `vector` object itself cannot be serialized? Serializing arrays is another conundrum. One solution is to write a header in the beginning of every serialized object that contains the number of elements. However, this won't work with reference counted objects. Most implementations of `std::string` are reference counted, which means that in the following code snippet, the five `string` objects share some of their data members:

```cpp
#include <string>
using namespace std;
void single_string()
{
  string sarr[4];
  string s = sarr[0];
  for (int i = 1; i< 4; i++)
  {
    sarr[i] = s;
  }
}
```

Reference counting is an implementation detail that is hidden from the users of the class; it is impossible to query the `string` object about how many strings it represents and to serialize this datum.

Handmade object persistence is becoming much more complicated than it seemed at first, isn't it? But that's not all yet. How might such a handmade persistence model represent templates? By simply storing specializations as ordinary objects, the model fails to represent the relationship that exists among the specializations. Worse yet, multiple inheritance and virtual inheritance are even more challenging. How can a handmade persistence model ensure that a virtual subobject is serialized only once, regardless of the number of its occurrences in the inheritance graph?

A Proposal for a Standardized Persistence Model

Most programmers probably give in at this point, and rightfully so. It is possible to come up with a solution even to the virtual base class problem, but as soon as this problem is solved, other special cases such as function objects, static data members, reference variables, and unions present more complexities. There is another drawback in the handmade persistence model: It is not standardized, and as such, programmers have to implement it on their own. The result is a lack of uniformity and varying levels of reliability and performance. Without standardized support for object persistence, a homemade persistence model is, at best, brittle and error prone. Obviously, without standardized object persistence it is impossible to ensure simple, portable, and efficient serialization and deserialization of objects.

Library-Based Extensions

What might such a standardized persistence model look like? There are two basic strategies. One is library-based, whereas the other relies on core language extensions (keywords and syntax). A library-based solution is advantageous in many respects. For example, it does not extend the core language, thus avoiding additional burden for programmers who do not intend to use persistent objects. In addition, a library can be replaced by a better implementation from another vendor without having to switch to a different compiler. This practice can be seen today with people who uninstall the original STL implementation—provided by the compiler vendor—and replace it with another one. Still, a library-based solution has to deal with the lack of language support for persistence, and it must face the same difficulties and complications that were demonstrated previously (the intricacies and vagaries of the most widely used object distribution frameworks, namely the Distributed Component Object Model (DCOM) and the Common Object Request Broker Architecture (CORBA), prove this point). STL might have never become what it is today without built-in support for templates and operator overloading. Furthermore, the language support for templates was extended in various ways to provide the necessary constructs for STL (see Chapter 2, "Standard Briefing: The Latest Addenda to ANSI/ISO C++," and Chapter 9). Similarly, the support for persistence requires core language extensions.

A New Constructor Type

The special member functions are automatically synthesized by the implementation if the programmer does not declare them explicitly and if the implementation needs them (see Chapter 4). Similarly, a language extension can be made so that another type of constructor, a *reconstituting constructor*, is either implicitly synthesized by the implementation when needed, or so that it can be declared by the programmer. As is the case with other constructor types, the programmers need to be allowed to override the default reconstituting constructor by defining it explicitly. The syntactic form of such a constructor must be distinct from all other constructor forms. In particular, a reconstituting constructor is not to be identified solely by its signature. In other words, the following

```
class A
{
//...
public:
  A(istream& repository ); //reconstituting ctor or an ordinary constructor
};
```

is not recommended. It might well be the case that the programmer's intention was to define an ordinary constructor that takes an `istream` object by reference and not a reconstituting constructor. Furthermore, such a convention might break existing code. A better approach is to add a syntactic clue that signifies a reconstituting constructor exclusively. For example, by preceding the symbol >< to the constructor's name

```
class A
{
//...
public:
  ><A(istream& repository ); //reconstituting constructor
};
```

the reconstituting constructor can take a single parameter of some stream type. This
parameter is optional. When the reconstituting constructor is invoked without an
argument, the implementation deserializes the object from a default input stream that
can be specified in the compiler's setting (similar to the default location of the standard header files). To automate the serialization process, a serializing destructor is also
necessary. How might such a destructor be declared? One solution is to add another
type of destructor so that classes can have two destructor types. This is, however, trou-
blesome because the object model of C++ is based on a single destructor per class.
Adding another type of destructor is ruled out then. Perhaps there is no need to
define a distinct destructor type. Instead, the existing destructor can do the serialization automatically: The compiler can insert into the destructor additional code that
performs the necessary serialization operations. (As you know, compilers already insert
code into user-defined destructors to invoke the destructors of base classes and
embedded objects.)

Automating the serialization process has drawbacks, too. Not every class has to be
serialized. The overhead of serializing an object should be imposed only when the user
really needs it. Furthermore, the possibility of encountering runtime exceptions during
serialization is rather high. A full hard disk, a broken network connection, and a corrupted repository are only a handful of the possible runtime exceptions that can occur
during the process of writing the contents of an object to a permanent storage
medium. However, throwing an exception from a destructor is highly undesirable (see
Chapter 6), so perhaps automatic serialization during object destruction is too risky.
Apparently, there is no escape from explicitly calling a member function to do the job.
There are other obstacles here: How to handle the creation and serialization of an
array of objects? How to synchronize changes in the definition of a class and the contents of an object that was serialized before the change took place? Every language
that supports object persistence deals with these difficulties in its own way. C++ can
borrow some of these ideas, too, or it can initiate innovative ideas.

This discussion gives you some feel of why language extensions are necessary, and
what kind of obstacles they overcome. However hypothetical this discussion might
seem, the evolution of C++ has been a democratic process. Many of the changes and
extensions were initiated by users of the language rather than Standardization committee members. STL is probably the best example of this. If you have a comprehensive
proposal for such an extension, you can present it to the Standardization committee.

Support for Concurrency

Concurrency is a generic term for multithreading and multiprocessing. Concurrent programming can effectively improve performance and responsiveness of an application, be it a word processor or a satellite homing system. C++ does not directly address the issues of multiprocessing, threads, and thread safety. It is important to note, however, that nothing in the Standard Library or the language itself *disallows* concurrency. Look at the example of exception handling: In a multithreaded environment, exception handling should be thread-safe, but a single-threaded environment can implement exception handling in a non–thread-safe manner; this is an implementation-dependent issue. Implementations are allowed to provide the necessary facilities for concurrency, and indeed many of them do so. Again, without direct support from the programming language, either by standardized libraries or by core extensions, the implementation of thread safety is more complicated and highly nonportable. There have been several proposals in the past for adding concurrency to C and C++. At present, however, none of these languages supports concurrency directly.

Multithreading

Multithreading, as opposed to multiprocessing, refers to the use of several control threads in a single process. Multithreading is therefore simpler to design and implement, and it enables the application to use system resources more effectively.

Because all threads in a process share the process's data, it is essential to synchronize their operation properly so that one thread does not interfere with another. For that purpose, *synchronization objects* are used. Various types of synchronization objects, such as mutex, critical section, lock, and semaphore offer different levels of resource allocation and protection. Unfortunately, the details and the characterizations of synchronization objects vary from platform to platform. A standard library of synchronization objects has to be flexible enough to enable users to combine platform-specific synchronization objects with standard objects. This is similar to the use of `std::string` and nonstandard string objects in the same program. Alternatively, the standard thread library could provide the basic interfaces of the synchronization objects, and the implementation would be platform-dependent. There is a problem with introducing multithreading support into the Standard, however: single-threaded operating systems such as DOS. Although these platforms are not very popular these days, they are still in use, and implementing a thread library on these platforms is nearly impossible.

Thread Safety

Perhaps the Standard can provide only the necessary features for thread safety and leave the other issues—such as synchronization objects, event objects, instantiation, destruction of threads, and so on—implementation-defined, as they are today. Thread safety ensures that an object can be used safely in a multithreaded environment. For example, the following thread-unsafe class

```
class Date
{
private:
  int day;
  int month;
  int year;
public:
  Date(); //current date
  ~Date();
     //accessors
  int getDay() const { return day; }
  int getMonth() const { return month; }
  int getYear() const { return year; }
   //mutators
  void setDay(int d)   { day = d; }
  void setMonth(int m)  { month = m; }
  void setYear(int y)   { year = y; }
};
```

can become thread-safe by applying the following changes to it: At the beginning of
each member function, a lock has to be acquired; in every return point of each member function, the lock has to be released.

The modified member functions now look like this:

```
void Date::setDay(int d)
{
  get_lock();
  day = d;
  release_lock();
}
void Date::setMonth(int m)
{
  get_lock();
  month = m;
  release_lock();
}
//etc.
```

This is tedious, and yet very simple to automate. The recurrent pattern is very rem-
iniscent of the *resource acquisition is initialization* idiom (discussed in Chapter 5, "Object-
Oriented Programming and Design"). You can define a class whose constructor
acquires a lock, and whose destructor releases it. For example

```
class LockDate
{
private:
  Date& date;
public:
  LockDate(const Date& d) : date(d) { lock(&d); }
  ~LockDate() { release(&d); }
};
```

A real-world lock class would probably be templatized. It would also provide time-outs and handle exceptions; however, the definition of `LockDate` suffices for this discussion. The member functions of `Date` can now be defined as follows:

```
int Date::getDay() const
{
  LockDate ld(this);
  return day;
}
 /...and so on
void Date::getDay(int d)
{
  LockDate ld(this);
  day = d;
 }
//etc.
```

This looks better than the original thread-safe version, but it's still tedious. Standard C++, however, goes only that far. A fully automated thread safety requires core language extensions.

It might not seem obvious from the example why language support for thread safety is necessary. After all, instantiating a local object in every member function is not unacceptably complicated or inefficient. The troubles begin with inheritance. Invoking a non–thread-safe inherited member function might have undefined results in this case. To ensure thread safety in inherited member functions as well, the implementer of `Date` has to override every inherited member function. In each override, a lock has to be acquired. Then, the parent member function is invoked, and finally, the lock is released. With a little help from the programming language, these operations can be made much easier.

Before Method and After Method

The CLOS programming language defines the concepts *before method* and *after method*. A before method is a sequence of operations that precedes the action of a method. An after method is a sequence of operations that succeeds the action of a method. Thus, each method (member function) in CLOS can be thought of as an object with a corresponding constructor and destructor. CLOS provides default before method and after method for each user-defined method. By default, the before method and after method do nothing. However, the user can override them to perform initialization and cleanup operations. Adopting this concept in C++ with slight modifications might simplify the implementation of thread-safe classes. One direction is to provide identical before method and after method for every member function of a class. That is, the before method and after method are defined only once, but they are automatically invoked by every member function of the class (except for the constructor and destructor). One of the benefits of this approach is that new member functions that are added to the class automatically become thread-safe, as do inherited member functions.

Extensible Member Functions

Several programming languages enable the user to compose inherited member functions in a derived class almost automatically. In C++, a member function of a derived class overrides rather than extends the corresponding member of the base class. It is possible to extend the inherited function by calling it explicitly before performing any other operations in the overriding member function (see Chapter 5). The following example (repeated here for convenience) shows how it is done:

```
class rectangle: public shape
{
  //...
  virtual void resize (int x, int y) //extends base's resize()
  {
    shape::resize(x, y);   //explicit call to the base's virtual function
    //add functionality
    int size = x*y;
  }
};
```

There are two problems with this approach. First, if the base class name changes, the implementer of the derived class has to find every occurrence of the old qualified name and change it accordingly.

Another problem is that some member functions are meant to be extended rather than overridden. The best examples are constructors and destructors (which, luckily, the compiler takes care of), but there are other such examples. The serialization and deserialization operations that were discussed previously also need to be extended rather than overridden in a derived class.

It is very tempting to solve the first problem by adding the keyword **super** to the language. Smalltalk and other object-oriented languages already have it. Why not let C++ programmers enjoy it as well? super refers to the direct base class. It can be used in the following manner:

```
class rectangle: public shape
{
  //...
  void resize (int x, int y) //extends base's resize()
  {
    super.resize(x, y);   //the name of the base class is not necessary anymore
    //add functionality
    int size = x*y;
  }
};

class specialRect: public rectangle
{
void resize (int x, int y) //extends base's resize()
  {
    super.resize(x, y);   //calls recatngle::resize()
    //add more functionality
  }
};
```

However, super is ambiguous in objects that have multiple base classes. An alternative solution is to add a different keyword to the language, extensible, that instructs the compiler to insert a call of the base member function in an overriding member function automatically. For example

```
class shape
{
public:
  extensible void resize();
}
class rectangle: public shape
{
  public:
  void resize (int x, int y) //extends base's resize()
  { //shape::resize() is implicitly invoked at this point
//add functionality
    int size = x*y;
  }
};

class specialRect: public rectangle
{
void resize (int x, int y) //extends base's resize()
  { //implicitly calls recatngle::resize()
    //...add more functionality
  }
};
```

extensible is a specialized form of virtual, so the latter is unnecessary. Surely, extensible solves the first problem: If the base class name changes, the implementer of the derived class does not have to change the definition of the member functions. The second problem is also solved here: After a member function is declared extensible, the compiler automatically sees that the corresponding member function of a derived class first invokes the member function of the base class.

Dynamically Linked Libraries

A typical C++ application consists of a statically linked executable that contains all the code and data of the program. Although static linking is efficient in terms of speed, it's inflexible: Every change in the code requires a complete rebuild of the executable. When a dynamically linked library is used, the executable does not need to be rebuilt; the next time the application is run, it automatically picks up the new library version. The advantage of dynamically linked libraries is a transparent upgrade of new releases of the dynamically linked library. However, this transparent "drop in" model breaks under the object model of C++ if the data layout of an object changes in the new release of the library; this is because the size of an object and the offset of its data members are fixed at compile time. There have been suggestions to extend the object model of C++ so that it can support dynamic shared libraries better. However, the costs are slower execution speed and size.

Rule-Based Programming

Many commercial databases support *triggers*. A trigger is a user-defined rule that instructs the system to perform specific actions automatically whenever a certain data value changes. For example, imagine a database that contains two tables, Person and Bank Account. Every row in Bank Account is associated with a record in Person. Deleting a Person record automatically triggers the deletion of all its associated Bank Account records. Rules are the equivalent of triggers in software systems. William Tepfenhart and other researchers at AT&T Bell Laboratories have extended C++ to support rules (*UML and C++: A Practical Guide to Object-Oriented Development*, p. 137). The extended language is called R++ (the R stands for "rules"). In addition to member functions and data members, R++ defines a third kind of class member: a rule. A rule consists of a condition and an associated action that is automatically executed when the condition evaluates to `true`. In C++, the programmer has to test the condition manually in order to decide whether the associated action is to be executed, usually by a `switch` statement or an `if` statement. In R++, this testing is automated—the system monitors the data members listed in the rule's condition, and whenever the condition is satisfied, the rule "fires" (that is, the associated action is executed). Rule-based programming is widely used in artificial intelligence, debugging systems, and event-driven systems. Adding this feature to C++ could considerably simplify the design and implementation of such systems.

Conclusions

Language extensions are needed to facilitate the implementation of operations that otherwise might be more difficult or even impossible. However, there is always a tradeoff involved. To use an analogy, adding an air conditioner to a car decreases its fuel efficiency and degrades its performance (*Principles of Programming Languages: Design, Evaluation and Implementation*, p. 327). Whether it is a beneficial tradeoff depends on various factors, such as the climate in the region where the car is used, the cost of fuel, the engine's power, and the personal preferences of its users. Note that the air conditioner can always be turned off to gain more power and increase the fuel efficiency. Ideally, new language features will not impose a performance penalty of any kind when they are not used. When the programmer deliberately uses them, they should impose as little overhead as possible or no overhead at all. There is, however, a notable difference between an air conditioner and language extensions: Extensions interact with one another. For example, the imaginary keyword `super` has an undesirable interaction with another language feature, namely multiple inheritance. A more realistic example is template's template arguments. The space between the left two angular brackets is mandatory:

```
Vector <Vector<char*> > msg_que(10);
```

Otherwise, the >> sequence is parsed as the right shift operator. In other situations, the interaction is much more complex: Koenig lookup, for instance, can have surprising results under some circumstances (as you read in Chapter 8, "Namespaces").

This chapter has presented three major proposals for language extensions: garbage collection, persistence, and concurrency. Suggestions for less radical extensions are extensible members and rules. None of these is to be taken lightly. The complexity involved in standardizing each of these is intensified even further when they interact with each other. For example, a persistence model becomes even more complicated in a thread-safe environment.

Considering the challenges that the designers of C++ have faced during the past two decades, you can remain optimistic. If you are familiar with the prestandardized implementations of container classes, RTTI, and exception handling of several well known frameworks, you are probably aware of how the standardized container classes, RTTI, and exception handling are much better in every way. This will also be the case if any of the features that are discussed here become part of the C++ Standard.

VI

Appendixes

Manual of Programming Style

Introduction

No two programmers are alike. Given identical design documents, the same software component can be written in various, sometimes radically different, ways. Programming is, after all, an intellectual creation that requires discipline, consistency, creativity, and vision, in addition to the necessary familiarity with the syntax rules of the language. Good programming style is not prescribed by standards—nor should it be; programming, after all, is an art, and as such, it cannot be dictated. Furthermore, every application domain emphasizes different conventions and styles. Thus, using a `goto` statement in structured programming is an anathema; however, in machine-generated code and in time-critical applications, `goto` has legitimate uses.

Coding Conventions

For many, a good programming style is synonymous with coding conventions. Preceding an *m* to a class member, affixing a *C* to a class name, and other such notations are instances of coding conventions. Coding conventions do not necessarily make a program more readable or easier to maintain. In fact, sometimes coding conventions engender the opposite results because programmers who use them have a hard time reading and understanding code written by other programmers who do not adhere to the same conventions. Another classic example of the conventions debate is the placement of curly braces: Should they appear on a separate line, as in

```
void f()
{
//...
}
```
or should they be placed as follows:
```
void f() {
//...
}
```

It's surprising to discover anew every time how such a trivial issue attracts so much fire and zeal.

That said, coding conventions are still important. They are necessary in large-scale software projects or in specific domain applications. For example, in a project that uses a compiler that does not support exception handling, proprietary error handling techniques might be required. Such techniques usually require the programmer's adherence to particular coding conventions and restrictions (for example, testing the return value of a function). Nonetheless, such conventions tend to be application-specific; as such, they are less useful as universal guidelines for C++ coding in general.

This appendix is not about writing conventions, nor is it about naming notations or quality assurance. Instead, it focuses on universal techniques and guidelines for good programming style. A good programming style consists of accurate and efficient usage of the language on the one hand, and abstention from coding styles that are cryptic, idiosyncratic, hard to maintain, inefficient, or incorrect on the other hand. There are some basic rules for good programming styles that are simple to follow: Avoiding deprecated features, using meaningful names, reusing existing and well-proven components instead of reinventing the wheel, and documenting are a few such rules. Other rules require more knowledge and experience from the programmer, as you will see in the following sections.

Design by Contract

The *design by contract* idiom states that the implementation of a component has to adhere to its externally observable behavior, and vice versa. In other words, the interface of a function, a class, and a member function needs to reflect as clearly and accurately as possible their services. The evolution of function prototypes from pre-Standard C (which did not have function prototypes at all), to ISO C (which defines prototypes as an option), and finally, to Standard C++ (in which prototypes are mandatory) demonstrates the importance of this idiom. Moreover, through the evolution of C++, function prototypes were extended to portray further behavior specifications. Thus, in addition to the signature and return value, a member function can also be declared as const as a guarantee that it will not change the state of its object. Exception specifications are another way of advertising the expected behavior. By guaranteeing the specified behavior in the interface, the implementation of a given component can vary across platforms and editions without affecting its users. Some of the language constructs were designed to document the programmer's intentions and guarantees explicitly, and to enforce the compiler's assistance in maintaining these guarantees.

const-Correctness

The const keyword embodies three distinct semantic properties: A const object cannot be modified, a const pointer to an object cannot change its address, and a const member function cannot change the state of its object. const-*correctness* refers to the proper usage of these qualifiers as a means of improving the quality and reliability of the software. This section describes the subtleties of the three semantic qualities of const and their applications.

const Objects

C++ borrowed the concept of const data types from Pascal. ISO C followed C++ and adopted const as a reserved keyword. An object that is not going to change its value during the program's execution needs to be explicitly declared as const. Not only does this document the programmer's intention, but it also allows the compiler to detect violations of this assertion. const does not imply runtime overhead. It is strictly a compile-time concept. In fact, const declarations can even boost performance because they enable the compiler to generate optimized code (as you saw in Chapter 12, "Optimizing Your Code." See also the sidebar "volatile Objects"). Following is an example of using const to ensure that an object is not modified:

```
#include <iostream>
#include <string>
using namespace std;

const string error_msg = "wrong input";

void login()
{
  string username;
  cout<< "enter your name: "<<endl;
  cin>>error_msg; //programmer's typo, should read cin>>username;
                  //however, detected by the compiler
  if (username == "")
    cout<<error_msg;
}
```

Passing const Arguments to Functions

Passing large objects by value as function arguments is very inefficient. On the other hand, passing them by reference enables the callee to change their values unexpectedly. To impede undesirable modifications to its arguments, therefore, the function needs to declare the corresponding parameter as const. For example

```
class File
{
//...
public:
  File& operator = (const File&);
};

void file_copy( const File & source, File & target)
{
  source = target;  // oops, should be: target = source
                    //fortunately, detected by the compiler
}
```

volatile Objects

const guarantees that the value of an object cannot be changed directly by the program. However, it can still be altered asynchronously—that is, by a way unknown to the compiler. For example, the current bit rate of a modem can be read directly from its port and stored in a const variable because it is not to be modified by the program. However, it can have different values during the execution of the program, due to the varying line conditions. The compiler might mistakenly assume that the value is immutable and store it in a machine register rather than fetch it from the modem port to enhance performance. The volatile qualifier instructs the compiler to read the value of the variable from its source every time it is accessed, instead of storing it in a faster processor register. The generated code might be less efficient in this case, but it is correct. Remember that the compiler can also store non-const variables in registers. In the following example

```
void func()
{
  for (int j = 0; j< 100; j++)
  {
    //...do something
  }
}
```

the compiler can store the variable j in a register, thereby eliminating the overhead of reading and writing its value on every iteration. In this case, the compiler's optimization strategy is both correct and efficient. Still, this optimization can be problematic in a multithreaded architecture. As you read in Chapter 14, "Concluding Remarks & Future Directions," a process's variables are shared among its threads. The compiler can store these variables in registers as an optimization; however, a thread's registers are invisible to other threads (a multiprocessor computer can allocate a separate processor for each thread). Now if one thread changes a variable that is kept in a register while another thread reads this variable from memory (where the old value is still kept), the two threads hold incompatible values of the same variable. Consequently, the program's behavior is undefined. By declaring such a variable as volatile, you ensure that it is never stored in a register; as a result, each thread always accesses the correct value.

const Member Functions

An object's state consists of the values of its nonstatic data members. The state of an object can be examined by invoking an *observer function*. An observer function is allowed to access the state of its object but it cannot alter that state. Observer functions are specified as const member functions of their class. By declaring a member function as const, the implementer is promising that the function can never change the state of an object. Applications in general are built upon infrastructure components that are supplied by a third party. Often, the users do not have access to the source code. The only available documentation consists of the declarations and prototypes in the header files. For example

```
class Person
{
private:
  int age;
  long social_security_n;
  //...
  void setAge (int Age);
  void setID(long ssn);
//observer functions
  int getAge () const;
  long getSocial_security_n () const;
};
```

Member functions that are not declared as const are allowed to change the state of their object, although they do not have to.

A common practice is to define a const version and non-const version of every member function that retrieves data members. For example

```
namespace std {
  template <class T, class Allocator = allocator<T> >
    class vector {
        //...
        public:
          reference       operator[](size_type n);
          const_reference operator[](size_type n) const;
          const_reference at(size_type n) const;
          reference       at(size_type n);
          reference       front();
          const_reference front() const;
          reference       back();
          const_reference back() const;
    };
  }
```

const Pointers

Like a const object, a const pointer holds a fixed address that cannot be changed. However, the object that is pointed to *can* be modified by such a pointer. For example

```
void f()
{
  int j = 10;
  int *const cpi = &j;   //cpi is a const pointer to a non-const int
  *cpi = 20;   //OK, j is assigned a new value
  cpi++;   //Error; cannot change cpi
}
```

The syntax of a const pointer to an object and a pointer to a const object can be confusing. Some programmers find it easier to read pointer declarations from right to left. For instance, the statement int *const cpi; declares a variable cpi to be a const pointer to an int. There is, however, a simpler rule: The sequence * const always denotes a const pointer. For example

```
int i;
unsigned int ui;
unsigned long int uli;
  // '* const' denotes a const pointer
  // therefore, the following three statements declare const pointers

int * const cpi = &i;
unsigned int * const cpui = &ui;
int long unsigned * const ppp = &uli;
```

Conversely, const * denotes a pointer to a const object:

```
// the following three statements declare pointers to
// const variables:

int const * pci;
const int *pci2;
unsigned const int * pci3;
```

It is also possible to combine the two. The following statement declares a const pointer to a const int. Again, the *const and const * tokens distinguish between a const pointer and a const object, respectively:

```
const int ci = 0;
int const * const cpci = &ci; //const pointer to const int
```

Examples of Using const Pointers

A simple memory model of an operating system can divide the address space into three parts as follows:

```
void * const uninitialized_memory = reinterpret_cast<void *> (0x0);
void * const user_data = reinterpret_cast<void *> (0x40000);
void * const readonly_mem = reinterpret_cast<void *> (0x800000);
```

The first memory region holds the address space from `0x0` to `0xffff`, in which uninitialized pointers are stored. The runtime system can treat every address in this range as a null pointer (the memory model of Windows 95 is based on a similar model). User data are stored in the following memory region. Finally, read-only data are stored in the memory addresses that are higher than `0x7fffff`. Any attempt to modify a variable whose address is higher than this value engenders a system exception.

In pre-Standard C++, an object's `this` was also a `const` pointer. (The standard now defines `this` to be a non-`lvalue` expression whose value is the address of its object.)

Using Exception Specifications

Specifying the possible exceptions of a function enables the user to handle these exceptions. Here again, a function's prototype provides the necessary information for proper usage and warns the user of the potential exceptions that the function might throw. In this respect, the function's prototype is similar to the user's manual of an electrical appliance, which explains how to use the appliance correctly and warns the users about the dangers of misuse. The runtime system enforces exception specifications and intercepts violations thereof.

Appending an Empty Exception Specification to the Special Member Functions

Some programmers append an empty exception specification to the constructor, copy constructor, assignment operator, and destructor of a class to explicitly state that these member functions do not throw any exceptions. For example

```
class C
{
public:
  C() throw();
  ~C() throw();
  C(const C&) throw();
  C& operator= (const C&); throw();
};
```

Notwithstanding the importance of documenting the function's behavior by specifying its potential exceptions, it is worth keeping in mind that the performance implications of an empty exception specification are implementation-dependent. On some implementations, this practice can improve performance because the compiler is free not to generate extra "scaffolding" code to support exception handling. On other implementations, the addition of empty exception specifications produces the opposite result. Therefore, it is recommended that you check the compiler's documentation first to make sure that empty exception specifications do not result in performance penalty. Note also that a constructor, a copy constructor, and the assignment operator usually perform operations such as calling operator `new` and constructing STL containers, which might throw exceptions. Therefore, don't use an empty exception specification unless all exceptions are handled inside these special member functions.

Using an Unnamed Function Parameter to Indicate Its Obsolescence

When an argument of a function is no longer used in the function body (in an upgraded version, for example), it doesn't have to be removed from the function's parameter list. It can instead become an unnamed argument. In the following example, the function WriteData() is used to support data streaming into various I/O devices, including 5.25" floppy disks. In its upgraded version, however, WriteData() no longer supports 5.25" disks. Removing the final parameter is not always a practical option. Users who link their application with a new binary library might still be using the old header file. Removing the parameter from the function declaration causes incompatibility between the old header file and the new one because the mangled name of the function differs in both cases (name mangling is discussed in Chapter 13, "C Language Compatibility Issues"). To ensure compatibility between the old and new versions of the same function, the final parameter doesn't have to be removed entirely. Rather, it can become unnamed:

```
void  WriteData(
                Floppy3_5& diskette,
                floppy5_25& ); //unnamed
```

Make Sure That Default Arguments of a Virtual Function Are Identical in All Levels of Derivation

Remember that whenever you are using default arguments in virtual functions, the default values in the overriding function must be identical to those of the corresponding member function in the base class. Otherwise, unexpected results might occur. For example

```
class Base
{
public:
  virtual void say (int n = 0) const { cout<<n;}
};

class Derived : public Base
{
public:
  void say (int n = 5) const { cout<<n;} //different default value; surprise!
};

void f()
{
  Base *p = new Derived;
  p->say();  //output is 0, not 5
}
```

Unlike virtual function calls, which are resolved at runtime, default arguments are resolved at compile time. In the preceding example, the static type of p is "pointer to Base." The compiler, therefore, supplies 0 as a default argument in the function call. However, the dynamic type of p is "pointer to Derived," which takes 5 as a default argument.

Because a base class and a derived class can be compiled separately, most compilers cannot detect such inconsistencies. Therefore, it is the programmer's responsibility to make sure that the default values of a virtual function match exactly in all levels of derivation.

Avoid Function-Like Macros and Macro Constants

In C, macros provide a means for avoiding the overhead of a full-blown function call, and they are also used in the implementation of generic functions and for defining constants. In C++, however, macros are to be avoided because they are type-unsafe, hard to debug, and can easily bloat the size of the executable file. C++ offers significantly better alternatives for macros: inline functions, template functions, const variables, and enum types.

Inline Functions

Function-like macros need to be replaced with inline functions; inline functions are safer because they enable type checking. Following is an example:

```
/* C-style inlining */
#include <string.h>
#define initialize(addr,size) memset((addr), 0, (size))


// C++
#include <cstring>
using namespace std;
inline void initialize(void * addr,size_t size) { memset(addr, 0, size); }
```

Inline functions are preferable to macros for several reasons. First, they can be overloaded:

```
inline void initialize(void * addr,size_t size) //general version
{ memset(addr, 0, size); }
inline void initialize(char * addr) //char * specific
{ memset(addr, 0, strlen(addr)+1); }
```

Second, unlike macros, inline functions can have default arguments:

```
inline void initialize(void * addr,size_t size, int initializer = 0)
{ memset(addr, initializer, size); }
```

Finally, macros are notoriously hard to debug. Inline functions, however, can be stepped into during debugging—just like ordinary functions.

const Variables and enum Types

Constant-like macros need to be replaced with const variables or enum types, both of which allow safe type checking and are easier to debug.

const Variables

Using #define to create macro constants is not recommended because the compiler usually cannot detect anomalies and type mismatches, as demonstrated in the following example:

```
#define OK   1. //OOPS! a double instead of int; undetected
```

Using const int prevents such type errors:

```
const int OK = 1; //compiler's type checking applied
```

Another benefit of using const variables rather than macros is the capability to examine their values during debugging.

Use enum Types to Create a Closed Set of Values

Creating a closed set of values with #define macros, as in the following example, is not recommended:

```
#define JAN 1
#define FEB 2
//...
#define DEC 12
```

Instead, use enum types for this purpose because they offer value abstraction and type-safety. enums are strongly-typed; therefore, only values from their enumerator list can be assigned to them. For example

```
enum Months
{
  Jan,
  //...
  Dec
};

enum Days
{
  Mon,
  //...
  Sun
};
void f()
{
  Days day = Mon;
  day = Jan; //error, type mismatch
}
```

enums are distinct types, so they can be used to overload functions:

```
void f(Months month);
void f(Days day);
int main()
{
  f(50); //error, type mismatch
  return 0;
}
```

In terms of performance, enum types are efficient because they are automatically converted by the compiler to an unspecified integral type. The compiler can optimize memory usage by compacting the enumerator list values in units that are smaller or larger than int. Furthermore, they can be stored in the machine's registers to create more efficient code.

There is another favorable aspect of using enums rather than #define macros: maintenance. Consider the following:

```
#define US_DOLLAR 1
#define GB_POUND 2
#define FINNISH_MARKKA 3
#define UNKNOWN 4
```

Adding a new value in between requires manual recalculation of all the subsequent constants, which is tedious and error prone. The compiler does not detect anomalies such as the following:

```
#define US_DOLLAR 1
#define GB_POUND 2
#define FINNISH_MARKKA 3
#define EURO 4 //new symbol inserted in between
#define UNKNOWN 4 //oops! forgot to increment value
```

It is true that the same problem can arise when using const int values. However, enum types automate the process:

```
enum currency
{
  US_DOLLAR,
  GB_POUND,
  FINNISH_MARKKA,
  EURO, //new symbol inserted in between
  UNKNOWN
};
```

Macros still have legitimate uses in C++ (in conditional compilation and #include guards), as you will see soon.

Be Cautious with Unsigned Integers

In many high-level languages, numeric types are always signed—and the programmer has no way of altering this attribute. C++ inherited from C the capability to control the "signedness" of integral types. Unsigned integers are sometimes unavoidable when dealing with raw binary data and in other low-level applications such as encryption, digital communication, and compression. Nevertheless, in conventional programming, unsigned is to be avoided in general. There are two main issues that are of concern here: eliminating possible bugs that can result from mixing signed and unsigned values, and the future maintenance problems that can arise due to the use of unsigned. A common—but wrong—practice is to use codes as unsigned integers. For example, a Geographic Information System (GIS) can have a lookup function that retrieves a city code by its name:

```
typedef unsigned int zip;
zip translate(const string& cityname);
```

translate() returns a city code from a lookup table. For new cities that do not have a code in the lookup table yet, zero is returned. Under normal usage conditions, this seems quite reasonable. But how do you handle a validation exception such as an illegal string? Negative values can be used to indicate error conditions; alas, translate() returns only positive values. This is a classic case of how the misuse of unsigned integers can limit possible future extensions.

Another problem with using unsigned integers is that they are automatically converted to signed, and vice versa, with a possible loss of their original value (although a good compiler might warn you about this). For example

```
void translate(unsigned int code, string& descr); //translate code to text
const int ERROR = -1;
//...additional codes
const int MEM_EXCEPTION_CODE = -100;
int init_GlobalSection();
int main()
{
  string err_description;
  if ( init_GlobalSection() == error)
    translate(MEM_EXCEPTION_CODE, //implicit signed to unsigned conversion;
              err_description);    //unexpected results
  return 0;
}
```

For these reasons, a signed integral type is usually a more portable, safe, and robust choice. Picking unsigned just because the language happens to have this feature is, at best, limiting; furthermore, doing so is a source of bugs.

Prefer References to Pointers

Even experienced C++ programmers who have prior experience with C tend to use pointers excessively, when references might be a better choice. Pointers might result in bugs such as the following:

```
struct Date {/**/};
bool isValid( const Date *pDate);

void f()
{
  Date *p = new Date;

  //...many lines of code
  delete p;       //p is now a dangling  pointer
  bool valid = isValid(p);  // undefined behavior
  p = NULL;
  valid = isValid(p); //null pointer dereferencing; disastrous
```

This example might seem contrived; unfortunately, however, such code does get written—and not necessarily by novices. When complex programs have to manage numerous pointers to various objects, the issue of ownership—that is, determining which part is responsible for the deletion of the pointers—can also become complicated and error prone. The use of references instead of pointers does not eliminate these problems entirely. However, it does eliminate two of the most notorious bugs that are associated with pointers—namely, null pointer dereferencing and dangling pointers—because a reference is always bound to an object, and it can never be null. It is therefore recommended that you use references instead of pointers whenever possible, and resort to pointers only for operations that are inherently pointer-based.

Arguments need to be passed to functions by reference with a const reference, which indicates an immutable argument, and a non-const reference, which indicates that the function is allowed to modify its argument. Some programming schools advocate that only immutable arguments are to be passed by reference, whereas modifiable arguments are to be passed as pointers. The claim is that pointers are more readable in this context; but this is just an old habit from C, which has no reasonable ground in C++.

Before Resorting To void *...

void pointers have special and legitimate uses that are very difficult to implement with any other type. Notwithstanding that, they suffer from the well-known ailments of pointers in general. Furthermore, void pointers usually have to be cast to some other pointer type before they can be used. Luckily, C++ offers higher level mechanisms for genericity that are both safer and more efficient.

Note

Following the "Prefer Automatic Storage to Free Store Whenever Possible" guideline that was discussed in Chapter 11, "Memory Management," you might discover that pointer-based operations are less frequently needed than you might initially think. For instance, examine the following partial class definition:

```
class PointerMisuse
{
private:
  CDC * m_pDeviceContext;
        //..
public:
  PointerMisuse();
  ~PointerMisuse();
};


PointerMisuse::PointerMisuse()
{
  m_pDeviceContext = new CDC; //is this really necessary?
}
PointerMisuse::~PointerMisuse()
{
 delete m_pDeviceContext;
}
```

Even experienced programmers are sometimes inclined to this programming style. Worse yet, classes like this are widely used in many commercial frameworks. Is the use of pointers and dynamic memory allocation really necessary here? It isn't. This class can be rewritten as follows:

```
class ProperUse
{
private:
  CDC * m_pDeviceContext;
  CDC cdc;
          //..
public:
  ProperUse();
};


ProperUse::ProperUse()
{
  m_pDeviceContext = &cdc;
}
```

Not only is this version safer (remember that dynamic memory allocations might fail), it is also simpler and more efficient. Note that the use of pointers now becomes redundant, and the member m_pDeviceContext is not needed anymore; however, to ensure backward compatibility with existing code, it is still used.

Templates

The significant advantages of using function templates and class templates rather than
void pointers are discussed in detail in Chapter 9, "Templates." Templates are type-safe,
completely generic, and high-level.

Inheritance

For a function or algorithm that can be applied to a family of related types, a common
base class from which all other related types are derived can serve the purpose. For
example

```
class WindBase
{
public:
  virtual void Create()=0;
  virtual void Destroy() = 0;
};
class Frame: public WindBase
{
public:
  void Create();
  void Destroy();
};
class View: public WindBase
{
public:
  void Create(); void Destroy();
};

void RegisterWindow(const WindBase &anyWindow);
```

Limit the use of void pointers to very low-level operations exclusively.

Use **typedef** Judiciously

typedefs can be used to enhance portability by hiding the underlying type of an
abstract entity. For instance, when maximal precision of a floating point is required, a
single typedef can be used universally even though its underlying representation is
machine-dependent:

```
#ifdef _WIN32
  typedef  double astronomicalUnit; //maximal precision on this environment
#else
  typedef long double astromonicalUnit; //this machine has higher precision
#endif
astromonicalUnit au;
```

A typedef can also improve readability by hiding complicated syntactic constructs
such as pointers to functions, pointers to class members, and unwieldy template declarations. On the other hand, excessive use of unnecessary typedef declarations can
result in less readable code. Therefore, typedef needs to be used judiciously.

Place a `default` Label in Every `switch` Statement

A `switch` statement needs to always contain a `default` label to handle exceptional values. Even with a seemingly "safe" set of values, which are not likely to be modified, it is still a good idea to place a default label just in case. Consider the following example:

```
//Month.h file
enum Month
{
  Jan,
  Feb,
  //...etc.
  Dec
};


//Month.cpp file

int daysInMonth(Month month)
{
  int result = 0;
  switch (month)
  {
    case Jan:
      result = 31;
    break;
    case Feb:
      result = 28;
    break;
    //...Mar to Nov go here
    case Dec:
      result = 31;
    break;    //no default
  } //end switch
  return result;
}
```

Now suppose that another programmer needs to extend the enumerator list of `Month` in the following manner:

```
//file Month.h re-edited
enum Month
{
  Jan,
  Feb,
  LeapFeb, //newly added
  Mar,
  //...etc.
  Dec
};
```

Consequently, the preceding `switch` statement will return the wrong result, `0`, for the month of type `LeapFeb`. The astonished user might have a better clue as to where the problems lies if the `switch` statement includes a `default` label:

```
switch (month)
{
//...
default:
  cout<<"unsupported month value; check this switch statement!";
break;
}
```

Even without extending the enumerator list of Month, daysInMonth() can still return unexpected results in the following cases:

```
Month m; //forgot to initialize
int days;
days = daysInMonth(m) //oops, m has an undefined value
```

Avoid Using Double Underscore in Identifiers

Names that contain a double underscore (__) and names that begin with an under-score followed by an uppercase letter are reserved for C/C++ implementations. Remember that C++ programs are transformed by the compiler. Consequently, new identifiers, which were not declared by the programmer, are inserted into the source file. In order to avoid name conflicts, the compiler-generated identifiers are usually decorated with a double underscore; so it is recommended that you do not prefix underscores to user-declared identifiers.

Avoid Using Deprecated Features

Chapter 2, "Standard Briefing: The Latest Addenda to ANSI/ISO C++," listed the deprecated features in the Standard. These features are not to be used in new code; furthermore, it is recommended that you remove them from legacy code if possible. Some of the deprecated features that are still widely used in new commercial libraries and frameworks are a typedef BOOL and the macros TRUE and FALSE. In addition to the inherent disadvantages of this practice (which were described in Chapter 2), using a typedef instead of the built-in bool type can cause maintenance problems in the future. It might be a worthwhile investment for programmers to familiarize themselves with the list of deprecated features and their recommended substitutions.

Use New Cast Operators Instead of C-style Cast

The C-style cast was not deprecated by the Standardization committee due to its widespread use in existing code. Still, its use in new code is not recommended due to its noticeable drawbacks. The new cast operators are preferable because they are safer and more readable.

Remember to Update Comments When the Code is Changed

The importance of comments cannot be over-emphasized. Yet there is only one thing worse than an undocumented source file: a misleadingly documented source file. A detailed description of a member function that no longer exists in a class or a documentation of a default constructor that now appears to be taking three mysterious arguments can turn software maintenance into a nightmare. Often, such out-of-sync comments render software components unusable. So whenever you change your code or reedit a machine-generated source file, remember to update the comments appropriately or remove them altogether.

Use Numerous Access Specifiers When It Can Improve Readability

There is no limit to the number of access specifiers—`private`, `protected`, and `public`—that a class can have. When large classes are declared, it is useful to repeat the access specifier frequently to improve readability; for example, after a page break, as in

```
class DatabaseTable { //a class representing a table in a relational database
private:
  int rows;
  string tableName;
  int fieldsPerRecord;
  Date created;
        //page break/full screen here
private:
  Date lastSorted
public:
  DatabaseTable(const DatabaseTable& other);
  DatabaseTable();
  DatabaseTable& operatot = (const DatabaseTable&);
  ~DatabaseTable();
public:
  //... rest of member functions
};
```

The repetition of access specifiers does not impose any performance overhead, so you can use as many specifiers as needed.

Use #include Guards

The same file can be #included in different source files that are compiled together. For example

```
// filename calendar.h
  //..declarations
// calendar.h
```

```
// filename Time.h
#include "calendar.h"
class Time
{
//...
};
// Time.h

// filename Date.h
#include "calendar.h"
class Date
{
//...
};
// Date.h

#include "Time.h" // Time.h contains #include "calendar.h"  directive
#include "Date.h" // Date.h also contains #include "calendar.h" directive
int main()
{ //compilation errors due to repeated inclusion of calendar.h
  Date d;
  Time t;
}
```

However, to #include a file more than once during a compilation session causes the compiler to issue error messages on repeated definitions. In order to avoid compile time errors, every header file needs to have an #include guard to ensure that it is scanned only once in a single compilation session:

```
//file calendar.h
#ifndef CALENDAR_H // is this file #included the first time ?
#define CALENDAR_H true
//declarations, namespace definitions, typedefs and any other stuff goes here:
#endif
```

The first time calendar.h is scanned during compilation, its contents are read and the macro CALENADR_H is defined. Thereafter, its contents are ignored. This is one of the few legitimate uses of macros in C++. Although some compilers now offer an automated mechanism that prevents repeated file inclusion during a compilation session, it is still recommended that you use #include guards to ensure portability. All standard headers have such #include guards too.

Infrastructure Components Should Trust Their Users

Infrastructure functions and classes that are used extensively need to follow the "trust the programmer" policy. That is, they are not to perform additional error checking. This policy is widely used in the Standard Library. For example, strcpy() does not check for null pointer arguments; it might be safer if strcpy() did so. However, the incurred runtime overhead might be unacceptable for many applications. Similarly, the overloaded operator [] in STL containers is meant to be as efficient as a built-in array subscript. If it performed additional checking for out of range subscripts, it couldn't be as efficient. In other words, the Standard Library trusts that the users know what they are doing. Nonetheless, it is important to document these assumptions; for example

```
namespace std
{
template<class T, class traits = char_traits<T>,
              class Allocator = allocator<T> >
  class basic_string {
  public:
  //...
  basic_string(const T* s, // 1)s should never be a null pointer
                          // 2) s must point to a null-terminated char array
              const Allocator& a = Allocator() );
  //...
  };
}
```

It is the responsibility of higher-level applications to apply a rigorous check before invoking infrastructure functions. For example

```
string writeToString (int symbol)
{
  const char *p = getDescription(symbol);
  if (p) // make sure that p is not null
  {
    return string(p);
  }
  return string();
}
```

Use Type Affixes in Hard Coded Literals

The type of hard coded literals needs to be specified explicitly through the use of the desired type affixes. This ensures that the compiler will figure out the correct type of the literal. In addition, type affixes make the code more readable and portable.

Integer Affixes

The letter L, when affixed to a number, indicates a long integer. In addition, the letter U indicates an unsigned type:

```
1000L  // constant is a long rather than an int
1000U  // constant is an unsigned int
```

These affixes can be used together:

```
1000UL // unsigned long
```

These affixes are not case sensitive, and their order is immaterial:

```
1000lu // also unsigned long
```

Hexadecimal and Octal Literals

A *hexadecimal literal* is indicated by the prefix 0x:

```
int n =0x1000; // decimal value of n is 4096
```

A sequence of one or more octal digits that is preceded by 0 (zero) is an *octal literal*. For example

```
n = 01000; // decimal value of n is 512
```

When using octal literals, beware of the following common pitfall:

```
const int warning = 10;
const int error = 100,
switch (status)
{
case 010   // OOPS, decimal value is 8, not 10
   handle_warning ();  // unreachable code!
   break;
case 100:
   handle_error ();
   break;
default:
   break;
}
```

In the preceding example, the programmer's intention was to use a uniform, fixed size format of three digits in all the case labels. However, the compiler treated each zero-preceded label as an octal number rather than as a decimal number.

Character and String Literals

A *character literal* is defined as follows:

```
const char  c = 'a';
```

A *string literal* is a sequence of zero or more quoted characters:

```
"string literal";
```

A wide character string literal is preceded by the letter L:

```
L"wide string literal";
```

Floating Literals

A *floating literal* consists of a *digit sequence*, followed by a decimal point and an optional fraction:

```
0.  // a double
1.5 // also a double
```

In addition, the suffixes F or f can be used for clarity:

```
0.f  // a double
1.5F // also a double
```

The suffix L or l indicates a `long double` type:

```
1.5L  // long double
```

Floating literals with scientific notation are indicated by a fractional constant or a digit sequence, followed by an *exponent part* and an optional floating suffix:

```
double light_speed = 3.0E+5;
```

When to Use a Pure Virtual Member Function

A pure virtual function is merely an interface. It can be thought of as a policy-enforcing mechanism. You use a pure virtual function when subclasses implement the same interface in completely different manners. For example, a persistence interface can have a `Write()` operation to store the state of an object. Yet, each class that implements this interface performs individual operations to store its state into a file:

```
class persistent
{
public:
  virtual void Write () = 0;
};
class Clock: public persistent
{
public:
  void Write() {...} // implement the interface
};
class Date: public persistent
{
public:
  void Write() {...} // implement the interface
};
```

Avoid Improper Inheritance

Using public inheritance with two classes that do not fully comply with the is-a relationship (although they might be somehow related to one another) is a common design mistake. For example, deriving a class that encapsulates a memory buffer from class `string` is a design flaw:

```
class mem_buff: public string {/**/};
```

Indeed, these classes share some resemblance: They have a contiguous sequence of addressable bytes in memory, and they might have similar iterating operations. Nonetheless, using public inheritance is too strong a statement about the relationship between the two: It implies, for example, that a function that takes a `string` object can also take a `mem_buffer` object. There are, however, some crucial differences between these classes. A null character is a string terminator, but a memory buffer does not treat it as a terminator. Furthermore, a `string` can hold printable characters, whereas memory buffers can hold any character type. Such improper inheritance relationships can result in serious maintenance problems. In this case, private inheritance—or better yet, a simple containment relationship—is more suitable. The fact that two classes happen to share some functionality does not imply that they should be publicly derived from one another.

Conclusions

High quality software begins with proper analysis, accurate design, implementation, and testing. This appendix has presented some guidelines for self-documenting coding and safer programming. Two additional guidelines follow: First, read code that is written by others. You'll be surprised to discover how much you can learn from others' experience. Similarly, let others read your code and comment on it. This is another great way to learn from other people's experiences, and to share your experience with others.

B

C++ Keywords

STANDARD C++ RESERVES 63 KEYWORDS, 32 of which are ISO C keywords. C++ keywords that are also ISO C keywords are **bold** (see Table B.1).

Table B.1   **Standard C++ Keywords**

asm	**do**	**if**	**return**	**typedef**
auto	**double**	inline	**short**	typeid
bool	dynamic_cast	**int**	**signed**	typename
break	**else**	**long**	sizeof	**union**
case	**enum**	mutable	**static**	**unsigned**
catch	explicit	namespace	static_cast	using
char	export	new	**struct**	virtual
class	**extern**	operator	**switch**	**void**
const	false	private	template	**volatile**
const_cast	**float**	protected	this	wchar_t
continue	**for**	public	throw	**while**
default	friend	**register**	true	
delete	**goto**	reinterpret_cast	try	

In addition, C++ defines 11 reserved alternative representations of operators and punctuators (see Table B.2).

Table B.2 **Alternative Representations**

and	and_eq	bitand	bitor	compl	
not	not_eq	or	or_eq	xor	xor_eq

Index

pointers, 238, 264
prototypes, 268
special member, 321
templates, 174, 176–177, 184
try blocks, 25, 128
virtual, 98, 336
virtual member, 72, 287–288
wrappers, 274–275

G

garbage collector, 242

generic programming, 8, 188

gigantic classes, 92

global flags, 115

global objects, 125

goto statements, 272

H

handlers, 118

handling
error codes, 114
errors, 114
implementing mechanisms, 117
terminating programs, 115
exceptions, 25, 116
advanced, 125
misuses, 131
global flags, 115

hashed associative container, 293

header files, 188

headers
C standard, 34
standard names, 158

heterogenic lists, 190

hexidecimal literals, 335

hierarchy
classes, 300
exception handlers, 126

holds-a relationship, 101

I

I/O streams, 31

if statements, 29

ill-formed program, 14

implementaion-dependent behavior, 15

implementation details, 93

implementation-defined behavior, 15

implementation-required initializations, 71

implementing
assignment operator, 75
copy constructors, 75
error handling mechanisms, 117
function objects, 205
reference counting, 215

implicit casting, 269

implicit int declaration, 34

implicitly-declared constructors, 69

implicitly-defined assignment operators, 72

improper inheritance, 336

#include guards, 332

inheritance, 87, 89, 101, 329
assignment operator, 73
improper, 336

J – K

L

time-critical applications, 299

toggling
exception handling support, 131
RTTI, 144

translation units, 13

triggers, 310

trivial constructors, 58

true const, 20

type
affixes, 334
info, 137

type-fields, 99

typecast operators, 18

typedef, 329

typedef boolean, 23

typeid operators, 137-139, 145

typename keyword, 30, 183

U

undefined behavior, 15

unions, 261
anonymous, 241, 261
initialization, 236
memory, 261

units, 13

unnamed function parameters, 322

unnamed namespaces, 33, 157

unsigned integers, 326

unspecified behavior, 15

unwinding stacks, 117, 119

user convenience, 294

user-defined conversions, 46

user-defined operators, 51

using declarations, 33, 101, 150

using directive, 150

utilities, 190

V

values, 14

variables
declarations, 269
if statements, 29
local static, 239-240
register, 262-263
scoping rules, 28

vector container class, 191

vectors, 198, 201

version control, 155

viewing bool variables, 24

virtual base downcasting, 143

virtual base class destructors, 96

virtual constructors, 71

virtual destructors, 79

virtual functions, 263

virtual inheritance, 107-108, 289

virtual member functions, 72, 336
access specifications, 98
extending, 97
support, 287-288

void pointers, 176, 269

volatile objects, 241, 318

W - Z

Macmillan
FREE Personal Bookshelf
ONLINE

Get FREE books and more...when you register this book online for our Personal Bookshelf Program

http://register.quecorp.com/

 Register online and you can sign up for our *FREE Personal Bookshelf Program*...unlimited access to the electronic version of more than 200 complete computer books—immediately! That means you'll have 100,000 pages of valuable information onscreen, at your fingertips!

 Plus, you can access product support, including complimentary downloads, technical support files, book-focused links, companion Web sites, author sites, and more!

 And you'll be automatically registered to receive a *FREE subscription to a weekly email newsletter* to help you stay current with news, announcements, sample book chapters, and special events, including sweepstakes, contests, and various product giveaways!

 We value your comments! Best of all, the entire registration process takes only a few minutes to complete, so go online and get the greatest value going—absolutely FREE!

Don't Miss Out On This Great Opportunity!

QUE® is a brand of Macmillan Computer Publishing USA.

For more information, please visit *www.mcp.com*